New Casebooks

POETRY

NOVELS AND PROSE

DRAMA

(continued overleaf)

MARLOWE Edited by Arraham Oz
REVENGE TRAGEDY Edited by Stevie Simkin
SHAKESPEARE: *Antony and Cleopatra* Edited by John Drakakis
SHAKESPEARE: *Hamlet* Edited by Martin Coyle
SHAKESPEARE: *Julius Caesar* Edited by Richard Wilson
SHAKESPEARE: *King Lear* Edited by Kiernan Ryan
SHAKESPEARE: *Macbeth* Edited by Alan Sinfield
SHAKESPEARE: *The Merchant of Venice* Edited by Martin Coyle
SHAKESPEARE: *A Midsummer Night's Dream* Edited by Richard Dutton
SHAKESPEARE: *Much Ado About Nothing* and *The Taming of the Shrew*
    Edited by Marion Wynne-Davies
SHAKESPEARE: *Othello* Edited by Lena Cowen Orlin
SHAKESPEARE: *Romeo and Juliet* Edited by R. S. White
SHAKESPEARE: *The Tempest* Edited by R. S. White
SHAKESPEARE: *Twelfth Night* Edited by R. S. White
SHAKESPEARE ON FILM Edited by Robert Shaughnessy
SHAKESPEARE IN PERFORMANCE Edited by Robert Shaughnessy
SHAKESPEARE'S HISTORY PLAYS Edited by Graham Holderness
SHAKESPEARE'S ROMANCES Edited by Alison Thorne
SHAKESPEARE'S TRAGEDIES Edited by Susan Zimmerman
JOHN WEBSTER: *The Duchess of Malfi* Edited by Dympna Callaghan

GENERAL THEMES

FEMINIST THEATRE AND THEORY Edited by Helene Keyssar
POSTCOLONIAL LITERATURES Edited by Michael Parker and
    Roger Starkey

New Casebooks Series
Series Standing Order
ISBN 0–333–71702–3 hardcover
ISBN 0–333–69345–0 paperback
(*outside North America only*)

You can receive future titles in this series as they are published by placing a standing order. Please contact your bookseller or, in case of difficulty, write to us at the address below with your name and address, the title of the series and the ISBN quoted above.

Customer Services Department, Macmillan Distribution Ltd
Houndmills, Basingstoke, Hampshire RG21 6XS, England

New Casebooks

OTHELLO

WILLIAM SHAKESPEARE

EDITED BY LENA COWEN ORLIN

First published 2004 by
PALGRAVE MACMILLAN
Houndmills, Basingstoke, Hampshire RG21 6XS and
175 Fifth Avenue, New York, N.Y. 10010
Companies and representatives throughout the world

PALGRAVE MACMILLAN is the global academic imprint of the Palgrave Macmillan division of St. Martin's Press, LLC and of Palgrave Macmillan Ltd. Macmillan® is a registered trademark in the United States, United Kingdom and other countries. Palgrave is a registered trademark in the European Union and other countries.

ISBN 0–333–63356–3 hardback
ISBN 0–333–63357–1 paperback

This book is printed on paper suitable for recycling and made from fully managed and sustained forest sources.

A catalogue record for this book is available from the British Library.

Library of Congress Cataloging-in-Publication Data
Othello / edited by Lena Cowen Orlin.
    p. cm. – (New casebooks)
    Includes bibliographical references (p.) and index.
    ISBN 0–333–63356–3 (cloth) — ISBN 0–333–63357–1 (paper)
    1. Shakespeare, William, 1564–1616. Othello. 2. Othello (Fictitious character) 3. Tragedy. I. Orlin, Lena Cowen. II. New casebooks (Palgrave Macmillan (Firm)).

PR2829.O8 2003
822.3′3—dc21   2003053281

10 9 8 7 6 5 4 3 2 1
13 12 11 10 09 08 07 06 05 04

Printed in China

Contents

Acknowledgements

The editor and publishers wish to thank the following for permission to use copyright material:

Denise Albanese, for 'Black and White, and Dread All Over: The Shakespeare Theatre's "Photonegative" *Othello* and the Body of Desdemona' from *A Feminist Companion to Shakespeare* (ed.) Dympna Callaghan (2000) pp. 226–47, by permission of Blackwell Publishing Ltd.

Harry Berger, Jr., for 'Impertinent Trifling: Desdemona's Handkerchief', *Shakespeare Quarterly*, 47 (1996) 235–50. Copyright © 1996 by the Folger Shakespeare Library, by permission of The Johns Hopkins University Press.

Lynda E. Boose, for ' "Let it be Hid": The Pornographic Aesthetic of Shakespeare's *Othello*' from *Women, Violence, and English Renaissance Literature: Essays Honoring Paul Jorgensen* (eds.) Linda Woodbridge and Sharon Beehler, Medieval and Renaissance Texts and Studies, Vol. 256 (2003) pp. 243–68. Copyright © 2003 Arizona Board of Regents for Arizona State University, by permission of the Arizona Center for Medieval and Renaissance Studies.

Michael D. Bristol, for 'Charivari and the Comedy of Abjection in *Othello*', *Renaissance Drama*, n.s. 21 (1990) 3–21, by permission of Northwestern University Press.

Elizabeth Hanson, for 'Brothers of the State: *Othello*, Bureaucracy, and Epistemological Crisis' from *The Elizabethan Theatre XIV: Papers given at the International Conference on Elizabethan Theatre held at the University of Waterloo, Ontario, in July 1991* (eds.) A. L. Magnusson and C. E. McGee (1996) pp. 27–48, by permission of P. D. Meany Publishers.

Barbara Hodgdon, for 'Race-ing *Othello*: Re-Engendering White-Out' from *Shakespeare the Movie: Popularizing the Plays on Film,*

TV, and Video (eds.) Lynda E. Boose and Richard Burt, Routledge (1997) pp. 23–44, by permission of Taylor & Francis Books Ltd.

Alan Sinfield, for 'Cultural Materialism, *Othello* and the Politics of Plausibility' from *Faultlines: Cultural Materialism and the Politics of Dissident Reading* by Alan Sinfield (1992) pp. 29–51. Copyright © 1992 The Regents of the University of California, by permission of the University of California Press and Oxford University Press.

Jyotsna Singh, for 'Othello's Identity, Postcolonial Theory and Contemporary African Rewritings of *Othello*' from *Women, 'Race' and Writing in the Early Modern Period* (eds.) P. Parker and M. Hendricks, Routledge (1994) pp. 287–99, by permission of Taylor & Francis Books Ltd.

Every effort has been made to trace the copyright holders but if any have been inadvertently overlooked the publishers will be pleased to make the necessary arrangement at the first opportunity.

General Editors' Preface

The purpose of this series of New Casebooks is to reveal some of the ways in which contemporary criticism has changed our understanding of commonly studied texts and writers and, indeed, of the nature of criticism itself. Central to the series is a concern with modern critical theory and its effect on current approaches to the study of literature. Each New Casebook editor has been asked to select a sequence of essays which will introduce the reader to the new critical approaches to the text or texts being discussed in the volume and also illuminate the rich interchange between critical theory and critical practice that characterises so much current writing about literature.

In this focus on modern critical thinking and practice New Casebooks aim not only to inform but also to stimulate, with volumes seeking to reflect both the controversy and the excitement of current criticism. Because much of this criticism is difficult and often employs an unfamiliar critical language, editors have been asked to give the reader as much help as they feel is appropriate, but without simplifying the essays or the issues they raise. Again, editors have been asked to supply a list of further reading which will enable readers to follow up issues raised by the essays in the volume.

The project of New Casebooks, then, is to bring together in an illuminating way those critics who best illustrate the ways in which contemporary criticism has established new methods of analysing texts and who have reinvigorated the important debate about how we 'read' literature. The hope is, of course, that New Casebooks will not only open up this debate to a wider audience, but will also encourage students to extend their own ideas, and think afresh about their responses to the texts they are studying.

John Peck and Martin Coyle
University of Wales, Cardiff

Introduction

LENA COWEN ORLIN

To trace the course of critical thinking about Shakespeare in the late twentieth century, one could scarcely do better than to take *Othello* as a case study. The play registers all the concerns of the newly politicized readings of the last decades: gender, power, sexuality, race. It was a key text in the works that introduced poststructuralist theory to the interpretation of English literature of the Renaissance. As a play that survives in multiple versions, including a quarto printing of 1622 and the Folio printing of 1623, it participates in debates about authorial revision, scribal corruption and textual transmission. It has as lively a record on stage and screen as in criticism, and this performance history intersects urgently with the continuing legacies of empire and enslavement. The play's broadest plot outlines remain sufficiently recognizable that it informs popular understandings of sensational current events. These, too, are matters of interpretation for the Shakespearean scholars of recent years, who in all these various ways have looked beyond formalist criticism to write about the kinds of work literature does in culture.

For centuries, *Othello* has demonstrated its emotional power on stage. Remarkably enough, we have a reaction to the play from 1610, when it was performed in Oxford. One Henry Jackson noted of the (male) actor who played Desdemona that 'when she was killed she was even more moving, for when she fell back upon the bed she implored the pity of the spectators by her very face'. Samuel Pepys saw the play in 1660 and recorded in his diary that 'a very pretty lady that sat by me, called out, to see Desdemona smothered'. This is the first of many descriptions of an audience member interrupting *Othello*'s last scene with audible horror or a conspicuous impulse to

1

prevent the tragic denouement. In 1822, an armed soldier at a Baltimore production shouted, 'It will never be said that in my presence a confounded Negro has killed a white woman!' Fortunately the soldier's shooting skill was poor enough that the actor playing Othello was injured only in the arm. At a performance in New York in 1943, director Margaret Webster detected a female voice from the audience whispering repeatedly 'Oh God, don't let him kill her ... don't let him kill her ...'. Responses like these could not be more distinct from the first *critical* appraisal of the play, Thomas Rymer's notoriously peevish observation of 1693: 'So much ado, so much stress, so much passion and repetition about an Handkerchief!'[1]

Modern criticism of *Othello* essentially begins with A. C. Bradley, who in 1904 displayed emotion comparable to that of the play's most vocal witnesses: 'Of all Shakespeare's tragedies', he wrote, '*Othello* is the most painfully exciting and the most terrible'. Bradley lastingly shaped the canon of English literature by designating four of Shakespeare's tragedies as the most important, and he included *Othello* in that top four (along with *Hamlet*, *Macbeth* and *King Lear*). And yet *Othello* has seemed to sit fairly uneasily among its fellows, even in Bradley's account of things. He complained that *Othello* lacks any 'suggestions of huge universal powers working in the world of individual fate and passion'.[2] There are various additional reasons why *Othello* can seem diminished by its comparison to the other great tragedies. The play has a domestic focus, comic structures, a constricted time frame, and an 'other' at its centre who, despite being the title character, has fewer lines than his antagonist, Iago. It is now also possible to recognize that earlier critics may have been unsettled about the play's canonical stature for the very reason that it attracts so much attention today: its address of hot-button problems like violence towards women and race-based hatred. In other words, personal discomfort with these issues may have been displaced into critical devaluations of the play.[3]

Bradley's analysis of *Othello* dominated scholarly dialogue about the play at least until the 1980s. Even those who disagreed with him felt compelled to engage with him. F. R. Leavis, for example, famously quarrelled with Bradley's depiction of Othello as a man of noble character. For years, critics located themselves either in Bradley's camp or in that of Leavis. In the last quarter of the twentieth century, however, what some have described as a 'revolution' in literary criticism introduced theories, methods and interests that dislodged *Othello* from the old interpretive boxes of character criticism, genre studies and literary appraisal. Different readers would mark the start of the revolution at different points, but one sure place to begin is with Lynda E. Boose's 'Othello's Handkerchief: "The Recognizance and Pledge of Love"' (1975).[4] 'Othello's Handkerchief' disengaged itself from character analysis and showed the enormous significance of that which Rymer had dismissed as trivial, opening up the rich potential for meaning in Othello's gift to his wife. As Boose pointed out, the strawberries embroidered on white linen are emblematic of virgin blood on nuptial sheets. The colour imagery of the handkerchief thus resonates throughout the play, especially as Desdemona asks to have her wedding sheets placed on the bed that will become her deathbed. In this, the 'trivial' handkerchief is central to the play's themes of marriage and justice.

OTHELLO AND FEMINIST CRITICISM

'Othello's Handkerchief' importantly introduced feminist politics to Othello criticism. Also in 1975, Juliet Dusinberre's Shakespeare and the Nature of Women lauded Shakespeare's creation of strong and articulate female characters, especially in his romantic comedies.[5] This ground-breaking book pioneered what has since been termed 'first-generation' or 'first-wave' feminist criticism, which aimed to make a place on the critical agenda for the topics of women in society and in literature. With scholars like Dusinberre and Lisa Jardine in England and Carol Thomas Neely and Coppélia Kahn in North America, feminist criticism was from the start an international movement. Over the next ten years, most publications in this vein took a psychoanalytic approach to Shakespeare's characters, many developed from Freudian theories of family structures. The match seemed like a 'natural' one, because Freud had made gender and sexuality central subjects of interpretation and because he had explained so many of his relational models through examples from Shakespeare. As Madelon Gohlke Sprengnether also noted, both Freudian psychology and Elizabethan culture were patriarchal in nature. First-wave feminist authors identified instances in Shakespeare's plays that may have disrupted some patriarchal assumptions.

Most characteristic of feminist work on Othello at this time were essays on Desdemona that contested earlier criticism by championing her. Just as Leavis and others had found character flaws in Othello that accounted for his tragedy, so some critics had located

part of the responsibility with Desdemona. The first source of discomfort was her intimate scene with Emilia and her speculation that
Lodovico seems 'a proper man' (4.3). Eighteenth- and nineteenth-
century productions, fully committed to an innocent and pathetic
Desdemona, had deleted that discussion, along with her Willow
Song, as unseemly. By the twentieth century, critics were willing to
judge her more harshly and to include the scene as inculpatory evidence. There was a suspicious enthusiasm in Marvin Rosenberg's
summation of the case against her:

> Yet she too is partly responsible for the catastrophe. She has taken the
> initiative in marriage, has virtually proposed to Othello; she has
> deceived her father, has eloped against his wishes with a man of
> another race and color. She is certainly not 'proper'; and she too
> is touched with the erotic ambience of the play: when she listens to
> Iago's rowdy jokes on the Cyprus quay, when she lets Emilia discuss
> the virtues of adultery, in her love play with Othello, and in her
> undressing and bedroom scenes. She 'meddles' in her husband's busi-
> ness, presses him to reinstate his dismissed officer – presses him at the
> worst moment, when he most needs understanding. Finally, she lies to
> him, and destroys their hope of love.[6]

Others looked censoriously at Desdemona's final exoneration of
Othello (which in an earlier time had won sentimental approval for
its forbearance). Shirley Nelson Garner (1976), Sprengnether
(1980), Ann Jennalie Cook (1980) and Irene Dash (1981) came to
Desdemona's defence. Garner and Cook invoked a feminist reading
of the virgin/whore dichotomy in order to argue that Desdemona
was no more the goddess of Cassio's over-idealization than she was
the slut of Iago's slander.[7] Just how far we've now come from these
positions is illustrated in the essay by Harry Berger, Jr. (chapter 4) in
this collection.

Three first-wave feminist works were particularly influential. First,
Carolyn Ruth Swift Lenz, Gayle Greene and Carol Thomas Neely
edited a collection of essays, *The Woman's Part: Feminist Criticism
of Shakespeare* (1980) which showed how large and active the
new community of feminist scholars was. *Othello* featured in this
landmark of Shakespeare scholarship through Neely's own essay on
'Women and Men in *Othello*: "What should such a fool/Do with so
good a woman?"' (revised from a version of 1978). Like other first-
wave feminists, Neely wrote in appreciation of Desdemona's character and criticized the values and perspectives of male characters.

Second, in *Man's Estate: Masculine Identity in Shakespeare* (1981), Coppélia Kahn discussed the misogyny represented in Iago, in the play's double standard, and in its patriarchal view of marriage. Third, the clearest articulation of the relationship between feminist politics and literary criticism was brought forward by Linda Bamber, in *Comic Women, Tragic Men: A Study of Gender and Genre in Shakespeare* (1982).[8]

In subsequent years, feminist criticism was modified in significant ways. There was a prevailing sense, for example, that a more rigorous historical specificity was required, and general acknowledgement that even Shakespeare could not escape being a man of his time. Such concerns about anachronism and presentism in feminist analysis coincided with a larger movement towards the historicization of literary studies. Second-wave feminism, therefore, drew as much on social, economic and cultural history as on feminist theory. Literary texts were read in tandem with legal proscriptions on and conduct manuals for early modern women. At this stage, *Othello* was best represented by Peter Stallybrass's essay on 'Patriarchal Territories: The Body Enclosed', which appeared in a widely celebrated collection, *Rewriting the Renaissance: The Discourses of Sexual Difference in Early Modern Europe* (1986). This volume moved feminist criticism to a new level of theoretical sophistication and interpretive influence. Another key article was Karen Newman's ' "And wash the Ethiop white": Femininity and the Monstrous in *Othello*' (1987), which incorporated the subject of race into feminist analysis.[9] A number of the practitioners of second-wave feminism, though, have gone on to leave Shakespeare behind. In one of its most fertile branches, feminist scholarship has set out to rediscover writings by Renaissance women. Textual editors have been particularly important in this phase, as they make long-lost works newly available for research and pedagogy. The search for 'Shakespeare's sisters' continues to remake the canon of English literature.

Meanwhile, third-wave feminism moves the understanding of Shakespeare in three new directions. First, it often strikes a balance between the partisan politics that most characterized first-wave feminism and the victims' discourse that sometimes marked second-wave feminism. It acknowledges the manifold restrictions on women in early modern England while demonstrating how ineffective patriarchal doctrine sometimes was in circumscribing their daily lives. Second, it recognizes that masculinity is as much a construct as is femininity, and as subject to historical particularization. For this reason, critical practice in this field is now called 'gender studies' as often as feminist criticism. Third, it analyses the ways in which female gender – whether that of early modern women or of Shakespeare's women characters – intersects with other categories of difference, like class, ethnicity, age and region. In this valence it is sometimes termed 'difference feminism'. For such readings, *Othello* is a key Shakespearean text, with Emilia and Bianca as critical to an understanding of Jacobean gender politics as is Desdemona. Susan Snyder and Nina Rulon-Miller, for example, have interrogated Bianca's identification as 'a courtesan' in the First Folio's list of *dramatis personae*. This is certainly not how the character self-identifies; in fact, Bianca denies that she is a strumpet. If the label 'courtesan' was, as is most likely, added in the printing house rather than authored by Shakespeare, that fact provides a way of talking less about Bianca's individual character and more about how misogyny stereotypes women. And in *Othello*, as Lisa Jardine has pointed out, it stereotypes every one of them: Desdemona, Emilia and Bianca are all at various times accused of unchastity.[10] This is a theme that Lynda E. Boose elaborates in chapter 1 in this collection.

OTHELLO AND NEW HISTORICISM

In the same year that *The Woman's Part* gave evidence of the arrival of feminist criticism in Shakespeare studies, *Renaissance Self-Fashioning: From More to Shakespeare* was published (1980).[11] Stephen Greenblatt's monograph was the most significant book of the decade among Shakespeareans. Its influence has also extended into the twenty-first century and among scholars outside the field of Shakespeare. *Renaissance Self-Fashioning* introduced the mode of interpretation Greenblatt called 'New Historicism', and, in a chapter on 'The Improvisation of Power', *Othello* was central to the inception of this critical approach, as well. Greenblatt describes Othello as having fashioned his own identity through the tales he tells at Brabantio's house and before the Venetian Senate. These constructions are narrative and performative, but they are subverted both unintentionally by Desdemona's submission to them and deliberately by Iago's malign improvisations upon them. In this way *Othello* is crucial to Greenblatt's notion of an expanding sense of human identity in the Renaissance, as something that could be constructed and something that could be manipulated.

In its way of approaching texts, New Historicism distinguished itself from the New Criticism, which read literature in isolation from other cultural phenomena as an aesthetic object responsive to formalist analysis. So dominant had been New Criticism that those who practised it held something of a monopoly on the denomination 'critics', while those who continued to invoke historical perspectives were more likely to be called 'scholars'. These earlier historicists, though, had confined social, economic and political research to the realm of 'backgrounds' or 'contexts'. New Historicists revoked such privileging of literature, placing Shakespeare's great plays next to tracts on witchcraft, medical treatises and other contemporary works with small claim to aesthetic merit. Most often contested as an 'old' historicist is E. M. W. Tillyard, whose idea of history had been a history of ideas. Tillyard was politically conservative, unresistant and empirical in his descriptions of Tudor concepts of order and his convictions regarding the orderliness of Tudor society. Greenblatt and other New Historicists like Louis Montrose were unpersuaded that history can be so knowable, so tidy and so progressive. If, in the event, history cannot be captured in the standard methods of exhaustive research and statistical models, then it remains for historical meaning to be discovered in the telling event or marginal text. In hands less skilled than those of Greenblatt and Montrose, this has sometimes been labelled anecdotalism.

New Historicism claims some affinity with Marxist analysis, but it is most significantly aligned with the work of French theorist Michel Foucault and is influenced also by anthropologist Clifford Geertz. The title of Greenblatt's chapter on *Othello* indicates his Foucauldian interest in power: how it circulates, how it works to contain subversion, how it creates the illusion of individual freedoms of will and choice, how even the possessor of power is formed by its discourses and stratagems. New Historicists also attribute power to literature itself. Where Tillyard, for example, had figured poetry and drama as unproblematizing 'mirrors' of culture, New Historicists argue that literature performs important work in its culture. Montrose has referred to 'the Textuality of History, the Historicity of Texts'.[12]

The contours of New Historicism are fuzzier than those of some other critical approaches, in part because Greenblatt has resisted over-theorizing his practice. In fact, in subsequent years, he has come to refer to it as a 'cultural poetics' instead. Perhaps partly in consequence of its resistance to delimitation, though, New Historicism has interpenetrated successfully with other modes of criticism. Work like Montrose's ' "Shaping Fantasies": Figurations of Gender and Power in Elizabethan Culture' (1983) impacted feminist scholarship profoundly and empoweringly.[13] In the mid-1980s there was nonetheless a rift between New Historicism and feminism, as feminists decoded masculinist biases in the characteristic topics, themes and vocabularies of New Historicism. But the general historicization of literary studies that was impelled by the New Historicism had as strong an impact on feminism as on any other approach.

OTHELLO AND CULTURAL MATERIALISM

New Historicism is also often related to cultural materialism, a critical practice that is similarly motivated to read literature in culture, to analyse the relations of subversion and containment, and to interrogate the idea that there can be individual freedom in culture and outside acculturation. For cultural materialists, too, E. M. W. Tillyard was a flashpoint. Far more famously and pointedly than did any New Historicist, Jonathan Dollimore challenged Tillyard, as well as A. C. Bradley, T. S. Eliot and others, in his ground-breaking *Radical Tragedy: Religion, Ideology and Power in the Drama of Shakespeare and his Contemporaries* (1984). The next year, Dollimore co-edited with Alan Sinfield the important collection *Political Shakespeare: New Essays in Cultural Materialism* (1985).[14] With Dollimore and Sinfield as its founding voices, cultural materialism, like New Historicism, made its first marks in Shakespeare studies.

There were crucial differences between the two practices, however. The leading voices of New Historicism are North American while those of cultural materialism are British. Cultural materialists have displayed less pessimism about the potential for subversion to effect social change. In fact, much of the edge and energy in their work derives from a political activism in which the more scrupulously scholarly New Historicism has seemed uninterested. Cultural materialists are explicitly Marxist, indebted in the first instance to Raymond Williams and Fredric Jameson. New Historicists, true to their original denomination, locate literary texts fairly strictly within their original moment of production. Cultural materialists are far more concerned with the ideological work that literature, and especially such canonical literature as that by Shakespeare, effects in the present. Sinfield titled one of his better known essays 'Give an account of Shakespeare and Education, showing why you think they are effective and what you have appreciated about them. Support your comments with precise references' (1985). The irreverence is characteristic, but so, too, is the ambition to enter into dialogue with contemporary culture. The iconic stature of Shakespeare in Great Britain makes him irresistible as a subject for materialist analysis by British critics. As Jameson wrote, 'The encounter between Shakespeare and radical (or Marxist) criticism and theory is a two-way street: we find ourselves asking not merely what such critical theory has to tell us about Shakespeare ... but also what Shakespeare has to tell us about radical criticism'.[15]

Othello, however, was not one of the first texts to which the leading cultural materialists turned, and so the play has a somewhat shorter history in this arena than it has had in others. The most significant cultural-materialist intervention in *Othello* studies is represented in chapter 2 by Alan Sinfield. This comes from his stimulating 1992 book *Faultlines*, titled for a key stratagem of materialist analysis. Sinfield argues that the social order 'inevitably produces within itself' 'conflict and contradiction'. These constitute the gaps or 'faultlines' for which the materialist critic searches and from which dissident readings emerge. One such faultline, Sinfield illustrates, is the sexual double standard, as Emilia recognizes in *Othello*. Because of it, women have the power to 'produce a crisis in the patriarchal story' through their choice of a marriage partner, as Desdemona does, or by committing adultery, as Othello fears she does. In this essay, Sinfield also engages in illuminating ways with others of the critics discussed here, including New Historicists and first-wave feminists.

The interest of the cultural materialists in dissidence, resistance and subcultures means that they have made far more room in their practice for issues of gender, race, class and, especially, sexuality than did many New Historicists. The New Historicists' attention to power and authority often resulted in a top-down approach to history. By contrast, Dollimore and Sinfield are themselves major voices in the fields of gender studies and queer theory. And, from the first, there were critics who identified themselves as feminist cultural materialists. Dollimore and Sinfield's collection on *Political Shakespeare* included Kathleen McLuskie's influential 'The Patriarchal Bard', which focused on *King Lear* and *Measure for Measure*. Of more immediate relevance to this collection, there is 'Desire's Excess and the English Renaissance Theatre: *Edward II, Troilus and Cressida, Othello*' (1992), written by prominent materialist feminist

Catherine Belsey. In 1991, the American critic Valerie Wayne published a collection on *The Matter of Difference: Materialist Feminist Criticism of Shakespeare*, to which she contributed the rigorously positioned 'Historical Differences: Misogyny and *Othello*'. On Wayne's reading, there was a variety of attitudes towards women and marriage in the Renaissance, and *Othello*, too, represents a range of ideological positions on the subject. Iago's misogyny embodies but one strand. This was marked as problematic in the period – though it was also kept alive by every effort to stigmatize it. Similarly, Wayne warned, readers of *Othello* who focus too narrowly on Iago's misogyny risk reproducing it.[16]

OTHELLO AND POSTSTRUCTURALISM

Most of the critical practices discussed to this point depend to greater or lesser degrees on the poststructuralist practice of deconstruction. Alan Sinfield, for example, participates in deconstructing *Othello* when he says that we must refuse 'to help the text into coherence' rather than recognize the gaps and fissures that keep it from holding strictly together. Earlier criticism had worked to compel a piece of literature to make sense, often by reducing it down to a central or unifying thesis that was sometimes referred to as 'organic'. But Sinfield maintains that to undertake this sense-making process in *Othello* too often implicates readers in forming conclusions like the following: Othello is gullible 'because' people of colour are simple-minded, Desdemona becomes submissive 'because' women are weak, and Iago is malignant 'because' he is latently homosexual. To deconstruct a text is to foreground rather than to suppress the passages that invalidate this kind of reductive 'logic'. In the internal contradictions of a text can be found its dissident meanings. Texts do not require deconstruction, according to leading theorists; they require the recognition that they have already deconstructed themselves.

Jacques Derrida, the French philosopher who coined the term 'deconstruction', has also suggested that thought is organized by difference, in dichotomous pairs. Just to list some of the most obvious – black and white, male and female, cause and effect – is to recognize how apt they are to the structures of *Othello*. So, too, is the fact that, as Derrida further recognizes, these dichotomies are simultaneously hierarchies. In each pair, one is privileged, often in multiple and sometimes in quite subtle ways. If deconstructive critics seek to reverse the polarities, they do so briefly and for immediate effect, but with the more important objective of erasing the boundaries that hold them separate.

Othello was not a central text in the development of deconstruction, nor was any work of Shakespeare's. Rather, deconstruction was imported into the field by those influenced by Derrida's thought. It has since been employed to produce a range of critical effects in readings of *Othello*, as a short list of essays from the mid-1980s demonstrates. For example, Christopher Norris's 'Post-Structuralist Shakespeare: Text and Ideology' appeared in a major venue for the new critical approaches, *Alternative Shakespeares*, edited by John Drakakis (1985).[17] Just as F. R. Leavis chose *Othello* as the exemplary text for his 'primer for criticism', so Norris took the critical history of *Othello*, and especially Leavis's famous attack on A. C. Bradley, as his own case study for outlining a manifesto of poststructuralist practice. Norris argues that by contesting Bradley on his own ground – that is, by arguing with Bradley's reading of Othello's character – Leavis fell into the particular jeopardy of character criticism, which leaves critics 'no choice but to occupy positions already taken up by characters in the play'. In this way, Leavis's vitriol towards Bradley replicates the 'drama' played out between Othello and Iago. The dichotomy of Bradley and Leavis, on Norris's view and in deconstructive terms, is no dichotomy at all.

More influentially, two poststructuralist essays from the 1980s have provided rewarding perspectives on the play itself. Patricia Parker co-edited *Shakespeare and the Question of Theory* with Geoffrey Hartman (1985). As with *The Woman's Part* and *The Matter of Difference*, here, too, the editor of a collection of essays took *Othello* for the subject of her own contribution, 'Shakespeare and Rhetoric: "Dilation" and "Delation" in *Othello*'.[18] Parker teases out the exfoliating significances of 'dilate' and 'delate', which include amplification, delay and accusation. In this essay, the use of close reading and an emphasis on rhetoric show the relationship between deconstruction and formalism – like the New Critics, many deconstructionists avoid looking outside the text to such contexts as history or biography. But where New Criticism sought ambiguity and irony as elements of a work's coherent effects, deconstructionists like Parker find contradiction, irresolution and irreducibly multiple meanings.

The work of Joel Fineman represents poststructuralism in another of its aspects, as influenced by the thought of French psychoanalytic theorist Jacques Lacan. Fineman's 'The Sound of O in *Othello*: The Real of the Tragedy of Desire' (1988) focuses on language in the play, and especially the sound on which Othello's name begins and ends, to discuss the issues of will, desire and Shakespeare's literary personae. This essay was subsequently reprinted in a collection on what Fineman termed 'the subjectivity effect' in literature.[19] There, he brought to bear on Shakespeare's sonnets the Freudian insight that we are not agents in control of our own discourse. The speaker of the sonnets, in Fineman's reading, is not a pre-existing subject but rather an after-effect of linguistic production. The continuing interest in early modern subjectivities is represented in Elizabeth Hanson's chapter in this collection.

OTHELLO AND POSTCOLONIAL CRITICISM

Patricia Parker went on to co-edit a second collection, *Women, 'Race,' and Writing in the Early Modern Period* (1994), for which she again contributed an essay on *Othello*: 'Fantasies of "Race" and "Gender": Africa, *Othello*, and Bringing to Light'. Her co-editor, Margo Hendricks, has also published on the play, in ' "The Moor of Venice", or the Italian on the Renaissance English Stage' (1996). With other authors like Dympna Callaghan, Michael Neill, Jyotsna Singh and Virginia Mason Vaughan, Hendricks and Parker have brought to *Othello* important advances in our understanding of concepts of 'race' in the Renaissance.[20]

Dympna Callaghan titled her essay, 'Othello Was a White Man' (1996), for the infamous remarks of a Miss Preston: 'It is true the dramatist paints him black, but this shade does not suit the man. It is a stage decoration, which *my taste* discards; a fault of colour from an artistic point of view. ... Shakespeare was too correct a delineator of human nature to have coloured Othello *black*, if he had personally acquainted himself with the idiosyncrasies of the African race. ... Othello *was* a *white* man'. M. R. Ridley, the editor of what was for years the preferred text of the play for academics, wrote condescendingly of this 'reductio ad absurdum' from the 'lady writing from Maryland'. He then went on to offer his own thoughts on the subject, in a manner that has become thoroughly notorious:

> There are more races than one in Africa, and that a man is black in colour is no reason why he should, even to European eyes, look sub-human. One of the finest heads I have ever seen on any human being was that of a negro conductor on an American Pullman car. He had lips slightly thicker than an ordinary European's, and he had

somewhat curly hair; for the rest ... he might have sat to a sculptor for a statute of Caesar, or, so far as appearance went, have played a superb Othello.

In 'Othello and the "Plain Face" of Racism' (1987), Martin Orkin wrote on this and other instances of racial bigotry in the earlier critical tradition.[21] Like feminist criticism, with its defences of Desdemona, race studies and postcolonial criticism in their first phases were concerned to expose and overturn the long record of colour prejudice in readings of Othello.

As currently practised, postcolonial criticism has three aspects. First, it continues to investigate the complex history of European concepts of race, nation and difference. Othello makes a challenging subject of analysis, because it involves the English idea of Moors – which may have been geographic or may have been religious – as well as English images of peoples from Venice, Africa, Barbary, Cyprus and Turkey. Some of these ideas and images were formed in the sensational travel and 'discovery' narratives published in Shakespeare's time; these certainly lay behind Othello's exoticized personal history. As postcolonial critics have shown, the contact histories of the early modern period had ideological uses in England as well as educational ones. Global exploration coincided with an era of growing national consciousness, and a signal method of self-definition was to differentiate what was English from what was not English. Because this was an evolving process, it is difficult to fix not only what Jacobeans might have imagined a Moor to be but also what being a Moor meant to them. The chapter by Emily Bartels in this collection speaks to this issue.

Postcolonial criticism also, second, studies the modern reception of Shakespeare's plays in non-European countries, especially among native populations in Africa, the Caribbean, Latin America, Australia, New Zealand and India. Shakespeare was introduced into regions colonized by England as a vital element of British 'civilizing' projects. In consequence, Shakespeare now constitutes a sort of universal language even in the aftermath of decolonization. But postcolonial critics look at the way Shakespeare has been appropriated for local uses that the colonizers would never have planned for. Through borrowings and adaptations, Shakespeare serves as a medium of cultural exchange, introducing non-Western works and perspectives into the Western literary tradition. Jyotsna Singh analyses two reworkings of Othello in her chapter in this collection.

Third, the issues of race and colonialism also come urgently to the forefront in discussions of *Othello*'s performance history. In chapter 8 in this collection, Barbara Hodgdon examines two staged (later filmed) interpretations of *Othello*, one performed in South Africa and one in England, but both given colonial settings. Also in this collection (chapter 9), Denise Albanese, like Hodgdon, addresses the central casting issue of the play, which is the race of the actor playing the title role. Up to the 1980s Othello was typically played by a white actor in blackface. One of the most famous was Laurence Olivier, who, in an intriguing display of the circulation of academic criticism in larger culture, based his characterization on F. R. Leavis's old portrayal of Othello's 'simple-mindedness'.

OTHELLO IN PUBLIC CULTURE

In his autobiography, Olivier describes the process of preparing himself to play the part of Othello by anointing his body with 'Max Factor 2880, then a lighter brown, then Negro No. 2, a stronger brown.... Then the great trick: that glorious half-yard of chiffon with which I polished myself all over until I shone'. He represents himself as having fallen deeply under the spell of his own metamorphosis: 'the black, black sheen that covered my flesh and bones, glistening in the dressing-room lights.... I am, I...I am Othello'. Then, too abruptly, he interrupts the threatened loss of his own identity in this mystified otherness: 'but Olivier is in charge. The actor is in control'.[22]

Olivier's transparent anxiety about maintaining his (civilized) control over a (savage) character is not unique. In a metadramatic film of 1934, *Men Are Not Gods*, an actor playing Othello decides to dispose of his wife in order to pursue another woman; he has the opportunity to hand because his wife is playing Desdemona, and so he attempts to disguise murder as an onstage accident during the play's violent closing scene. The implications of this fantastic adaptation of *Othello* are more explicit in its remake, the 1948 film *A Double Life*. In the latter film, for which lead actor Ronald Colman won an Academy Award, it was the very experience of playing Othello that plunged the actor into a murderous psychosis.

The premise behind each film seems to be exactly that about which Olivier was so anxious: the terrible superstition among white people that to inhabit darker skin is to turn savage, to lose control and reason. One of the few black actors to play the part before the

1980s, Paul Robeson was described in early performances as having 'ceased to be human and become a gibbering primeval man'. As his performance developed, however, he was faulted on the very grounds that he was *insufficiently* 'savage'. One reviewer, who commented pejoratively that 'the core of violence is lacking', seemed to share a general belief that for an actor to be convincing in the part he must be, in Ridley's old words, 'sub-human'. In chapter 3 in this collection, Michael D. Bristol discusses Othello's race as an accident of the text, in that it is not required to motivate the tragedy. But he recognizes, as all responses to *Othello* continue to show, that race is essential to its meanings.

Men Are Not Gods and *A Double Life* are aspects of *Othello's* afterlife in contemporary society. This has become an important site of investigation in Shakespeare studies. If *The Merchant of Venice* has particular resonances in Germany and if Caliban has had a sympathetic meaning in Africa, *Othello* has featured regularly in American popular culture. Two examples of its continuing circulation return us to the point with which reactions to *Othello* began: the emotional power of the play. In the collision of its issues – sex, race, violence – race most often appears to be the incendiary element.

In 1991, for the first instance, the George H. W. Bush White House nominated Clarence Thomas to fill a vacancy on the United States Supreme Court.[23] Thomas's confirmation hearings in the US Senate notoriously included an investigation into charges that he had sexually harassed a professional colleague, Anita Hill. Hill had worked for Thomas and had been denied a promotion by him. Various analogies were deployed during the Senate hearings, all of them competing to mould public and congressional opinion about the conflicting testimonies regarding Thomas and Hill. Thomas's supporters, for example, sought to depict Hill as a scorned woman with a 'fatal attraction' (a reference to the 1987 movie in which Glenn Close's character turns violently vindictive when Michael Douglas's character tries to end an affair with her). Thomas's up-from-poverty personal history was strategically exaggerated when he was termed the 'black Horatio Alger' (an allusion to the series of nineteenth-century juvenile novels that preached the rewards of hard work). This analogy's effectiveness was mitigated by the fact that Hill's own success story was at least as compelling. Thomas also did what has since been called 'playing the race card', probing the unhealed wounds of the country's racial history by calling the Senate proceedings a 'high-tech lynching'. And Senator Alan Simpson introduced yet another narrative construction by quoting from *Othello*:

> I tell you I do [think] Shakespeare would love this. This is all Shakespeare. This is about love and hate and cheating and distrust and kindness and disgust and avarice and jealousy and envy – all those things that make that remarkable bard read today. But, boy, I tell you one thing came to my head and I just went and got it out of the back of the book, *Othello*. Read *Othello* and don't ever forget this line. 'Good name in man and woman dear, my Lord' – remember this scene – 'is the immediate jewel of their souls. Who steals my purse steals trash; T'is [sic] something, nothing; T'was [sic] mine, t'is [sic] his and has been slave to thousands. But he that filches from me my good name robs me of that which not enriches him and makes me poor indeed.' What a tragedy! What a disgusting tragedy!

The remarks raise obvious questions. Did Simpson realize he was quoting Iago and not Othello? Had he (or a staffer) simply found *Othello* under 'reputation' in *Bartlett's Familiar Quotations* and seized upon it without knowing its context? *Othello* may have seemed apt because Thomas was black, but could there have been any intention to invoke the parallel that both had white wives (given what happens to Desdemona)? Virginia Thomas was seated prominently throughout the hearings, just behind her husband.

All this suggests ignorance or ineptitude on Simpson's part. In fact, as Peggy Anne Russo has suggested, the *Othello* analogy may have been shrewdly deployed for reasons peculiar to its local context. As she observes, the two opposing camps had 'abandoned the search for veracity and focused instead on motives for mendacity'. For Thomas's supporters, it was an inspired stroke to depict Hill as Iago and, thus, imaginatively to impute to her Iago's motives for malignancy. A few months earlier, the Washington Shakespeare Theatre, then located a block away from the seat of Congress, had staged a celebrated production of *Othello* with Avery Brooks as the title character and Andre Braugher as Iago. African-American director Harold Scott had cast African-Americans in both roles as a way, he said, of making Othello's susceptibility to Iago's 'poison' more credible. For many Washingtonians, in other words, their most recent encounter with *Othello* would have featured a black Iago. For the analogical purposes of Thomas's allies, race trumped gender, making the connection between Iago and Hill more plausible. Moreover, as Russo also points out, for those inside the Beltway, 'personal ambition makes a better bedfellow with power politics than does passion'. Evocation of *Othello* worked to deflect attention away from sexual harassment allegedly committed by Thomas and to professional frustration putatively felt by Hill when she was not promoted. Hill was re-narrativized as 'bent on revenge not because of thwarted passion but because of thwarted ambition'.

Thomas was approved as a Supreme Court justice, but over ten years later American popular opinion remains profoundly divided as to whether his or Hill's was the true story. This irresolution, Russo concludes, could indicate that no one of the many shaping narratives in circulation proved 'conclusive'. In particular, because other regions of the country had no immediate reference point in the Washington Shakespeare Theatre production, the analogy to *Othello* proved too murky to carry a full burden of explanatory significance beyond Capitol Hill. This would not be the case three years later, when *Othello* once again informed a national scandal, the trial of O. J. Simpson for the murder of his ex-wife Nicole Brown Simpson.

In chapters 8 and 9, both Barbara Hodgdon and Denise Albanese refer to what was called 'the trial of the century' in America. Nicole Brown Simpson and Ronald Goldman were brutally killed outside the home she had occupied since divorcing her husband. Simpson was a retired football hero, sometime actor and sports-caster, and celebrity spokesperson. Under suspicion for the murder, Simpson refused to surrender himself to police, who trailed him through one long afternoon for what was always termed a 'low-speed chase' along the highways of Los Angeles. The police exercised caution because Simpson's friend, at the wheel of Simpson's white Ford Bronco, reported that O. J. was crouched with a gun to his head in the back. As the 'chase' progressed, crowds gathered on highway overpasses holding makeshift signs of sympathetic identifi-cation: 'Save the Juice' ('Juice' had been his nickname as a Heisman Trophy-winning running back) and 'Run, O. J., Run' (this was the slogan for a Hertz advertising campaign that had punned visually on Simpson's football technique).

The story of celebrity, scandal, violence and suspense was gripping, and for some time unraced. Few people were aware that Simpson's ex-wife had been white. Colour was not introduced into the narrative until a television anchor made the connection to *Othello*: a black man marries a white woman, murders her, and commits suicide. Simpson did not kill himself, but he penned a rambling suicide note: 'If we had a problem, it's because I loved her so much' ('speak / Of one that lov'd not wisely, but too well'), and 'Please think of the real O. J. and not this lost person' ('That's he that was Othello; here I am').

The trial was a media extravaganza. After sitting through nine months of evidence, arguments and sensation, on 2 October 1995 the jurors acquitted Simpson in short order. One of his lawyers, Johnnie Cochran, had played 'the race card' with conspicuous success. He was aided in no small part by revelations of the bigotry of L. A. policeman Mark Fuhrman, the Simpson trial's Iago. Later, the families of the victims, the Browns and the Goldmans, brought a civil suit against Simpson. On 4 February 1997, he was judged guilty of committing battery and wrongful death. With opposite verdicts in the criminal and civil courts, this case, like that of Clarence Thomas, was left publicly unresolved. Private opinions tended to divide along racial lines. Meri Nana-Ama Danquah, however, decoded a shared national investment in O. J. Simpson's story: he 'more than any other black hero or celebrity, embodies the idea, the dream, the illusion – call it whatever you want – that we as a nation have transcended race'.[24] Simpson had been so successful a pitchman because, as he said, 'Hertz told me in all their surveys that I was colorless'. But this trial for a brutal act of violence re-raced him. And it proved, as *Othello* continues to prove and as responses to *Othello* continue to prove, how much race still matters. *Othello*'s meanings in contemporary culture are far from exhausted.

THIS COLLECTION

The essays in this volume follow from the works that revolutionized Shakespeare study in the 1980s. They demonstrate the play's continued currency in the classroom and in public culture. There are essentially two clusters: one on the topics of gender and marriage, with essays by Lynda E. Boose, Alan Sinfield, Michael D. Bristol, Harry Berger, Jr., and Elizabeth Hanson; and one on race and reception, with essays by Emily Bartels, Jyotsna Singh, Barbara Hodgdon, and Denise Albanese. This is a small selection of new approaches to *Othello*; for more on the play's critical history, suggestions for 'Further Reading' are appended.

NOTES

1. Jackson and Pepys are excerpted by Gamini Salgado (and Jackson is translated by him from the Latin) in *Eyewitnesses of Shakespeare: First Hand Accounts of Performances 1590–1890* (London: Sussex University

Press, 1975), pp. 30, 49. For the Baltimore soldier, see Edward Pechter, *Othello and Interpretive Traditions* (Iowa City: University of Iowa Press, 1999), p. 12, and see the analysis by Michael D. Bristol in this collection. Julie Hankey quotes Margaret Webster in *'Othello': Plays in Performance* (Bristol: Bristol Classical Press, 1987), p. 1. Rymer is quoted frequently; see, for instance, Lynda E. Boose, 'Othello's Handkerchief: "The Recognizance and Pledge of Love" ', *English Literary Renaissance*, 5 (1975), p. 360.

2. A. C. Bradley, *Shakespearean Tragedy: Lectures on 'Hamlet', 'Othello', 'King Lear', 'Macbeth'*, 2nd edn. (1905; New York: St. Martin's Press, 1967), pp. 176, 185.

3. Estelle W. Taylor charged in 1984 that the 'uneasiness' of *Othello's* most influential critics – not only Bradley but also F. R. Leavis, T. S. Eliot, and others – was in fact 'a form of racism'. 'Treating Othello as if he were a man of their acquaintance or a case study', she wrote, these readers used common racial stereotypes to describe him: a 'savage', a 'black puppet', and a 'fool'. Newer, more political and more theoretical ways of reading literature have developed strategies for resisting this sort of character criticism – though they are not interested to argue, as Taylor does, that Othello has been unfairly denied his stature as a tragic hero. See 'The Masking in *Othello* and Unmasking the Criticism of *Othello*', *Shakespeare Newsletter* (Winter 1984), 42.

4. Cited above, note 1.

5. Juliet Dusinberre, *Shakespeare and the Nature of Women* (London: Macmillan, 1975).

6. Marvin Rosenberg, *The Masks of 'Othello': The Search for the Identity of Othello, Iago, and Desdemona by Three Centuries of Actors and Critics* (Berkeley: University of California Press, 1961), pp. 6, 7.

7. S. N. Garner, 'Shakespeare's Desdemona', *Shakespeare Studies*, 9 (1976), 233–52. Ann Jennalie Cook, 'The Design of Desdemona: Doubt Raised and Resolved', *Shakespeare Studies*, 13 (1980), 187–96. Madelon Gohlke [Sprengnether], ' "And when I love thee not": Women and the Psychic Integrity of the Tragic Hero', *Hebrew University Studies in Literature*, 8 (1980), 44–65. Irene Dash, 'A Woman Tamed: *Othello*', chapter 5 of *Wooing, Wedding, and Power: Women in Shakespeare's Plays* (New York: Columbia University Press, 1981), pp. 103–30.

8. Carol Thomas Neely, 'Women and Men in *Othello*: "What should such a fool / Do with so good a woman?" ' in *The Woman's Part: Feminist Criticism of Shakespeare*, ed. Carolyn Ruth Swift Lenz, Gayle Greene and Carol Thomas Neely (Urbana: University of Illinois Press, 1980), pp. 211–39. Coppélia Kahn, *Man's Estate: Masculine Identity in Shakespeare* (Berkeley: University of California Press, 1981). Linda Bamber, *Comic Women, Tragic Men: A Study of Gender and Genre in Shakespeare* (Stanford: Stanford University Press, 1982).

9. Peter Stallybrass, 'Patriarchal Territories: The Body Enclosed', in *Rewriting the Renaissance: The Discourses of Sexual Difference in Early Modern Europe*, ed. Margaret W. Ferguson, Maureen Quilligan and Nancy J. Vickers (Chicago: University of Chicago Press, 1986), pp. 123–42. Karen Newman, ' "And wash the Ethiop white": Femininity and the Monstrous in *Othello*', in *Shakespeare Reproduced: The Text in History and Ideology*, ed. Jean E. Howard and Marion F. O'Connor (New York and London: Methuen, 1987), pp. 142–62.

10. See Susan Snyder's 'A Modern Perspective' in the New Folger Library *Othello*, ed. Barbara A. Mowat and Paul Werstine (New York: Washington Square Press, 1993), p. 296, and, for a thorough review of Bianca's critical history, Nina Rulon-Miller, '*Othello*'s Bianca: Climbing Out of the Bed of Patriarchy', *The Upstart Crow*, 15 (1995), 99–114. And see Lisa Jardine, ' "Why should he call her whore?": Defamation and Desdemona's Case', in *Addressing Frank Kermode: Essays in Criticism and Interpretation*, ed. Margaret Tudeau-Clayton and Martin Warner (London: Macmillan, 1991).

11. Stephen Greenblatt, *Renaissance Self-Fashioning: From More to Shakespeare* (Chicago: University of Chicago Press, 1980).

12. Louis Montrose, 'The Politics and Poetics of Culture', in *The New Historicism*, ed. H. Aram Vesser (New York and London: Routledge, 1989), p. 21.

13. Louis Montrose, ' "Shaping Fantasies": Figurations of Gender and Power in Elizabethan Culture', *Representations*, 1:2 (Spring 1983), 61–94.

14. Jonathan Dollimore, *Radical Tragedy: Religion, Ideology and Power in the Drama of Shakespeare and his Contemporaries* (Brighton: Harvester Press, 1984). Jonathan Dollimore and Alan Sinfield, eds., *Political Shakespeare: New Essays in Cultural Materialism* (Manchester: Manchester University Press, 1985).

15. Fredric Jameson, 'Radicalizing Radical Shakespeare: The Permanent Revolution in Shakespeare Studies', in *Material Shakespeare: A History*, ed. Ivo Kamps (London: Verso, 1995).

16. Kathleen McLuskie, 'The Patriarchal Bard: Feminist Criticism and Shakespeare: *King Lear* and *Measure for Measure*', in *Political Shakespeare: New Essays in Cultural Materialism*, ed. Jonathan Dollimore and Alan Sinfield (Manchester: Manchester University Press, 1985), pp. 88–108. Catherine Belsey, 'Desire's Excess and the English Renaissance Theatre: *Edward II, Troilus and Cressida, Othello*', in *Erotic Politics: Desire on the Renaissance Stage*, ed. Susan Zimmerman (New York and London: Routledge, 1992), pp. 84–102. Valerie Wayne, 'Historical Difference: Misogyny and *Othello*', in *The Matter of Difference: Materialist Feminist Criticism of Shakespeare*, ed. Valerie Wayne (Ithaca: Cornell University Press, 1991), pp. 153–79.

17. Christopher Norris, 'Post-Structuralist Shakespeare: Text and Ideology', in *Alternative Shakespeares*, ed. John Drakakis (London and New York: Methuen, 1985), pp. 47–66. This volume was succeeded by *Alternative Shakespeares II*, edited by Terence Hawkes (London: Routledge, 1996).

18. Patricia Parker, 'Shakespeare and Rhetoric: "Dilation" and "Delation" in *Othello*', in *Shakespeare and the Question of Theory*, ed. Patricia Parker and Geoffrey Hartman (New York and London: Methuen, 1985), pp. 54–74.

19. Joel Fineman, 'The Sound of O in *Othello*: The Real of the Tragedy of Desire', *October*, 45 (1988), 76–96. Joel Fineman, *The Subjectivity Effect in Western Literary Tradition: Essays toward the Release of Shakespeare's Will* (Cambridge, MA: MIT Press, 1991).

20. Some key works by these authors include: Dympna Callaghan, ' "Othello Was a White Man": Properties of Race on Shakespeare's Stage', in *Alternative Shakespeares II*, ed. Terence Hawkes (London and New York: Routledge, 1996), pp. 192–215; Margo Hendricks, ' "The Moor of Venice", or the Italian on the Renaissance English Stage', in *Alternative Shakespeares II*, pp. 193–209; Michael Neill, 'Unproper Beds: Race, Adultery, and the Hideous in *Othello*', *Shakespeare Quarterly*, 40 (1989), 383–412; Patricia Parker, 'Fantasies of "Race" and "Gender": Africa, *Othello*, and Bringing to Light', in *Women, 'Race' and Writing in the Early Modern Period*, ed. Margo Hendricks and Patricia Parker (London: Routledge, 1994), pp. 84–100; Virginia Mason Vaughan, *'Othello': A Contextual History* (Cambridge: Cambridge University Press, 1994).

21. M. R. Ridley, 'Introduction' to the Arden Shakespeare *Othello*, ed. M. R. Ridley (London: Methuen, 1958), p. li. Martin Orkin, '*Othello* and the "Plain Face" of Racism', *Shakespeare Quarterly*, 38 (1987), 166–88.

22. Quoted by Barbara Hodgdon (chapter 8 in this collection), p. 194.

23. For the following discussion I am indebted to (and also quote Alan Simpson from) Peggy Anne Russo, '*Othello* Goes to Washington: Cultural Politics and the Thomas/Hill Affair', *Journal of American Culture*, 17:4 (Winter 1994), 15–22.

24. Meri Nana-Ama Danquah, 'Why We Really Root for O. J.', *Washington Post*, 3 July 1994, C9.

1

'Let it be Hid': The Pornographic Aesthetic of Shakespeare's *Othello*

LYNDA E. BOOSE

> Utter my thoughts? Why, say they are vile and false:
> As where's that palace, whereinto foul things
> Sometimes intrude not? who has a breast so pure,
> But some uncleanly apprehensions
> Keep leets and law-days, and in session sit
>   With meditations lawful?
>   (*Othello* 3.3.140–5)[1]

The final act of *Othello* visually confronts its audience with what is arguably the most unforgettable stage tableau in all of Shakespeare. Before the forces of institutional morality burst in and feebly attempt to assert control over the chaos of the bedroom, the audience has been led into the forbidden space of this hitherto offstage room – the imagined chamber towards which the play has always pointed, the place which it has repeatedly eroticized, and the space which until now it has kept discreetly hidden, blocked from audience view behind one of a number of fictive doors that we have consented to imagine. In the closing act, when the final door to the play's last bedroom figuratively swings open, we are allowed/compelled to be the only witnesses to the act of erotic violence that we have already been induced to see: Desdemona strangled on her wedding sheets, dying in suggestive paroxysms in the violent embrace of the alien black husband.

22

All Shakespearean tragedy ends with control returning to the representative forces of social order. But in the other tragedies, those forces are not only considerably more successful, but they conclude the play by paying tribute to, not trying to erase and avoid, the tableau of tragic violence: Hamlet is elevated to the stage like a soldier and given funeral accolades; Lear's endurance receives an awed encomium from the play's survivors; Octavius Caesar grudgingly orders that tribute be paid to Antony and Cleopatra before ordering everyone back to Rome; and even the spiked head of the slaughterous Macbeth is implicitly honoured as it is raised up to tower over the victors below. By contrast, the ending of *Othello* provides no eulogy but only what New Cambridge editor Norman Sanders calls 'Cassio's lip service remark, "For [Othello] was great of heart", standing for the final panegyric'.[2] Moreover, beyond even the omitted tribute, what this play's concluding spokesman presents as formula for the reassertion of order is an explicit indictment of not only the tragic loading on the bed but those who watch it – the viewers who are, implicitly, the play's own audience: 'The object poisons sight, / Let it be hid' (5.2.365–6). The play then concludes in aversion and avoidance, with Lodovico beating a hasty retreat, determined to cover up the picture on the bed and then go 'straight aboard, and to the state' (371), avoiding as quickly as possible that condemned sign of a now hidden sign, the bed and its euphemized 'loading' (F) or 'lodging' (Q1 and 2) that are together said to poison sight.

In the final moments of this play, the 'object' of such consternation and that which infects its watchers is ultimately identified as the 'work' of Iago, the figure from whom most of the play's ubiquitous commands to 'look ... watch ... see' have emanated and the nasty little fellow to whom an audience owes a substantial amount of its own fascination with this particular Shakespeare tragedy. From *Othello*'s opening scene, the audience's ears have been filled with references to 'looking', usually spoken by Iago and repeatedly phrased in either the imperative that commands the listener's visual attention, or in rhetorical questions that solicit it while simultaneously assuming compliance. The 'look' command, since Iago's initial use of it on Brabantio, has been, throughout the play, directed towards an increasingly sexualized image, yet an image that, until the final act, has been available only through the participatory act of imagining it. Only with Lodovico's last use of the ubiquitous injunction – 'Look on the tragic loading of this bed' (364–5) – does the command make contact with its at-last literal and concrete referent, the sexual scene now elevated in mute display on the play's at-last visible bed. But precisely as the fetishized object of aesthetic gratification becomes visually available to its viewers, that same spectacle is suddenly condemned, enclosed, and the watchers of it, rebuked – 'the object poisons sight, / Let it be hid'. And at this moment, the inclusive implication of Iago's earlier rhetorical questions, such as the one that appears here as epigraph, should likewise become clear. To Othello's increasingly voyeuristic demands to 'Make me to see't, or at the least so prove it...' (3.3.370), where proof becomes merely an after-thought to seeing, and to his pleas for a 'satisfaction' that is increas-ingly bound up with 'ocular proof', Iago had responded with a damning question that explicitly implicates the audience in his tawdry pact: 'Would you, the supervisor, grossly gape on? / Behold her topped?' (3.3.395–7). By the end of this play, the audience – the ultimate 'super-visors' of it – have indeed grossly gaped.[3]

Yet in taking the audience through that final fictive door and into the bedroom space to be discovered within the voyeuristic fantasy they came to see, this tragedy fulfils the aesthetic conditions which, again in Iago's voice, it had explicitly laid out:

> What then? How then?
> What shall I say? Where's satisfaction?
> It is impossible you should see this,
> Were they as prime as goats, as hot as monkeys,
> As salt as wolves in pride, and fools as gross
> As ignorance made drunk. But yet, I say,
> If imputation and strong circumstances,
> Which lead directly to the door of truth,
> Will give you satisfaction, you might have't.
>   (3.3.401–9)

As most academics who teach Shakespeare know, the question the observant student wants to ask is the prurient one that is built into the text of this play: whether Othello and Desdemona did or did not consummate their marriage. The question is unavoidable. It is layered into the dynamics of the drama in a way that it is not, for instance, in *Romeo and Juliet*. Because we know what happened in Juliet's bedroom, the consummation never becomes an issue of obsessive curiosity to the audience. The dramatic construction of *Othello*, however, seduces its readers and watchers into mimicking Iago's first question to Othello: 'Are you fast married?' (1.2.11). What is important is not any presumed answer to the question, which can probably be argued either way. What is important is the fact that we need to ask it.

If *Hamlet* is, as Stephen Booth has famously said, a play about an audience that can't make up its mind,[4] then *Othello* is one about an audience that finds itself aroused by, trapped within and ultimately castigated for its prurience. And the audience implied by this play and structured into it from its opening scene is definitively masculine in gender: from Iago's arousal of the first male watcher of the play with his injunction to 'Look to your house, your daughter, and your bags' (1.1.80), men are the lookers and women are the objects to be looked at, trapped within and constructed by the pornographic images transmitted inside of an increasingly lethal circuitry of male discourse that is constructed by and itself constructs this play's disturbing male bond.

The dynamic linking any play to its audience is no doubt inherently a voyeuristic suture. But *Othello* exploits that linkage more relentlessly than does any other play in the canon. And although images of erotic violence enacted on a bed may be all too familiar by the twenty-first century to make us uneasy with what they invite, my own rough survey of pre-Shakespearean playscripts suggests that *Othello* may have been one of the first (extant) plays of its kind in English drama.[5] Although in pre-*Othello* plays an audience might hear about some salacious act that had occurred offstage, texts and prop records indicate that before *Othello* the bed had, in general, been restricted on stage to its use as a deathbed – as a place for kings like Henry IV to die. *A Woman Killed With Kindness* and the arbour scene in *The Spanish Tragedy* might both be candidates for the first sexually suggestive stagings of the bed with the woman on it. But nothing extant prior to *Othello* approximates its use as a staging area for sexual violence, a kind of drama that collapses the poles of the word 'death' and brings to full representation the orgasmic undertones always present in the Elizabethan use of this term.[6] And Shakespeare's apparent transgression of the previously observed limits of stage decorum may itself have served as something of a catalyst to open the way for the sex and violence sensationalism that shortly afterwards flooded the Jacobean and later the Restoration stage.

In *Othello*, Shakespeare seems to have been shaping a new kind of dramaturgy. Through a dramatic construction that critics from A. C. Bradley on have uneasily recognized as being somehow 'different' from that of the other major tragedies,[7] this play holds up a mirror that mercilessly exposes the complicity of the audience's spectatorship.

On the first two of the three successive bridal nights of the play's construction, Othello and Desdemona are isolated behind the bedroom door while the audience of watchers is turned over to the control of Iago, positioned as participants in the increasingly violent, masculine anti-epithalamion he orchestrates without. The spatial design solicits attention inward. More damningly, however, the voyeuristic desire for *dramatic* satisfaction aroused by the construction of the first two nights compels the action of the climactic third one and implicates the play's watchers in the amorphous 'cause' that Othello's lines allude to as he enters the bedroom on the final night, bringing with him not only the violence from the street outside but, at long last, the voyeuristic desires of the audience: 'It is the cause, it is the cause' (5.2.1).

It is in the bedroom where this play consummates its union with its audience – and that same space of viewer gratification is where the play likewise dis-covers the audience as its 'guilty creatures sitting at a play', left at the end of the fantasy castigated for their voyeurism and, as the forces of moral order exit for Venice, dramatically abandoned within the indicted fantasy. Characteristically, in what one might even call nearly a condition of Shakespearean tragic catharsis, a Shakespeare tragedy always provides, at closure, a viable secondary figure in whom the masculine desires of the audience may find a sufficiently heroic site for transfer and displacement.[8] But in *Othello*, there is no Horatio, no Macduff, no Edgar, no Octavius, nor are there any other mitigatingly heroic rituals available to absorb the masculine anxieties that this tragedy seems designed to arouse. The figure who occupies the requisite structural position in *Othello* is Cassio, but Cassio's all too apparent character weaknesses plus the fact that the play leaves him disabled and implicitly rendered impotent by the wound in his thigh, all work to disqualify him as any kind of acceptable model. By refusing to provide any such escape hatch, the play leaves its audience trapped within a highly problematic identity polarized between Othello and Iago. And it seems likely that this uncomfortable male position is the key gender factor that, along with the racial factor, has worked to give *Othello* a special place in the 400 years of Shakespearean cultural legacy.

In performance, *Othello* has been simultaneously one of the most popular of all the plays and one that has also disturbed its audiences in peculiarly noteworthy ways, confronting them as it does with the taboo issues of not only sexual violence but the ugliness of racism played off against the deepest white racist fears of miscegenation.[9]

Yet another factor that no doubt accounts for the peculiar anxieties that have historically attended *Othello* is the way it substantively differs from its counterparts in its refusal to gratify the audience's need for the retributive justice that is an important condition for the dispersal of anxiety and aggression that is in drama called catharsis. Not only do the forces of political order refuse to legitimate the role of *Othello*'s watchers, but they refuse to mete out any genuine retribution to the salacious little villain whose 'work' has lured the audience into the space of condemnation. With the exceptions of Aaron the Moor and Iago, all of Shakespeare's tragic villains repent their evil; but Aaron is sentenced to a horrific death, while Iago – as opposed to all other villains in the tragedies – exits the play neither killed on stage nor with any such condign punishment even suggested. What ultimately is most problematic about Iago is the audience's own relation to him – something that might be called, in D. H. Lawrence's phrase, 'the fascination of the revulsion'.

Despite the fact that from the play's opening scene the audience has been aware of the sordidly vicious, misogynist and racist nature of the vision that this 'Ensign' holds up as a standard for all men to rally around, it is nonetheless to this same jocularly obscene, inexplicably attractive force of malignity that all male characters in the text are drawn and to whom an audience owes a large amount of its theatrical pleasure. It is Iago who repeatedly stands at the fictive boundary of the play, talking to the audience, confiding in them and luring them into a tawdry complicity that depends upon their tacit consent to be given access to what Iago alternately calls his 'heavenly shows' and 'dangerous conceits [that] are in their natures poisons' (3.3.331). Through such consent, an audience yields to Iago, much as does Othello, the role of leading them inward into the doubly represented space of the play's forbidden, offstage room and the mind's unacknowledgeable fantasies. Iago plays the pander who opens the door to the listener's pornographic imagination. And through the figure of Iago, Shakespeare's play mirrors a specific triad of concerns – political, social and literary – that had suddenly emerged into cultural consciousness at the end of the sixteenth century as a result of England's recent contact with a type of literature we would today label pornography.[10] Far more than a genuine 'character' with discernably coherent motivation, Iago is a role, a strategy within the *Othello* text that shapes this play's construction.

Pornography in its original literary manifestation is by definition male-authored and subscribed – not only authored by a male but subscribed by a culture which deprecates the feminine and invests the masculine with sexual desire accompanied by fear, guilt and loathing of female sexuality. Although its ideological functions are undoubtedly numerous, the primary job that pornographic literature fulfils in its unacknowledged bond with a culture is providing a medium for reconstituting and circulating the society's norms about male power and male dominance. Its special authority lies in the way that it codes itself inside of transgressive, often violent sexual narratives that only seem to oppose the cultural authority by which they are tacitly enabled. As a medium for reifying masculine dominance, pornography has been, correspondingly, a medium for constructing feminine subservience, often in narrative forms of erotic bondage.

Since pornography as a genre is thus a primary carrier for all the culture's erotic 'master plots' and often repeats the very same stories that recur in romance and other institutionally more legitimate forms, pornography has a way of lurking beneath, and tacitly working as pattern for, the only erotic fantasies the culture knows how to construct – the kinds of fantasies defined by the gendered polarization of both cultural and physical power that underlie and seep into Desdemona's thrilled desire to be 'subdued / Even to the utmost pleasure of my lord' (1.3.246–7), or her determination to be passive, unprotesting, obedient and ever the 'gentle Desdemona' even when she is subjected to Othello's physical abuse. What may be valuable about pornography as an excavation site is that perhaps especially here, where the culture's erotic narratives transgress the legitimate, can we clearly see the shape of things that constitute the legitimate. Desdemona has fallen in love with stories about Othello that are the essence of romance – stories in which he appears as the conquering warrior bearing tales of a world that she, in fulfilling the archetype of her role as 'a maiden never bold; / Of spirit so still and quiet that her motion / Blushed at herself' (1.3.94–6), can experience only vicariously, through loving such powerful men. In part, she falls in love with romance itself, as culture has implicitly trained her to do by guaranteeing that heterosexual desire will be circulated and endlessly reconstituted through such stories of male heroism, male power, male conquest. Yet these same tacitly authorized stories about warrior/lovers, daughters eloping at midnight with exotic dark strangers, commanding males who sweep women away into exotic lands to discover erotic delight, are also the groundwork for tales we would recognize as pornographic. In fact, influenced by his loss of territorial control in his presumed loss of Desdemona's body, Othello begins to renarrate his epic story of martial conquest from the grounds of the pornographic, where the female body becomes a sexual topos to be multiply 'occupied' by men and further devalued by sexual congress with 'pioners', who belonged to a class of soldier so low that dishonourable discharge was often considered a preferable alternative.[11]

> I had been happy if the general camp,
> Pioners and all, had tasted her sweet body
> So I had nothing known ...
> Farewell! Othello's occupation's gone.
> (3.3.346–8; 358)

Moreover, the Othello and Desdemona story of the black male and white woman is itself a primary site for pornographic narration and one that has, since the lewdly racist images in Iago's scene one descriptions to Brabantio, already been suggested to the audience as available for just such kind of generic appropriation.

Because of pornography's inherently deflective logic and its defensive fantasy that construes all women as insatiably carnal, pornography as a genre frequently disguises itself as an exposé of women's lust, often structured as a dialogue between two women confessing to one another the 'pranks / They dare not show their husbands. Their best conscience / Is not to leav't undone, but keep't unknown' (3.3.203–5). Within the deflected logic of this formula, the lustful female speakers created by the pornographic author do indeed become the 'fair papers' and 'goodly books' that were made to write 'whore' upon, for 'pornography' itself means, literally, a written story of whores. And this was the form in which pornography first arrived in England in 1584 under the title of Pietro Aretino's *I Ragionimenti*. In Aretino's dialogues, the male fantasy is displaced into the voices of an older and a younger woman debating the merits of becoming a nun, a wife or a courtesan; the conversation is, of course, merely an excuse to describe and revel in the graphic porntopia fictionalized here as the older woman's experiences.

Prior to 1584, Aretino had been known in England only as a political satirist and poet, and had even been compared to Tasso and Petrarch by none other than Gabriel Harvey. Then word began to come from continental sources about Aretino's other productions, in particular, his obscene sonnets on the positions of love written to accompany the erotic drawings of Giulio Romano, which were standardly referred to in Italian treatises as 'I Modi', but which are coded in all English references as either 'the postures' or 'the pictures'.[12] In 1584, the *Dialogues* were published by John Wolfe, Harvey's own publisher. Shortly afterwards, Aretino moved from being known as the 'divine Aretine' to being the exemplar of the obscene, or, more colourfully put, 'an Italian ribald, [who] vomits-out the infectious poyson of the world, [so that] an Inglish horrel-lorrel must licke it vp for a restoratiue'.[13] The impact of *I Ragionimenti* can perhaps be measured by the fact that the form which pornography took for the next 150 years across Europe was Aretino's dialogue between two women, an emulation that has led modern biographers to call Pietro Aretino, appropriately enough, the 'father' of modern pornography.

By connecting Shakespeare's conception of Iago to that other Venetian scoundrel, Aretino, I am not implying that Shakespeare necessarily used Aretino as a source for *Othello*, nor that Iago should be read as an allusion to him. In Shakespeare's own time Aretino's name had come to be a layered metaphor that not only represented a certain type of salacious text and its aroused reader's response, but provoked a volley of self-legitimating political responses from various state and social institutions reacting against this newly available form of moral transgression. Shakespeare's play re-presents that mirror. And to enable that representation, the text includes not Arch-imago, the arch image-maker of Spenser's *Faerie Queene* whose dream pictures of a lascivious Una abed with the squire cause Red Crosse Knight to betray his quest, but a dramatically viable character named I-ago, the picture-making Imago whose occupation as 'Ensign' locates him as the bearer of signs within the play and bearer as well of a certain ugly cultural standard that rallies its followers into a male bond formed around the time-honoured misogyny and racism that the 'Ancient' both disseminates and perpetuates.

No doubt because Shakespeare's culture did recognize its own image in what it denounced as an invasion of literary obscenity from Italy, Aretino was not only well known by the 1590s – he was infamous. So much so that David McPherson has argued that the deluge of works in the 1590s depicting Italian diabolism owes its impetus more to England's contact with Aretino than with Machiavelli.[14] Within a decade of Aretino's arrival, suddenly writers like Thomas Nashe and John Marston began experimenting with a type of literature that cannot be defined as generically belonging to either the Elizabethan bawdy or the Ovidian sensual. This new type – works like Nashe's *The Choice of Valentines; or, Nashe, his Dildo*, and both Marston's *Metamorphosis of Pigmalion's Image* and *The Scourge of Villanie* – bear the graphic stamp of Aretino. And it was this newly transgressive literature that provided, as well, a rich opportunity for the moralists, theologians and satirists like Joseph Hall, Gabriel Harvey and, ironically enough, again John Marston to excoriate in print. Quite probably, what had popularized Aretino as the exemplar of the obscene was the use that had been made of him in the scurrilous Harvey–Nashe pamphlet wars where Harvey had attacked Nashe's immoral writings by calling him the 'English Aretine'. Ben Jonson's allusions are those that best illustrate the dual pleasure and outrage that constitute the poles of the English response to Aretino. In *The Alchemist*, Sir Epicure Mammon devises a pleasure palace to excite his moribund sexual fantasies by imagining it will be

> Fill'd with such Pictures as Tiberius took
> From Elephantis, and dull Aretine
> But coldly imitated.
> (*The Alchemist* 2.2.43–5)

In *Volpone*, however, Corvino lashes out at

> some young Frenchman, or hot Tuscan blood
> That had read Aretine, conned all his prints,
> Knew every quirk within lusts labyrinth
> And were professed critic in lechery.
> (*Volpone* 3.7.59–62)[15]

Running parallel with this newly sexualized literature and the printed attack on it, the last years of Elizabeth's reign were marked by a likewise abrupt increase in censorship designed to halt circulation of these two newly emergent literary forms – forms which, we might add, were becoming frequently indistinguishable from one another. In 1599, the official censors of the press issued orders to ban such works as John Hall's *Virgidimiarum*, Marston's *Pigmalion's Image* and *The Scourge of Villanie*, Marlowe's *Elegies*, Davies's *Epigrams*, the Harvey–Nashe pamphlets, and certain books 'against women', apparently a reference to Robert Tofte's *Of Marriage and Wyving* and *The XV Joyes of Marriage*, thought to be an earlier version of *The Batchelars Banquet*, also translated from the French by Tofte.[16] Although the books characterized as being 'against women' were actually witty arguments designed to make women so disgusting as to discourage men from marriage and the state's concern to ban them almost certainly reflected its desire to protect not women but the patriarchal institution through which they were subordinated, the list nonetheless rather neatly draws together graphic sexuality, verbal invective and misogyny as the elements the state found it expedient to suppress. They are also the three interests bound together in England's emerging pornography – a pornography that never became original, but contributed only one new element to the genre – the imprint of scatological revulsion.

By censorship, the state acknowledges the power possessed by the censored object. But it is safe to assume that the reaction of the Elizabethan state was political, not altruistic, and intended to protect its own authority to set limits. One may assume that in suddenly enacting an unexpected ban on certain popular literature, the state was legitimizing its authority by asserting it, reifying its not-to-be-questioned social boundaries by redrawing them. And these political concerns are likewise what Lodovico and the state representatives speak to when they conclude the play by ordering redistribution of property rather than eulogy, and censorship rather than the condign retribution we have come to expect from Shakespearean tragedy. Instead of anything that would ritually mark or affirm some connection between the society and the dead bride and groom whom Lodovico has reduced to the 'loading on the bed', the final movement is invested in taking things away, in dissociating the state from the sign of transgressive excess that lies on the bed. Having seized upon and redistributed the house and fortunes of the man who has been depersonalized back to 'the Moor', Lodovico turns to address the Iago problem. When he does so, however, it is within a syntax that makes 'torture' merely parallel with the logistics of organization and reserves its imperative emphasis for the authority of enforcement.

> To you, lord governor,
> Remains the censure of this hellish villain:
> The time, the place, the torture, O, enforce it!
> (5.2.363–5)

Not only is the audience's need for retribution left wholly ignored and Iago's punishment turned over to the questionably capable hands of Cassio, the new 'lord governor', but as Lodovico and company depart abruptly for Venice, the audience ends up left behind, positioned inside the play's inner space, confronting the condemned fantasy object while Iago exits alive and dangerous and still a part of the highly civilized culture of which he is a subterranean part. In a rhetoric of sound and fury that actually signifies very little, the state pronounces Iago a 'hellish villain' and a 'Spartan dog'. But it is never implied (though a remarkable number of critics have inferred) that the state either can or wants to kill Iago. As the rational structures attempt to reestablish the boundaries that have been violated, it becomes increasingly clear, through all that is *not* being said and done, that the violation the Venetian representatives are most concerned to enclose is the excessive passion of Desdemona and Othello, the sign of which they order hidden. When the officials on stage finally provide the overdue indictment of Iago, the language in which it is framed – which accuses Iago of having created a 'work' that is itself an 'object' that 'poisons sight' and must 'be hid' – is both descriptively odd and grossly inadequate to encompass the enormity of his crimes. What Lodovico's phrasing makes Iago sound guilty of is having crafted a piece of unseemly and socially offensive art.

Lodovico's sentence likewise dramatizes precisely what the state has always done with pornography – overtly torture and suppress, but covertly ensure its existence. The state's 'cunning cruelty' for Iago will be, as Lodovico says in a rather revealing construction, to 'torment him much and hold him long' (5.2.335). But if we have learned anything from this play, we should recognize that as a fantasy content, as the voyeur's aroused imagination, and indeed as a literary genre, pornography is fed, not starved, by prohibition. Like Iago, it must be denied promotion to be aroused to action; its life depends on its suppression.

The writer who seems best to have understood such seeming paradoxes inherent in the demands of the emerging form was John Marston, whose *Metamorphosis of Pigmalion's Image* deliberately experiments with masturbatory strategies of inhibited desire which stimulate the reader's arousal by creating a friction with it. As Marston's poem leads its male reader towards the given object of desire, the centripetal figure of the waiting female body, it alternately arouses him with prurient questions much like Iago's and then prohibits his access by refusing to show what the reader has been led to imagine, a denial technique that – like Iago's 'pursed up' thoughts, his 'stops' and 'close denotements' (3.3.127)[17] – only guarantees that the aroused reader will demand the voyeuristic satisfaction of 'Make me to see it'. At the end of *Pigmalion*, a seeming reversal unexpectedly appears in appended verses entitled 'The Authour in prayse of his precedent Poem', where suddenly the poet radically switches his stance and, in the voice of the moralist, scathingly attacks his readers as 'lewd Priapians' whose prurience has been 'tickled up' by the poem which the author now disclaims as a piece of 'chaos indigest' which he 'slubbered up' to 'fish for fools' – who are, of course, his readers. The poem and its annexed verses together constitute the paradox of pornography's split mentality, the seeming contradiction of Iago's dual stance. By appropriating the voice of the moralist disgusted by what he graphically describes, the strategy neutralizes the guilt of the sexualist and allows the two psychic figures to co-exist in the reader. Only *because of* such a split can the moralist revel in what he simultaneously decries and the voluptuary be whipped for the pleasures that arouse him. The split is most vividly illustrated in *Othello* by Othello's vacillating stances during the bedroom murder. Having erotically murdered the seducing strumpet he sees on the bed, Othello then priggishly aligns himself with Iago as another 'honest man ... [who] hates the slime / That sticks on filthy deeds' (148–9).

Important to understanding the voice in which the pornography of late sixteenth-century English literature speaks is the recognition of how the genre, although originally appropriated from the Italian, nonetheless reflects its own particular origins. As distinct from the pleasure principle of its Italian progenitor, the idiom of English pornography is invested in the language of slime, poison, revulsion, disgust, garbage, vomit, clyster pipes, dung and animality that emerges in Iago's every mention of sex and eventually displaces the Othello music. Moreover, it is an idiom that English pornography borrowed from the *moralists* who began writing against sexualized literature. It is likewise the language that John Marston, more than any other writer, contributed to English satire in his 1598 *The Scourge of Villanie*, which purports to be an attack on sexual writing, spoken in the voice of the moralist.[18] In the Juvenalian coarseness of the *Scourge* persona, Marston seems to have opened up new rhetorical strategies for the satirists to explore; moreover, his newly coarsened language of sexual bluntness likewise provided a rich muck-pit for drama to mine and may well have provided a 'father tongue' not only for Iago but for such characters as Thersites, Bosola and other Jacobean malcontents who – along with Marston's own dramatic scourgers of sexual vice – emerged on the English stage shortly thereafter. The persona-speaker of *The Scourge* is, very much like Iago, a bluntly honest man who hates 'the slime of filthy sensuality' which he endlessly describes in snarling ejaculations at

> *Aretine's* filth, or of his wandering whore ...
> of *Ruscus* nastie lothsome brothell rime
> That stinks like Ajax froth, or muck-pit slime
> (xi.II.144, 146–7)

Out on this salt humour, letchers dropsie,
Fie, it doth soyle my chaster poesie ...
(xi.II.155–6)

Marston's bitter Scourge persona is pornographic, but he fails to
lure his readers into complicity. Shakespeare's exuberant Iago makes
his watchers have to admire his success, disarming an audience even
as he appalls them with his witty images of lewd jocularity, comically
memorable pictures like 'the old black ram tupping ... ' that are carefully interlarded among his passages of scatological bluntness. And
in Iago's prurient descriptions of Desdemona, he does not so befoul
the whole image that desire will turn to revulsion; he just soils her
enough in the making to render her carnally available to his listening audience's fantasies. From the opening scene of this play, to be a
spectator is to be invited into an Iago-orchestrated world of images
centred upon the availability of Desdemona's body – the locus
where, inexorably, the action of the drama likewise leads.

If contemporary analysis of pornography agrees on anything, it
may be the recognition that beneath the overt sexuality and apparent life impetus of the pornographic script, its true objective is not
sex but death – and in particular, death experienced as erotic com-
pletion. This hidden truth is, in Shakespeare's drama, the Turk that
invades the palace, and Iago's role is to solicit it and make men 'turn
Turks'. Beneath Iago's salacious script and its 'pageant to keep men
in false gaze' (1.3.19), the target of the fantasy is the figure whom
the script has violently eroticized since its opening moment, the one
it eventually succeeds in isolating behind its bedroom door, and the
one it finally stifles into silence. She is Iago's target, she becomes
Othello's, and she is likewise the voyeuristic object that the language
of the play has endlessly invited the audience to violate. Even her
identity as the appropriate target has been available to the audience
since first hearing her name.

It was, after all, *Des-demon* who first transgressed against the
boundaries of patriarchal enclosure, creating a fissure in two of its
most sacred texts by self-authorizing her own marriage and then
disrupting the state's discourse of sanctioned aggression with a
counterclaim that privileged her own 'downright violence' and the
right to live with the man she married. Her arrival into the Venetian
Council in 1.3 visually and verbally represents what her intrusion
threatens: to drive wedges into the structures of the masculine
paterfamilias of authority and unity. It is thus appropriately through

Brabantio, the father, that the culture transmits the warning that becomes a rallying cry. Under the banner that 'she has deceiv'd her father [and] may do thee' (1.3.293), the men of this play repeatedly regroup and bond into a shared identity that progressively isolates the object of desire and resignifies it as an object of mutual threat. Along with Desdemona herself, the watchwords are carried to Cyprus by the Ensign: 'She has betrayed her father ... '. The echoed warning informs the strange logic of Othello's conviction that 'she must die, else she'll betray more men' (5.1.6); and it reifies itself once more even in the parodically deflected eulogy that Gratiano speaks when he enters the bedroom and looks at Desdemona, murdered on her bed. Gazing at the figure of his dead niece, Gratiano, too, aligns himself with the patriarchal text and, instead of eulogizing the tragedy of this young bride, his words condemn Desdemona as the implicit agent of her father's death: 'Poor Desdemona, I am glad thy father's dead; / Thy match was mortal to him, and pure grief / Shore his old thread atwain ... ' (5.2.205–7).

The pervasive idea of women as the ultimate threat to the masculine world finally transforms every performance in the play into the misogynistic violence that utterly overwhelms *Othello*'s concluding act. While Othello goes from the male violence outside in the street, emblematically bringing it with him into the bedroom to execute the 'fair devil' within, Bianca simultaneously magnetizes blame for the violence outside when, ignoring her own safety, she rushes out in the street to save Cassio. It is Iago who directs both forms of aggression. But it is Cassio's silent complicity as he psychologically bonds with his attackers that confirms Iago's script. And though his injuries are not so severe as to prevent him from defending Roderigo (whom he tried to kill the previous night) from accusation, Cassio – whose life was actually saved by Bianca's intervening presence – says nothing in Bianca's behalf as Iago turns blame for the attack on her. What ultimately happens to Bianca is not explicit within the text, but the issue is hardly irrelevant in terms of the overall ideas explored within this play. Moreover, the text does provide an inference that is both the logical one for the situation and one which fits the play's larger pattern of a disturbing parallel among its three women/three men/three couples. Since Iago is in total command and literally directing this scene, what happens to Bianca lies wholly within his control. After sending Cassio off to a surgeon, Iago – with the Venetian authorities his audience – moves to solidify his accusations against Bianca by once again invoking the regime of male looking at a female body and reading it for signs of its presumptive guilt.

What, look you pale? –
Stay you, good gentlewoman; look you pale, mistress?
Do you perceive the gestures of her eye?
Nay, an you stir, – we shall have more anon:
Behold her well I pray you, look upon her,
Do you see, gentlemen? nay, guiltiness
Will speak, though tongues were out of use.
                              (5.1.103–9)[19]

When a remarkably calm Bianca rejects his subsequent reading of
her body and its guilt ('He [Cassio] supp'd at my house, but I therefore shake not'), Iago seizes upon the authoritative language of an
arresting officer – 'O did he so? I charge you go with me' (119), and
concludes the scene by asserting further legal control over her as he
orders her to come with him, 'Come, mistress, you must tell's another
tale'. From this reference in conjunction with those above – that 'we
shall have more anon' and 'guiltiness / Will speak, though tongues
were out of use' – Iago seems to allude to a confession that the authorities will forcibly extract from Bianca even if she initially refuses to
speak it. By inference, Bianca, undefended by Cassio and under a
charge from Iago that goes unchallenged by the Venetian authorities,
is being hauled off to prison. My inference of such callous treatment
seems further justified by the fact that neither Cassio nor the authorities make any move to exonerate or lift the accusation from her in
the play's final scene, even after they know of Iago's guilt from the
letter found on Roderigo's body. Bianca exits the play under accusation
and, is, in fact, never spoken of again.

In this play it isn't just Othello who calls the woman he loves a
'whore' – it is every male in the drama who has any narrative relationship with a woman. Moreover, it is always Iago's innuendoes, the
Ensign's presence and its implicit call for the rallying of the male
bond, that prompt each man to do so. Iago labels all three women
in the play whores, and by the end of the fourth act Othello has
denounced Emilia as a 'simple bawd' and 'subtle whore' (4.2.20, 21).
But in ways that form a disturbing parallel with Othello's willingness
to call Desdemona a whore, Cassio, around Iago, sniggeringly characterizes the woman with whom he has sexual relations a 'customer',
a 'monkey', a 'bauble' and a 'fitchew' (4.1); Roderigo, around Iago,
believes that the Desdemona he idealizes is available for sexual purchase
had he but jewels and gold enough to buy her; and even her father,
influenced by Iago's smutty pictures, is willing publicly to brand his
own daughter as a woman who, having 'betrayed' his incestuous
fantasies by marrying Othello, will now betray her husband and,

ergo, become a whore. In this tragedy, not only Desdemona but all the women are the 'fair papers' on which the men of the play write 'whore'. And for the women, the consequences of such male inscription are lethal.

Within the *Othello* text the 'whore' that all the men imagine and with which term they so quickly brand the women they love is a label that, for the women, is so threatening that all three of them circle warily around it, so desperate to extricate themselves from its condemnation that they willingly displace it onto other women as if such displacement would stand as proof of their own purity. In the final night scene between Desdemona and Emilia, as both women nervously try to suppress their half-conscious knowledge of the coming violence that lies heavy in the air, their dialogue compulsively cycles back, again and again, to sexual fidelity. Interestingly enough, as each of the women tries to come to terms with the loathing she feels projected at her by her husband, each seems implicitly to consider the possibility that she might have made – or might make – some other choice. But such a possibility, while perhaps discursively acceptable and even consciously accessible as a topic among Shakespearean males,[20] is for the women always already framed within the dangerous cultural binary of virgin and whore. Moreover, that binary clearly acts not only as an external inhibitor but, even more problematically, as a set of stringent rules that culture has trained all women, even those who represent such widely different social classes as do the three in *Othello*, to internalize. And thus, in the Desdemona–Emilia exchange, no sooner is the thought of infidelity even partially expressed than it is instantly retracted and quickly displaced onto some imagined other woman, the presumptive 'whore' whose existence must be theorized in order to carry the transferred guilt of the speaker's unacknowledgeable fantasies and thereby confirm the position of virtue from which she must always be seen – by herself as well as others – to speak.

The women's scene takes place shortly after Othello, having hit Desdemona and humiliated her in front of the shocked Venetian ambassadors, has ordered her to bed. From the digressive Willow Song in which Desdemona sings forlornly about a woman deserted by her love, her dialogue shifts in jarring transition to the sudden observation that 'This Lodovico is a proper man' (4.3.35), to the logically unrelated question she keeps pushing at Emilia about the supposedly unimaginable existence of women so vile as ones who could possibly 'abuse their husbands / In such gross kind' (61–2).

Its almost Pinteresque construction suggests that the absent connectives that would lend it logical coherence lie in precisely such an interplay of denial, repression and displacement. And Desdemona's sequence is then immediately followed by a similar, though much more conscious one from Emilia. Beginning with an initially candid acknowledgement that 'There be some such[women], no question' (62) and the admission that she could even imagine herself doing such a deed, Emilia's dialogue then likewise becomes suggestively entangled with guilt and repression. Retracting her earlier candour she next insists that if she ever did commit adultery, she would 'undo't when I had done it' (70–1), and then reconstructs the imagined act as something she might do not for herself but only to better her husband – she might 'make her husband a cuckold', but it would be only 'to make him a monarch' (74–5). Emilia's attempt to contain her resentment inside of the accepted double standard is, however, only partially successful, and thus she concludes this scene with an angry outburst that essentially justifies a woman's adultery by insisting that women, too, have affections, desires for sport, and frailty. And yet, even though she has, in effect, already admitted that sexual infidelity is an entirely thinkable option and one that she could potentially imagine herself committing, in the very next scene when she hears Iago frame his accusation of Bianca in terms of 'this is the fruit of whoring' (5.1.115), Emilia immediately disavows that dangerously liberated space with which she had flirted just moments before and reclaims the position of moral superiority by joining with her husband in denouncing/chastising Bianca with 'Fie, fie upon thee, strumpet!' (120) – an appellation which Bianca, too, then instantly displaces by equating herself with Emilia in insisting that she is 'of life as honest / As you, that thus abuse me' (121–2).

In this play's darkly pessimistic exploration of sex and gender bonds, such painful ironies abound. While the three women blame problems in their relationships with men on some imagined other woman and simultaneously go either or almost to the death in defence of the men with whom they are bonded, the three men repeatedly affirm the actually lethal male bonds among them and either kill their mates or silently refuse to testify in their behalf. Not just Desdemona but to greater degrees likewise Emilia and Bianca clearly recognize that some kind of problem exists within their marital/sexual bond. But the condition of the heterosexual bond in this play seems to require that women must locate the problem not within the males with whom they are joined or even within the internal dynamics of the relationship. Instead, the problem must be externalized and projected elsewhere, almost inevitably onto another female. Thus Bianca, instead of challenging Cassio's insulting query, 'What do you mean by this haunting of me?', transfers her anger into a jealous accusation that the handkerchief he has given her to copy is 'some minx's token' or something he has had from some 'hobby-horse' (4.1.143; 151–2). The presumptive other woman rather than Cassio receives the opprobrium; and once that site has absorbed the anger, what Cassio receives is Bianca's invitation to supper.

This pattern of gender-conditioned deflection is, moreover, reified by its parallel in the reactions of both Emilia and Desdemona. Desdemona's Willow Song – always understood as a site onto which she transfers her own senses of despair and abandonment and intuition of her own death – is also a complex site where, having run out of all of the earlier, impersonal excuses through which she has tried to account for the irrational rage being projected at her by her husband, she at last struggles with the issue of blame. Having retracted the line '*Let nobody blame him, his scorn I approve, – *' with the interjection 'Nay, that's not next' (4.3.51–2), she replaces it with '*I call'd my love false love; but what said he then? ... If I court moe women, you'll couch with moe men*' (54, 56). Albeit the accusation occurs only in deflected form inside of the fictional voices of a song, Desdemona does here at last, for a moment, replace self-accusation with an accusation of a male/Othello figure. But even her accusation that he is a 'false love' is couched in terms of a presumptive infidelity with some implied other woman, and as she elucidates the accusation further by allowing him to respond, even the recognition that his rage is based on a belief in her infidelity is tangled up with his threat to 'couch with more women'. Not even the outspoken Emilia proves capable until the play's final scene of facing the genuine rage she harbours against her husband. That wives may fall is, she vigorously asserts, their husbands' faults. But the fault that she finds – one which seems wide indeed of Iago, whose contempt for women is so legion as to make sexual infidelity the least believable of perhaps any accusation – again implicates the ubiquitous other woman: if men 'slack their [sexual] duties' it is because they 'pour our treasures into foreign laps'. And wives' infidelities are thus justified because husbands have 'change[d] us for others' (4.3.87–8; 97). Desdemona's fatal flaw, it has often been argued, is her extreme passivity, her refusal to read Othello's anger and confront it with anger of her own at his abuse. Yet Bianca and Emilia – neither of whom could be accused of passivity – fare no better, and, in ways that echo Desdemona, each of them goes almost to the death in defence of men who routinely treat them with contempt. Bianca's and Desdemona's abjection might be excused by the fact that they are in love. But the fact that Emilia's actions are disappointingly similar argues for a strongly gendered pattern that this play goes to considerable lengths to construct. For despite Emilia's clear dislike of her husband and resentment at his contempt, she nonetheless strives to win his approval by stealing the handkerchief, and even when his villainy is revealed so thoroughly as to make any excuse impossible, her dumb-founded iteration, 'My husband ... my husband ... my husband?' (5.2.141; 148; 150), exposes the difficulty she has not so much in recognizing his viciousness but in revising her own determined refusal to confront it.

When Emilia does at last break through her own model of the obe-dient wife and comes into the bedroom to assert the strident truth of her accusations against men, for a brief but critical moment we sud-denly have a genuine, awakened 'woman reader in the text'.[21] But the moment is emphatically short-lived. Clearly, no one on stage wants to hear the brazen, accusing truth of Emilia's revelations; and thus an entire roomful of able-bodied men stands there, dumbly mute, as Iago viciously acts for them all in silencing the only remain-ing female voice. After threatening his wife and demanding her silence on five different occasions during a fifty-line exchange on stage, when Iago finally draws his sword on her, the only reaction from the men on stage is Gratiano's comment, 'Fie, / Your sword upon a woman?' (5.2.225). In Q1 and Q2 the stage directions (which do not appear in F) indicate that Othello, outraged at Iago's betrayal, 'runnes at Iago. Iago kills his wife'. But in no text are there directions to indicate that Gratiano, Montano or Othello makes any attempt to protect Emilia, although in almost all *Othello* produc-tions the director adds in a mighty struggle on stage which Iago breaks through and manages to stab his wife despite heroic attempts to stop him. The addition seems unwarranted, not only by the lack of prior language or directions that suggest any kind of struggle to protect Emilia, but also by what follows. As Emilia falls, Gratiano's only response is 'The woman falls, sure he has kill'd his wife' and 'He's gone, but his wife's kill'd' (237; 239). Moreover, although the bond between the two women receives the powerful affirmation of Emilia's dying request to be laid next to her mistress,[22] since none of the men ever verbally responds to her plea or says another word about her, we have no idea whether it is ever honoured or whether her body lies ignored on the floor and the men simply step over it as the scene continues. Even when the Venetian authorities indict Iago, the murder of his wife is apparently an act not deemed criminal enough to warrant inclusion and it thus goes unmentioned, despite the fact that it is Iago's one crime which all of the men on stage actually witnessed. As was likewise true of Bianca, all reference to Emilia simply disappears.

As violence once more erupts in the bedroom and the audience witnesses yet the second murder of a wife by her husband, the room on stage defined by the bed progressively becomes a semiotic space of collective misogynist aggression, presided over by the representatives of Venetian culture, orchestrated by the Imago of that society and venting itself on the now not one but two women who finally lie dead within that space, their bodies trapped in death even as in life inside of the voyeuristic apparatus of cultural meanings. It is usually assumed that Othello's final lines, 'Killing myself, to die upon a kiss' (5.2.360), direct that the final 'loading' on the bed and the object that poisons sight must be the tableau of the black man on the bed, on top of the white woman, and thus dying 'upon' a kiss. Consequently, most texts include the stage direction, '*He falls on the bed and dies*'. In actuality, the only authoritative stage directions that have Othello falling on the bed occur much earlier, at line 199, just prior to Emilia's 'Nay, lay thee down and roar', and that direction occurs in the two Quartos but not in Folio. At the moment of Othello's suicide at line 360, Q1 directs only '*He dies*' and Folio simply says '*dies*'.[23]

Given the ambiguities about just which bodies besides Desdemona's constitute the bed's final loading, the staging of this scene actually includes several possibilities: Desdemona's body alone; Othello's and Desdemona's together; a trio of Othello's, Desdemona's and Emilia's; or the final bed that the play directs its audience to 'look' at could even contain just the bodies of the two women. But regardless of which possibility is staged, the signifying presence of the bed carries with it its own 'loading' of eroticized cultural meanings. And thus in the tableau to which this play leads, the effect threatens to become the cause; the tragic loading/lodging on the deathbed threatens to transform it back into a bed of sexual desire; and the image of victimization re-eroticizes the script with its indissociable invitation to audience voyeurism. On the one hand, the play's action accuses its audience. By the final act, refracted incidents of misogynistic violence become so repetitious that they collectively constitute a moral demand for the masculine consciousness of the play's targeted audience to look, see and confront the image of a collective cultural guilt. But while the action accuses, the picture seduces. What an audience is ultimately left gaping at does emblematically signify the culture's guilt. But it also signs the culture's desire. It demands that its audience 'look' at the bed. But the spectacle thus commanded to vision is the very same one that invites voyeuristic transfer. The picture mutely speaks. And the unease its silent tableau so clearly provokes from the men on stage perhaps makes the most expedient solution seem to be enclosure and exit – 'Let it be hid'.

Through both the ambivalence of the play's closing sign and the talent of the pornographic artist whose 'work' this is, the sexualist and the moralist within the watchers are ultimately assured of a coexistence within the text of *Othello*. And it is precisely that ambivalence that Lodovico unconsciously repeats when he orders the watchers of this play to 'look' at what 'poisons sight'. By the play's conclusion its supervisors have most certainly grossly gaped; but in doing so, they have further invested Iago's work with the collective power of the culture's own guilt, violence, prurience, desire and revulsion. Thus there could be, I suspect, no more appropriate a message for the creator of this 'work' to offer than the enigmatic hieroglyph with which Iago leaves Othello and *Othello*'s audience:

> Demand me nothing, what you know, you know;
> From this time forth I never will speak word.
> (304–5)

In every unacknowledged and unacknowledgeable way, not only Othello but likewise the audience does 'know what it knows', and what it knows is mutely signified by the sign on stage at close. Nor is it only the bond between Othello and Iago that remains unbroken at the end of the play, but likewise the bond that Iago has insinuated between himself and his watchers. If there is any comfort to be had, then surely it lies in Iago's final promise to never more speak word. And yet, by that same source of comfort the play ensures its audience's discomfort. For by that very promise, as Iago exits alive and 'yet unkilled', the play exposes the continued existence of a secret bond with its watchers and extends the implications of that bond far beyond the boundaries of any given performance.

This is a revised and expanded version of Lynda E. Boose's conference paper, ' "Let it be hid": Renaissance Pornography, Iago and

Audience Response', published in *Autour d'Othello*, ed. Richard
Marienstras and Dominique Goy-Blanquet (Paris, 1987), pp. 135–43.

NOTES

[Lynda E. Boose takes a feminist approach to the pornographic nature of
Iago's imagination and of *Othello* itself. Iago is not a character with enough
psychological substance to have a motive for malignancy, Boose argues.
Instead, Iago is a strategy for luring members of the audience into complicity with his project and into confrontation with their own prurience.
She shows how successful this strategy is. Like many earlier critics, she
describes how unusual *Othello* is both among Shakespeare's tragedies and
in Renaissance drama more generally. Unlike these critics, she emphasizes
such differences as the play's ending in erasure and avoidance, its refusal to
provide a survivor onto whom heroic identification can be transferred, and
its previously unexampled use of the stage property of a bed as a 'staging
area for sexual violence'. Boose also employs some of the techniques usually
associated with New Historicism to discuss state censorship of pornography
in the sixteenth century. This essay is a follow-up to her highly influential
1975 article on 'Othello's Handkerchief'. Ed.]

1. *Othello*, The Arden Shakespeare, ed. M. R. Ridley (London: Methuen,
   1958; rpt. 1960). Unless otherwise noted, all *Othello* quotations are
   from this edition.

2. Norman Sanders (ed.), *Othello*, New Cambridge edition (Cambridge:
   Cambridge University Press, 1984), Introduction, p. 20.

3. In 'Grossly Gaping Viewers and Jonathan Miller's *Othello*', *Shakespeare
   the Movie: Popularizing the Plays on Film, TV, and Video*, ed. Lynda E.
   Boose and Richard Burt (London: Routledge, 1997), pp. 186–97, I have
   earlier discussed the way that placing a mirror into the final bedroom
   scene and making the television audience have to peer into it in order to
   see the image of Desdemona lying on her bed draws attention to audience
   voyeurism. An excellent psychoanalytic study of the voyeuristic dynamic is
   Barbara Freedman's *Staging the Gaze: Postmodernism, Psychoanalysis,
   and Shakespearean Comedy* (Ithaca: Cornell University Press, 1991). See
   also Sheila T. Cavanagh's exploration of Spenser in *Wanton Eyes &
   Chaste Desires: Female Sexuality in 'The Faerie Queene'* (Bloomington:
   Indiana University Press, 1994).

4. Stephen Booth, 'On the Value of *Hamlet*', in *Reinterpretations of
   Elizabethan Drama: Selected Papers from the English Institute*, ed.
   Norman Rabkin (New York: Columbia University Press, 1969), p. 152.

5. I would welcome any information to the contrary, that is, prior to
   Othello, do early modern English playscripts exist in which the bed is
   explicitly used on stage for a place of erotic consummation?

6. See especially Michael Neill, 'Unproper Beds: Race, Adultery, and the Hideous in *Othello*', *Shakespeare Quarterly*, 40 (1989), 383–412.

7. See New Cambridge editor, Norman Sanders, for instance: 'It is the ending of the play that separates it most strikingly from the other tragedies. In the first place, there is no emphatic reestablishment of public order ... or even the gesture of picking up the pieces' (p. 20).

8. Harry Berger, Jr., in 'Text Against Performance: The Example of *Macbeth*', *Genre: Forms of Discourse and Culture* 15 (1982), 49–79, discusses the way MacDuff provides such a figure for the masculine desires of the audience.

9. It was only in the past decade or so that *Othello* critiques really began to take account of the crucial way that race and racism construct this play and the way that race, gender and sexuality function as linked discourses within it. Without suggesting that the following is an inclusive list, at least some of these important critiques are: Virginia Mason Vaughan, '*Othello*': A Contextual History* (Cambridge: Cambridge University Press, 1994); Karen Newman, ' "And Wash the Ethiop White": Femininity and the Monstrous in *Othello*', in *Shakespeare Reproduced: The Text in History and Ideology*, ed. Jean E. Howard and Marion F. O'Connor (New York and London: Routledge, 1987), pp. 143–62; Kim F. Hall, *Things of Darkness: Economies of Race and Gender in Early Modern England* (Ithaca: Cornell University Press, 1995); Dympna Callaghan, ' "Othello was a white man": properties of race on Shakespeare's stage', *Alternative Shakespeares*, vol. 2, ed. Terence Hawkes (London: Routledge, 1996), pp. 196–215; Ania Loomba, *Gender, Race, Renaissance Drama* (Manchester: Manchester University Press, 1989); Edward Pechter, '*Othello*' and Interpretive Traditions* (Iowa City: University of Iowa Press, 1999); Anthony Barthelemy, *Black Face, Maligned Race: The Representation of Blacks in English Drama from Shakespeare to Southerne* (Baton Rouge: Louisiana State University Press, 1987); Ruth Cowhig, 'Blacks in English Renaissance Drama and the Role of Shakespeare's *Othello*', in *The Black Presence in English Literature*, ed. David Dabydeen (Manchester: Manchester University Press, 1989), pp. 1–25; Jyotsna Singh, 'Othello's Identity, Postcolonial Theory, and Contemporary African Rewritings of *Othello*', in *Women, 'Race', and Writing in the Early Modern Period*, ed. Margo Hendricks and Patricia Parker (New York and London: Routledge, 1994), pp. 287–99; Patricia Parker, 'Fantasies of "Race" and "Gender": Africa, Othello, and bringing to light', also in Hendricks and Parker, pp. 84–100. See Singh in this collection, chapter 7.

10. I have discussed the intersection of these concerns in greater detail in 'The 1599 Bishops' Ban, Elizabethan Pornography, and the Sexualization of the Jacobean Stage', in *Enclosure Acts: Sexuality, Property, and Culture in Early Modern England*, ed. Richard Burt and

John Michael Archer (Ithaca: Cornell University Press, 1994), pp. 185–200.

11. See the New Cambridge edition notes for 3.3.347. As the ultimate threat against Lucrece's resistance, Tarquin had likewise invoked a similarly literal form of social class de-gradation by threatening to place Lucrece's (dead) body with a household servant's.

12. See David O. Foxon, *Libertine Literature in England, 1660–1745* (London: New Hyde Park, 1965), pp. 11–12. The most accessible version in English of the text and history of 'I Modi' is *I modi: The Sixteen Pleasures: An Erotic Album of the Italian Renaissance: Giulio Romano, Marcantonio Raimundi, Pietro Aretino, and Count Jean Frederic-Maximilien de Waldeck*, ed. and trans. with commentary by Lynne Lawner (Evanston: Northwestern University Press, 1988). For an excellent analysis of erotic texts in the Elizabethan era, see Ian Moulton, *Before Pornography: Erotic Writing in Early Modern England* (Oxford: Oxford University Press, 2000). And for studies of the intersecting concerns over gender and subjectivity underlying the period's attacks on the theatre, see especially Laura Levine, *Men in Women's Clothing: Anti-theatricality and Effeminization 1579–1642* (Cambridge: Cambridge University Press, 1994) and Katharine Eisaman Maus, 'Horns of Dilemma: Jealousy, Gender, and Spectatorship in English Renaissance Drama', *ELH*, 54 (1987), 561–84.

13. The phrase comes from one of Gabriel Harvey's attacks on Thomas Nashe. See *Pierce's Supererogation* in *The Works of Gabriel Harvey*, ed. A. B. Grosart (London, 1884), II, 91–6.

14. David McPherson, 'Aretino and the Harvey-Nashe Quarrel', *PMLA*, 84 (1969), 1551–8; p. 1551, n. 3. See also the excellent work of David O. Frantz in his article, ' "Leud Priapians" and Renaissance Pornography', *Studies in English Literature*, 12 (1972), 157–72, and his book, *Festum Voluptatis: A Study of Renaissance Erotica* (Columbus: Ohio State University Press, 1989).

15. Ben Jonson, *Three Comedies: Volpone, the Alchemist, Bartholomew Fair*, ed. Michael Jamieson (Baltimore: Penguin Books, 1966).

16. For details about the ban, see my article cited above in note 10.

17. F and Q2 (seconded by Rowe and Theobald) read 'dilations' for Q1's 'denotements', the reading which Capell chooses. Steevens finally added 'delations'. For a complex illumination of meanings, see especially Patricia Parker in 'Shakespeare and Rhetoric: "dilation" and "delation" in *Othello*', in *Shakespeare and the Question of Theory*, ed. Patricia Parker and Geoffrey Hartman (New York and London: Methuen, 1984), pp. 54–74.

18. John Marston, *The Scourge of Villanie*, in *The Poems of John Marston*, ed. Arnold Davenport, Liverpool English Texts and Studies

(Liverpool: Liverpool University Press, 1961). Davenport likewise sees Marston as instrumental in the creation of this new language of the Jacobean stage. See his introduction to *Poems*.

19. At line 104 Qq read 'gentlewoman' and F reads 'gentlemen'. Either is logical, but if the former, then Iago – perhaps physically – has probably here intercepted Bianca's move to follow Cassio and is addressing her (whom he earlier called 'strumpet') with deriding sarcasm. At line 106, Qq reads 'an you stirre' and F, 'if you stare'. Most editors follow the Q reading; Sanders further notes how the 'stir' reading here suggests that 'Iago has a hold on Bianca, who starts to struggle and is threatened by him'.

20. Linguistic evidence of such a powerful double standard exists, of course, in the fact that while female infidelity is marked by a number of pejorative, often powerfully punitive terms (such as 'whore', 'strumpet', etc.), in English and probably most other languages there are no counterterms for naming unfaithful males.

   Two Gentlemen of Verona provides a lighthearted example of the kind of licence for male infidelity that is stringently denied to women in Renaissance drama. Similarly, the young male lovers in *A Midsummer Night's Dream* are comic in their changeability; while conversely, Helena and Hermia both remain faithful, thus virtuous, and the comedy of the women's roles lies in the way Hermia projects her fury not at Lysander for his betrayal, but at Helena, the other woman to be despised for having stolen him. In terms of male licence within this implicit double standard, *All's Well that Ends Well* offers a much more pointed critique of the way that Bertram's credit with his peers goes up, not down, when he abandons his wife and is thought to have seduced the virginal Diana; even in the play's final scene where he is chastised for such bad behaviour, while Diana's revelations of supposed sexual congress threaten her with prison, Bertram's behaviour is ultimately always to be forgiven by not only the society but the betrayed wife herself. The one overall exception to this understood rule about gender and sexual fidelity may perhaps occur in *Antony and Cleopatra*. For while Antony follows the rule that allows males to violate the rule and thus lives within marital and sexual infidelities himself while raging at Cleopatra as a 'triple-turned whore' for the lovers she has enjoyed before him, Cleopatra is in some regards a unique Shakespearean female. While she remains virtuous and does not sexually betray Antony during the course of the play, she alone among Shakespearean heroines is at least allowed to chat happily with other women about her earlier lovers. Despite the exception, however, Cleopatra exists in an emphatically pre-Christian, pagan world, and, as Shakespeare makes clear, this world ends with Egypt's invasion by Octavius Caesar and his 'Roman thoughts'.

21. The phrase comes, of course, from Mary Jacobus's article, 'Is There a Woman in This Text?', *New Literary History*, 14 (1982), 117–54,

which was itself a feminist response to Stanley Fish, *Is There a Text in This Class? The Authority of Interpretive Communities* (Cambridge, Mass.: Harvard University Press, 1980). The first reading to recognize the implicitly feminist position from which Emilia speaks itself appeared in the first feminist collection of essays on Shakespeare: Carol Thomas Neely's 'Women and Men in *Othello*: "What should such a fool / do with so good a woman?"' in *The Woman's Part: Feminist Criticism of Shakespeare*, ed. Carolyn Ruth Swift Lenz, Gayle Greene and Carol Thomas Neely (Urbana: University of Illinois Press, 1980), pp. 211–39.

22. It is possible to read Emilia's lines as saying *either* that she wishes to have her body placed on the bed next to Desdemona's *or* that she is asking to be buried next to her mistress.

23. James R. Siemon offers an excellent reprise of the various complexities and multiple possibilities implicit in staging the final scene of *Othello*. See '"Nay, That's Not Next": *Othello* V.ii. in Performance, 1760–1900', *Shakespeare Quarterly*, 37 (1986), 39–51.

2

Cultural Materialism, *Othello* and the Politics of Plausibility

ALAN SINFIELD

''TIS APT AND OF GREAT CREDIT'

Cassio, in Shakespeare's *Othello*, is discovered in a drunken brawl. He laments: 'Reputation reputation, I ha' lost my reputation!' (2.3.254).[1] Iago replies, 'You have lost no reputation at all, unless you repute yourself such a loser' (2.3.261–3), but this assertion is absurd (though attractive), since reputation is by definition a social construct, concerned entirely with one's standing in the eyes of others. In fact, language and reality are always interactive, dependent upon social recognition; reputation is only a specially explicit instance. Meaning, communication, language work only because they are shared. If you invent your own language, no one else will understand you; if you persist, you will be thought mad. Iago is telling Cassio to disregard the social basis of language, to make up his own meanings for words; it is the more perverse because Iago is the great manipulator of the prevailing stories of his society.

Stephen Greenblatt has remarked how Othello's identity depends upon a constant performance of his 'story';[2] when in difficulty, his immediate move is to rehearse his nobility and service to the state. Actually, all the characters in *Othello* are telling stories, and to convince others even more than themselves. At the start, Iago and Roderigo are concocting a story – a sexist and racist story about how

49

Desdemona is in 'the gross clasps of a lascivious Moor' (1.1.126).
Brabantio believes this story and repeats it to the Senate, but Othello
contests it with his 'tale':

> I will a round unvarnish'd tale deliver,
> Of my whole course of love.
>   (1.3.90–1)

The tale is – that Othello told a story. Brabantio 'Still question'd me
the story of my life' (1.3.129), and this story attracted Desdemona.
She asked to hear it through, observing,

>   if I had a friend that lov'd her,
> I should but teach him how to tell my story,
> And that would woo her.
>   (1.3.163–5)

So the action advances through a contest of stories, and *the conditions of plausibility* are therefore crucial – they determine which
stories will be believed. Brabantio's case is that Othello must have
enchanted Desdemona – anything else is implausible:

> She is abus'd, stol'n from me and corrupted,
> By spells and medicines, bought of mountebanks,
> For nature so preposterously to err,
> (Being not deficient, blind, or lame of sense,)
> Sans witchcraft could not.
>   (1.3.60–4)

To Brabantio, for Desdemona to love Othello would be preposterous, an error of nature. To make this case, he depends on the plausibility, to the Senate, of the notion that Blacks are inferior outsiders.
This, evidently, is a good move. Even characters who want to support
Othello's story accept that he is superficially inappropriate as a husband for Desdemona. She says as much herself when she declares,
'I saw Othello's visage in his mind' (1.3.252): this means, he may
look like a black man but really he is very nice. And the Duke finally
tells Brabantio: 'Your son-in-law is far more fair than black'
(1.3.290) – meaning, Othello doesn't have many of those unpleasant
characteristics that we all know belong to Blacks, he is really quite
like a white man.

With the conditions of plausibility so stacked against him, two
main strategies are available to Othello, and he uses both. One is to

appear very calm and responsible – as the Venetians imagine themselves to be. But also, and shrewdly, he uses the racist idea of himself as exotic: he says he has experienced 'hair-breadth scapes', redemption from slavery, hills 'whose heads touch heaven', cannibals, anthropophagi 'and men whose heads / Do grow beneath their shoulders' (1.3.129–45). These adventures are of course implausible – but not when attributed to an exotic. Othello has little credit by normal upper-class Venetian criteria, but when he plays on his strangeness, the Venetians tolerate him, for he is granting, in more benign form, part of Brabantio's case.

Partly, perhaps, because the senators need Othello to fight the Turks for them, they allow his story to prevail. However, this is not, of course, the end of the story. Iago repeats his racist and sexist tale to Othello, and persuades him of its credibility:

> I know our country disposition well…
> She did deceive her father, marrying you…
> Not to affect many proposed matches,
> Of her own clime, complexion, and degree,
> Whereto we see in all things nature tends…
> (3.3.205, 210, 233–5)

Othello is persuaded of his inferiority and of Desdemona's inconstancy, and he proceeds to act as if they were true. 'Haply, for I am black', he muses (3.3.267), and begins to take the role of the 'erring barbarian' (1.3.356–7) that he is alleged to be. As Ania Loomba puts it, 'Othello moves from being a colonised subject existing on the terms of white Venetian society and trying to internalise its ideology, towards being marginalised, outcast and alienated from it in every way, until he occupies his "true" position as its other.'[3] It is very difficult not to be influenced by a story, even about yourself, when everyone else is insisting upon it. So in the last lines of the play, when he wants to reassert himself, Othello 'recognizes' himself as what Venetian culture has really believed him to be: an ignorant, barbaric outsider – like, he says, the 'base Indian' who threw away a pearl. Virtually, this is what Althusser means by 'interpellation': Venice hails Othello as a barbarian, and he acknowledges that it is he they mean.[4]

Iago remarks that the notion that Desdemona loves Cassio is 'apt and of great credit' (2.1.282); and that his advice to Cassio to press Desdemona for his reinstatement is 'Probal to thinking' (2.3.329). Iago's stories work because they are plausible – to Roderigo, Brabantio, the Senate, even to Othello himself. As Peter Stallybrass has observed, Iago is convincing not because he is 'superhumanly ingenious but, to the contrary, because his is the voice of "common sense", the cease-less repetition of the always-already "known", the culturally "given" '.[5] The racism and sexism in the play should not be traced just to Iago's character, therefore, or to his arbitrary devilishness, but to the Venetian culture that sets the conditions of plausibility.

THE PRODUCTION OF IDEOLOGY

I have spoken of stories because I want an inclusive term that will key in my theory to the continuous and familiar discourses of every-day life. But in effect I have been addressing the production of ideology. Societies need to produce materially to continue – they need food, shelter, warmth; goods to exchange with other societies; a transport and information infrastructure to carry those processes. Also, they have to produce ideologically (Althusser makes this argu-ment at the start of his essay on ideological state apparatuses).[6] They need knowledges to keep material production going – diverse tech-nical skills and wisdoms in agriculture, industry, science, medicine, economics, law, geography, languages, politics and so on. And they need understandings, intuitive and explicit, of a system of social rela-tionships within which the whole process can take place more or less evenly. Ideology produces, makes plausible, concepts and systems to explain who we are, who the others are, how the world works.

   The strength of ideology derives from the way it gets to be common sense; it 'goes without saying'. For its production is not an external process, stories are not outside ourselves, something we just hear or read about. Ideology makes sense for us – of us – because it is already proceeding when we arrive in the world, and we come to conscious-ness in its terms. As the world shapes itself around and through us, certain interpretations of experience strike us as plausible: they fit with what we have experienced already, and are confirmed by others around us. So we complete what Colin Sumner calls a 'circle of social reality': 'understanding produces its own social reality at the same time as social reality produces its own understanding'.[7] This is apparent when we observe how people in other cultures than our own make good sense of the world in ways that seem strange to us: their outlook is supported by their social context. For them, those frameworks of perception, maps of meaning, work.

The conditions of plausibility are therefore crucial. They govern our understandings of the world and how to live in it, thereby seeming to define the scope of feasible political change. Most societies retain their current shape, not because dissidents are penalized or incorporated, though they are, but because many people believe that things have to take more or less their present form – that improvement is not feasible, at least through the methods to hand. That is why one recognizes a dominant ideology: were there not such a powerful (plausible) discourse, people would not acquiesce in the injustice and humiliation that they experience. To insist on ideological construction is not to deny individual agency (though it makes individual agency less interesting). Rather, the same structure informs individuals and the society. Anthony Giddens compares the utterance of a grammatical sentence, which is governed by the lexicon and syntactical rules that constitute the language, but is individual and, through its utterance, may both confirm and slightly modify the language.[8]

Ideology is produced everywhere and all the time in the social order, but some institutions – by definition, those that usually corroborate the prevailing power arrangements – are vastly more powerful than others. The stories they endorse are more difficult to challenge, even to disbelieve. Such institutions, and the people in them, are also constituted in ideology; they are figures in its stories. At the same time, I would not want to lose a traditional sense of the power elite in the state exercising authority, through the ideological framework it both inhabits and maintains, over subordinate groups. This process may be observed in Shakespearean plays, where the most effective stories are given specific scope and direction by powerful men. They authorize scripts, we may say, that the other characters resist only with difficulty. Very often this does not require any remarkable intervention, or seems to involve only a 'restoration of order', for the preferences of the ruling elite are already attuned to the system as it is already running. Conversely, scripting from below by lower-order characters immediately appears subversive; consider Shylock, Malvolio, Don John, Iago, Edmund, Macbeth, Caliban. Women may disturb the system (I return to this shortly), and in early comedies they are allowed to script, sometimes even in violation of parental wishes, but their scripts lead to the surrender of their power in the larger story of marriage. Elsewhere, women who script men are bad – Goneril and Regan, Lady Macbeth, the Queen in *Cymbeline*. Generally, the scripting of women by men is presented as good for them. Miranda's marriage in *The Tempest* seems to be all that Prospero has designed it to be. In *Measure for Measure*, Isabella is given by the Duke the script she ought to want – all the men in the play have conspired to draw her away from an independent life in the convent. To be sure, these are not the scripts of men only. As Stephen Orgel remarks, the plays must have appealed to the women in the audience as well: these were the fantasies of a whole culture.[9] But insofar as they show the powerful dominating the modes in which ideology is realized, these plays record an insight into ideology and power.

The state is the most powerful scriptor; it is best placed to enforce its story. In *Othello*, the Duke offers Brabantio, for use against Desdemona's alleged enchanter, 'the bloody book of law' (1.3.67–70): the ruling elite have written this, and they decree who shall apply it. At the end of the play, Othello tries to control the story that will survive him – 'When you shall these unlucky deeds relate, / Speak of them as they are …' (5.2.342–3). However, the very last lines are spoken by Lodovico, the Venetian nobleman and representative of the Senate: 'Myself will straight aboard, and to the state / This heavy act with heavy heart relate'. The state and the ruling elite will tell Othello's story in the way they choose. They will try to control Iago's story as well, torturing him until he speaks what they want to hear: the state falls back on direct coercion when its domination of the conditions of plausibility falters. Through violence against Iago, the state means to make manifest his violence while legitimating its own.

The relation between violence and the ideological power of the state may be glimpsed in the way Othello justifies himself, in his last speech, as a good Venetian: he boasts of killing someone. Not Desdemona – that, he now agrees, was bad – but 'a malignant and a turban'd Turk', who 'Beat a Venetian, and traduc'd the state'. Othello says he 'took by the throat the circumcised dog, / And smote him thus' (5.2.352–7). And so, upon this recollection, Othello stabs himself, recognizing himself, for the last time, as an outsider, a discredit to the social order he has been persuaded to respect. Innumerable critics discuss Othello's suicide, but I haven't noticed them worrying about the murdered Turk. Being malignant, circumcised, and wearing a turban into the bargain, he seems not to require the sensitive attention of literary critics in Britain and North America. The character critic might take this reported murder as a last-minute revelation of Othello's long-standing propensity to desperate violence when people say things he doesn't like. But the violence here is not Othello's alone, any more than Venetian racism and sexism are particular to individuals. Othello's murder of the Turk is the kind of thing the Venetian state likes – or so we must assume, since Othello is in good standing in Venice as a state servant, and presents the story to enhance his credit. 'He was great of heart', Cassio enthuses (5.2.362), pleased that he has found something to retrieve his respect for Othello. In respect of murdering state enemies, at least, he was a good citizen.

It is a definition of the state, almost, that it claims a monopoly of legitimate violence, and the exercise of that violence is justified through stories about the barbarity of those who are constituted as its demonized others. For the Venetians, as for the Elizabethans, the Turks were among the barbarians.[10] In actuality, in most states that we know of, the civilized and the barbaric are not very different from each other; that is why maintaining the distinction is such a constant ideological task. It is not altogether Othello's personal achievement, or his personal failure, therefore, when he kills himself declaring, with respect to the Turk, that he 'smote him thus'. Othello becomes a good subject once more by accepting within himself the state's distinction between civilized and barbaric. This 'explains' how he has come to murder Desdemona: it was the barbarian beneath, or rather in, the skin. And when he kills himself it is even better, because he eradicates the intolerable confusion of finding both the citizen and the alien in the same body. Othello's particular circumstances bring into visibility, for those who want to see, the violence upon which the state and its civilization rest.

STRUCTURE AND INDIVIDUALS

My argument has reached the point where I have to address the scope for dissidence within ideological construction. 'The class which is the ruling material force is, at the same time, its ruling intellectual force. The class which has the means of material production at its disposal, has control at the same time over the means of mental production', Marx and Engels declare in *The German Ideology*.[11] The point is surely only sensible: groups with material power will dominate the institutions that deal with ideas. That is why people can be persuaded to believe things that are neither just, humane, nor to their advantage. The issue is pressed harder in modern cultural theory. In work deriving from Althusser and Foucault, distinct as those two sources are, ideological constructedness, not just of our ideas but of our subjectivities, seems to control the scope for dissident thought and expression. This is a key question: if we come to consciousness within a language that is continuous with the power structures that sustain the social order, how can we conceive, let alone organize, resistance?

The issue has been raised sharply by feminist critics, in particular Lynda E. Boose and Carol Thomas Neely. They accuse both New Historicism and cultural materialism of theorizing power as an unbreakable system of containment, a system that positions subordinate groups as effects of the dominant, so that female identity, for instance, appears to be something fathered upon women by patriarchy.[12] How, it is asked, can women produce a dissident perspective from such a complicit ideological base? And so with other subordinated groups: if the conditions of plausibility persuade black or gay people to assume subjectivities that suit the maintenance of the social order, how is a radical black or gay consciousness to arise?

Kathleen McLuskie's argument that *Measure for Measure* and *King Lear* are organized from a male point of view has received particular attention. There is no way, McLuskie says, to find feminist heroines in Regan and Goneril, the wicked women, or in the good woman, Cordelia. Feminist criticism 'is restricted to exposing its own exclusion from the text'.[13] The alternative feminist position, which we may term a humanist or essentialist feminism, is stated by Carolyn Ruth Swift Lenz, Gayle Greene and Carol Thomas Neely in their groundbreaking collection of essays, *The Woman's Part*. They believe feminist critics should, typically, be finding that Shakespeare's women characters are *not* male constructions – not 'the saints, monsters, or whores their critics have often perceived them to be'. Rather, 'like the male characters the women are complex and flawed, like them capable of passion and pain, growth and decay'.[14] This perspective is evidently at odds with the approach I am presenting. In my view, when traditional critics perceive Shakespearan women characters in terms of stereotypes, they are often more or less right. Such critics recognize in the plays the ideological structures that our cultures have been producing. My dispute with them begins when they admire the patterns they find and collaborate in rendering them plausible, instead of offering a critique of them. As McLuskie says, we should attend to 'the narrative, poetic and theatrical strategies which construct the plays' meanings and position the audience to understand their events from a particular point of view'.[15]

There are in fact two issues here. One is whether there is (for women or men) any such fullness of personhood as Lenz, Greene and Neely propose, or whether subjectivity is, as I have been arguing, an effect of cultural production. The other is the authority of Shakespeare: can we reasonably assume that he anticipated a progressive modern sexual politics? As McLuskie points out, he was working within 'an entertainment industry which, as far as we know, had no women shareholders, actors, writers, or stage hands'. Ultimately these issues converge: the idea that Shakespearean texts tune into an essential humanity, transcending cultural production, is aligned with the idea that individual characters do that. As Lynda Boose says, the question is whether the human being is conceived as inscribing 'at least something universal that transcends history, or as an entity completely produced by its historical culture'. Boose credits McLuskie with 'unblinkered honesty', but complains that one has 'to renounce completely one's pleasure in Shakespeare and embrace instead the rigorous comforts of ideological correctness'.[16] Maybe one does (try listening again to the words of most Christmas carols); but pleasure in Shakespeare is a complex phenomenon, and it may not be altogether incompatible with a critical attitude to ideology in the plays.

The essentialist–humanist approach to literature and sexual politics depends upon the belief that the individual is the probable, indeed necessary, source of truth and meaning. Literary significance and personal significance seem to derive from and speak to individual consciousnesses. But thinking of ourselves as essentially individual tends to efface processes of cultural production and, in the same movement, leads us to imagine ourselves to be autonomous, self-determining. It is not individuals but power structures that produce the system within which we live and think, and focusing upon the individual makes it hard to discern those structures; and if we discern them, hard to do much about them, since that would require collective action. To adopt the instance offered by Richard Ohmann in his book *English in America*, each of us buys an automobile because we need it to get around, and none of us, individually, does much damage to the environment or other people. But from that position it is hard to get to address, much less do anything about, whether we should be living in an automobile culture at all.[17]

I believe feminist anxiety about derogation of the individual in cultural materialism is misplaced, since personal subjectivity and agency are, anyway, unlikely sources of dissident identity and action. Political awareness does not arise out of an essential, individual, self-consciousness of class, race, nation, gender, or sexual orientation; but from involvement in *a milieu, a subculture.* 'In acquiring one's conception of the world one belongs to a particular grouping which is that of all the social elements which share the same mode of thinking and acting', Gramsci observes.[18] It is through such sharing that one may learn to inhabit plausible oppositional preoccupations and forms – ways of relating to others – and hence develop a plausible oppositional selfhood. That is how successful movements have worked.

These issues have been most thoroughly considered by recent theorists of lesbian identity. Judith Butler argues against a universalist concept, 'woman', not only on the ground that it effaces diversities of time and place, but also because it is oppressive: it necessarily involves 'the exclusion of those who fail to conform to unspoken normative requirements of the subject'.[19] Butler asks if 'unity' is indeed necessary for effective political action, pointing out that 'the articulation of an identity within available cultural terms instates a definition that forecloses in advance the emergence of new identity concepts in and through politically engaged actions'. For agency to operate, Butler points out, a 'doer' does not have to be in place first; rather, she or he is constructed through the deed. Identity develops, precisely, in the process of signification: 'identity is always already signified, and yet continues to signify as it circulates within various interlocking discourses'. So 'construction is not opposed to agency; it is the necessary scene of agency, the very terms in which agency is articulated and becomes culturally intelligible'. Identity is not that which produces culture, nor even that which is produced as a static entity by culture: rather, the two are the same process.

If these arguments are correct, then it is not necessary to envisage, as Neely does, 'some area of "femaleness" that is part biological, part psychical, part experiential, part cultural and that is not utterly inscribed by and in thrall to patriarchal ideology and that makes possible female discourse'.[20] 'Female discourse' will be the discourse that women work out together at a historical conjuncture, and it will be rendered plausible by social interaction, especially among women. Desdemona gets closest to seeing what is going on when she talks with Emilia (what she needs is a refuge for battered wives); Othello gets it wrong because he has no reliable friends with whom to check out his perceptions. Subcultures constitute consciousness, in principle, in the same way that dominant ideologies do – but in partly dissident forms. In that bit of the world where the subculture runs, you can feel confident, as we used to say, that Black is beautiful, gay is good: there, those stories work, they build their own kinds of interactive plausibility. Validating the individual may seem attractive because it appears to empower him or her, but actually it undervalues potential resources of collective understanding and resistance.

ENTRAPMENT AND FAULTLINES

While the ideology of individualism is associated mainly with traditional modes of literary criticism, the poststructuralist vein in recent cultural work, including New Historicism, has also helped to obscure the importance of collectivities and social location. A principal theoretical task in such work has been to reassess the earlier Marxist base/superstructure model, whereby culture was seen as a one-way effect of economic organization. (In apparent ignorance of this work, much of which has been conducted in Europe, J. Hillis Miller supposes that people of 'the so-called left' hold 'an unexamined ideology of the material base'.[21]) It was necessary to abandon that model, but in the process, as Peter Nicholls has pointed out, the tendency in New Historicism has been 'to replace a model of mechanical causality with one of structural homology'. And this works to '*dis*place the concepts of production and class which would initiate a thematics of historical change'. Homology discovers synchronic structural connectedness without determination, sometimes without pressure or tension. Hence 'the problem of ideology becomes a purely superstructural one'.[22] The agency that has sunk from view, following Nicholls's argument, is that, not of individuals, but of classes, class fractions, and groups. Yet Marx was surely right to envisage such collectivities as the feasible agents of historical change.

New Historicism has been drawn to what I call the 'entrapment model' of ideology and power, whereby even, or especially, manouvres that seem designed to challenge the system help to maintain it. Don E. Wayne says New Historicism has often shown 'how different kinds of discourse intersect, contradict, destabilize, cancel, or modify each other...seek[ing] to demonstrate how a dominant ideology will give a certain rein to alternative discourses, ultimately appropriating their vitality and containing their oppositional force'.[23] The issue informs the ambiguous title of *Renaissance Self-Fashioning*: Stephen Greenblatt's central figures aspired to fashion themselves, but he finds that their selves were fashioned for them. So Wyatt 'cannot fashion himself in opposition to power and the conventions power deploys; on the contrary, those conventions are precisely what constitute Wyatt's self-fashioning'.[24] Hence Carolyn Porter's complaint that the subordinate seems a mere discursive effect of the dominant in New Historicism.[25]

Of course, not all work generally dubbed 'New Historicist' takes such a line (not that of Louis Adrian Montrose). Nor is entrapment only here at issue – it arises generally in functionalism, structuralism and Althusserian Marxism. Greenblatt has recently denied proposing that resistance is always co-opted, and he is in my view right to say that his 'Invisible Bullets' essay has often been misinterpreted.[26] I associate the entrapment model with New Historicism neverthe-less, because its treatment there has been distinctively subtle, power-ful and pressured, and because it is, of course, not by chance that this aspect of New Historicism has been emphasized. The notion that dissidence is characteristically contained has caught the imagi-nation of the profession. Therefore, even while acknowledging the diversity and specificity of actual writing (which I draw upon fre-quently in the pages that follow), it is the aspect of New-Historicist thought that has to be addressed.

An instance that confronts the entrapment model at its heart is the risk that the legally constituted ruler might not be able to control the military apparatus. Valuable New-Historicist analyses, considering the interaction of the monarch and the court, have tended to discover 'power' moving in an apparently unbreakable circle – proceeding from and returning to the monarch. But although absolutist ideology represents the ruler as the necessary and sufficient source of national unity, the early modern state depended in the last analysis, like other states, upon military force. The obvious instance is the Earl of Essex's rebellion in 1601. With the queen aging and military success in Cádiz to his credit, it was easy for the charismatic earl to suppose that he should not remain subordinate. Ideological and military power threaten to split apart; it is a faultline in the political structure. Indeed, army coups against legitimate but militarily dependent polit-ical leaders still occur all the time. In the United States, during the Korean War, General Douglas MacArthur believed he could override the authority of President Harry S. Truman.

In *Macbeth*, Duncan has the legitimacy but Macbeth is the best fighter. Duncan cannot but delegate power to subordinates, who may turn it back upon him – the initial rebellion is that of the Thane of Cawdor, in whom Duncan says he 'built / An absolute trust'.[27] If the thought of revolt can enter the mind of Cawdor, then it will occur to Macbeth, and others; its source is not just personal

(Macbeth's ambition). Of course, it is crucial to the ideology of absolutism to deny that the state suffers such a structural flaw. Hence the projection of the whole issue onto a supernatural backdrop of good and evil, and the implication that disruption must derive, or be crucially reinforced, from outside (by the Weird Sisters and the distinctively demonic Lady Macbeth). Macbeth's mistake, arguably, is that he falls for Duncan's ideology and loses his nerve. However, this does not mean that absolutist ideology was inevitably successful – when Charles I tried to insist upon it there was a revolution.

Henry V offers a magical resolution of this faultline by presenting the legitimate king as the triumphant war leader. The pressure of aspiration and anxiety around the matter may be gauged from the reference to Essex by the Chorus of act 5. In the most specific contemporary allusion in any Shakespeare play, Henry V's return from France is compared first to Caesar's return as conqueror to Rome and then to Essex's anticipated return from Ireland:

> As, by a lower but by loving likelihood,
> Were now the general of our gracious empress,
> As in good time he may, from Ireland coming,
> Bringing rebellion broached on his sword,
> How many would the peaceful city quit
> To welcome him! much more, and much more cause,
> Did they this Harry.[28]

Notice the prudent qualification that this is 'a lower ... likelihood' insofar as Essex is but 'the general of our gracious empress'; Harry would be welcomed 'much more, and much more cause'. The text strives to envisage a leader whose power, unlike that of the queen, would be uncontestable, but yet at the same time that of the queen. Promoting Elizabeth to empress (of Ireland) seems to give her a further edge over her commander. Even so the comparisons refuse to stabilize, for Henry V himself has just been likened to a caesar, and Julius Caesar threatened the government after his triumphal entry into Rome. And Elizabeth becomes empress only through Essex's military success, and that very success would enhance his potential for revolt. With the city specified as 'peaceful', it seems only thoughtful to wonder whether it would remain so. However, faultlines are by definition resistant to the fantasies that would erase them. The epilogue to *Henry V* has to record that the absolutist pyramid collapsed with the accession of Henry VI, who, precisely, was not the strongest military leader. And Essex failed to mobilize sufficient support to bring Elizabeth within his power.

My argument is that dissident potential derives ultimately not from essential qualities in individuals (though they have qualities) but from conflict and contradiction that the social order inevitably produces within itself, even as it attempts to sustain itself. Despite their power, dominant ideological formations are always, in practice, under pressure, striving to substantiate their claim to superior plausibility in the face of diverse disturbances. Hence Raymond Williams's observation that ideology has always to be *produced*: 'Social orders and cultural orders must be seen as being actively made: actively and continuously, or they may quite quickly break down'.[29] Conflict and contradiction stem from the very strategies through which ideologies strive to contain the expectations that they need to generate. This is where failure – inability or refusal – to identify one's interests with the dominant may occur, and hence where dissidence may arise. In this argument the dominant and subordinate are structurally linked, but not in the way criticized by Carolyn Porter when she says that although 'masterless men' (her instance) may ultimately have been controlled, 'their subversive resistance cannot [therefore] be understood simply as the product of the dominant culture's power'.[30] It was the Elizabethan social structure that produced unemployed labourers, and military leaders, but it could not then prevent such figures conceiving and enacting dissident practices, especially if they were able to constitute milieux within which dissidence might be rendered plausible.

DESDEMONA'S DEFIANCE

Another key point at which to confront the entrapment model concerns the scope of women. *Othello*, like many contemporary texts, betrays an obsessive concern with disorder; the ideology and power of the ruling elite are reasserted at the end of the play, but equilibrium is not, by any means, easily regained. The specific disruption stems from Desdemona's marital choice.[31] At her first entrance, her father asks her: 'Do you perceive in all this noble company, / Where most you owe obedience?' She replies that she sees 'a divided duty' – to her father and her husband:

> I am hitherto your daughter: but here's my husband:
> And so much duty as my mother show'd
> To you, preferring you before her father,

So much I challenge, that I may profess,
Due to the Moor my Lord.
(1.3.179–89)

And to justify the latter allegiance, she declares: 'I did love the Moor, to live with him' (1.2.248).

This is a paradigm instance. For, in her use of the idea of a divided duty to justify elopement with an inappropriate man, Desdemona has not discovered a distinctive, radical insight (any more than Cordelia does when she uses it). She is offering a straightforward elaboration of official doctrine, which said that a woman should obey the male head of her family, who should be first her father (or failing that a brother or uncle), then her husband. Before marriage, the former; afterwards, the latter. Ideally, from the point of view of the social order, it would all be straightforward. The woman's transition from daughter to wife – from one set of duties to another – would be accomplished smoothly, with the agreement of all parties. But things could go wrong here; it was an insecure moment in patriarchy. The danger derived from a fundamental complication in the ideology of gender relations. Marriage was the institution through which property arrangements were made and inheritance secured, but it was supposed also to be a fulfilling personal relationship. It was held that the people being married should act in obedience to their parents, but also that they should love each other.[32] The 'divided duty' was not especially Desdemona's problem, therefore; it is how the world was set up for her.

The Reformation intensified the issue by shifting both the status and the nature of marriage. The Catholic church held that the three reasons for matrimony were, first, to beget children; second, to avoid carnal sin; and third, for mutual help and comfort. Protestants stressed the third objective, often promoting it to first place; the homily 'Of the State of Matrimony' says: 'it is instituted of God, to the intent that man and woman should live lawfully in a perpetual friendly fellowship, to bring forth fruit, and to avoid fornication'.[33] Thus protestants defined marriage more positively, as a mutual, fulfilling, reciprocal relationship. However, they were not prepared to abandon patriarchal authority; it was too important to the system. In *Arcadia*, Philip Sidney presents an ideal marriage of reciprocity and mutual love, that of Argalus and Parthenia: 'A happy couple: he joying in her, she joying in herself, but in herself, because she enjoyed him: both increasing their riches by giving to each other; each making one life double, because they made a double life one'. However, the passage concludes: 'he ruling, because she would obey, or rather because she would obey, she therein ruling'.[34] Does this mean that Parthenia was fulfilled in her subordinate role; or that by appearing submissive she managed to insinuate her own way? Neither seems ideal. In *The Anatomy of Melancholy*, Robert Burton displays a protestant enthusiasm: 'You know marriage is honourable, a blessed calling, appointed by God himself in paradise; it breeds true peace, tranquillity, content and happiness'. But the elaboration is tricky: 'The husband rules her as head, but she again commands his heart, he is her servant, she his only joy and content'.[35] The alternation of head and heart sounds reciprocal but is not, for we know that the head should rule the heart. Then the strong phrasing of 'servant' reverses altogether the initial priority, introducing language more appropriate to romantic love; and finally 'only joy and content' seems to privilege the wife but also places upon her an obligation to please. Coercion and liberty jostle together unresolved, and this is characteristic of protestant attitudes.

In fact, protestantism actually strengthened patriarchal authority. The removal of the mediatory priest threw upon the head of household responsibility for the spiritual life and devout conduct of the family. Also, there was a decline in the significance of great magnates who might stand between subject and monarch. From these developments, protestants devised a comprehensive doctrine of social control, with a double chain of authority running from God to the husband to the individual, and from God to the monarch to the subject. The homily 'Against Disobedience and Wilful Rebellion' derives earthly rule from God and parallels the responsibilities of the monarch and the head of household.[36] Indeed, the latter could be said to have the more important role. 'A master in his family hath all the offices of Christ, for he must rule, and teach, and pray; rule like a king, and teach like a prophet, and pray like a priest', Henry Smith declared in 'A Preparative to Marriage' (1591). This leaves little space for independence for offspring, or anyone else in the household. Smith says parents must control marital choice because, after all, they have the property: 'If children may not make other contracts without [parents'] good will, shall they contract marriage, which have nothing to maintain it after, unless they return to beg of them whom they scorned before?'[37] As with other business deals, it is wrong to enter into marriage unless you can sustain the costs. This was one extreme; at the other, only radicals like the Digger Gerrard

Winstanley proposed that 'every man and woman shall have the free liberty to marry whom they love'.[38] In between, most commentators fudged the question, suggesting that children might exercise a right of refusal, or that even if they didn't like their spouses at first, they would learn to get on. 'A couple is that whereby two persons standing in mutual relation to each other are combined together, as it were, into one. And of these two the one is always higher and beareth rule: the other is lower and yieldeth subjection', William Perkins declared.[39] The boundaries are plainly unclear, and conflict is therefore likely. Hence the awkward bullying and wheedling in the disagreements between Portia and Bassanio, Caesar and Portia, Othello and Desdemona, Macbeth and Lady Macbeth, Leontes and Hermione. Lawrence Stone says dutiful children experienced 'an impossible conflict of role models. They had to try to reconcile the often incompatible demands for obedience to parental wishes on the one hand and expectations of affection in marriage on the other'.[40] At this point, the dominant ideology had not quite got its act together.

Parental influence over marriage in early modern England is nowadays often regarded simply as an instance of the oppressiveness of patriarchy, but that is not quite all. The ambiguity of official doctrine afforded one distinct point at which a woman such as Desdemona could produce a crisis in the patriarchal story. 'Despite the economic and social mechanisms that reinforced parental authority, it was in marriage that parents were most often defied', Dympna Callaghan observes.[41] All too often, such defiance provoked physical and mental violence; at the least it must have felt very unpleasant. That is how it is when you disturb the system – the tendency of ideology is, precisely, to produce good subjects who feel uncomfortable when they transgress. But contradictions in the ideology of marriage produced, nevertheless, an opportunity for dissidence, and even before the appearance of Othello, we are told, Desdemona was exploiting it – refusing 'The wealthy curled darlings of our nation' (1.2.68). Her more extreme action – marrying without parental permission, outside the ruling oligarchy, and outside the race – is so disruptive that the chief (male) council of the state delays its business. 'For if such actions may have passage free', Brabantio says, 'Bond-slaves, and pagans, shall our statesmen be' (1.2.98). Desdemona throws the system into disarray – and just when the men are busy with one of their wars – killing people because of their honour and their property – proving their masculinity to each other.

To be sure, Desdemona was claiming only what Louis Montrose calls 'the limited privilege of giving herself',[42] and her moment of power ends once the men have accepted her marriage. But then dissident opportunities always are limited – otherwise we would not be living as we do. Revolutionary change is rare and usually dependent upon a prior build-up of small breaks; often there are great personal costs. The point of principle is that scope for dissident understanding and action occurs not because women characters, Shakespeare, and feminist readers have a privileged vantage point outside the dominant, but because the social order *cannot but produce* faultlines through which its own criteria of plausibility fall into contest and disarray. This has been theorized by Stuart Hall and his colleagues at the Centre for Contemporary Cultural Studies at the University of Birmingham:

> the dominant culture of a complex society is never a homogeneous structure. It is layered, reflecting different interests within the dominant class (e.g. an aristocratic versus a bourgeois outlook), containing different traces from the past (e.g. religious ideas within a largely secular culture), as well as emergent elements in the present. Subordinate cultures will not always be in open conflict with it. They may, for long periods, coexist with it, negotiate the spaces and gaps in it, make inroads into it, 'warrenning [sic] it from within'.[43]

Observe that this account does not offer to decide whether or not dissidence will be contained; it may not even be actualized, but may lie dormant, becoming disruptive only at certain conjunctures. But if ideology is so intricately 'layered', with so many potential modes of relation to it, it cannot but allow awareness of its own operations. In *Othello*, Emilia takes notable steps towards a dissident perception:

> But I do think it is their husbands' faults
> If wives do fall: say, that they slack their duties,
> And pour our treasures into foreign laps;
> Or else break out in peevish jealousies,
> Throwing restraint upon us; or say they strike us ...
> (4.3.86–90)

Emilia has heard the doctrine of mutual fulfillment in marriage, and from the gap between it and her experience, she is well able to mount a critique of the double standard. At faultlines, such as I am proposing here, a dissident perspective may be discovered and articulated.

The crisis over marital choice illustrates how stories work in culture. It appears again and again – in *A Midsummer Night's Dream*,

The Merchant of Venice, The Taming of the Shrew, Romeo and Juliet, Measure for Measure, King Lear, The Winter's Tale, The Tempest. Roughly speaking, in comedies parents are eventually reconciled to children's wishes; in tragedies (as in *Othello*), precipitate actions without parental authority lead to disaster. And in writing, on through the ensuing centuries until the late nineteenth century, the arranged- versus the love-match is a recurring theme in literature. This is how culture elaborates itself. In these texts, through diverse genres and institutions, people were talking to each other about an aspect of their life that they found hard to handle. When a part of our worldview threatens disruption by manifestly failing to cohere with the rest, then we reorganize and retell its story, trying to get it into shape – back into the old shape if we are conservative-minded, or into a new shape if we are more adventurous. The question of the arranged- versus the love-match died out in fiction in the late nineteenth century because then, for most people in Britain, it was resolved in favour of children's preferences, and therefore became uninteresting (but not, however, for British families deriving recently from Asia). The other great point at which the woman could disturb the system was by loving a man not her husband, and that is why adultery is such a prominent theme in literature. It upsets the husband's honour, his masculinity and (through the bearing of illegitimate children) his property. Even the rumour of Desdemona's adultery is enough to send powerful men in the state into another anxiety.

This is why it is not unpromising to seek in literature our preoccupations with class, race, gender and sexual orientation: it is likely that literary texts will address just such controversial aspects of our ideological formation. Those faultline stories are the ones that require most assiduous and continuous reworking; they address the awkward, unresolved issues, the ones in which the conditions of plausibility are in dispute. For authors and readers, after all, want writing to be interesting. The task for a political criticism, then, is to observe how stories negotiate the faultlines that distress the prevailing conditions of plausibility.

READING DISSIDENCE

The reason why textual analysis can so readily demonstrate dissidence being incorporated is that dissidence operates, necessarily, with reference to dominant structures. It has to invoke those structures to oppose them, and therefore can always, ipso facto, be discovered reinscribing that which it proposes to critique. 'Power relations are always two-way; that is to say, however subordinate an actor may be in a social relationship, the very fact of involvement in that relationship gives him or her a certain amount of power over the other', Anthony Giddens observes.[44] The inter-involvement of resistance and control is systemic: it derives from the way language and culture get articulated. Any utterance is bounded by the other utterances that the language makes possible. Its shape is the correlative of theirs: as with the duck/rabbit drawing, when you see the duck the rabbit lurks round its edges, constituting an alternative that may spring into visibility. Any position supposes its intrinsic *op*-position. All stories comprise within themselves the ghosts of the alternative stories they are trying to exclude.

It does not follow, therefore, that the outcome of the inter-involvement of resistance and control must be the incorporation of the subordinate. Indeed, Foucault says the same, though he is often taken as the theorist of entrapment. In *The History of Sexuality: An Introduction*, he says there is no 'great Refusal', but envisages 'a plurality of resistances ... spread over time and space at varying densities, at times mobilising groups or individuals in a definitive way'. He *denies* that these must be 'only a reaction or rebound, forming with respect to the basic domination an underside that is in the end always passive, doomed to perpetual defeat'.[45] In fact, a dissident text may derive its leverage, its purchase, precisely from its partial implication with the dominant. It may embarrass the dominant by appropriating its concepts and imagery. For instance, it seems clear that nineteenth-century legal, medical and sexological discourses on homosexuality made possible new forms of control; but, at the same time, they also made possible what Foucault terms 'a "reverse" discourse', whereby 'homosexuality began to speak in its own behalf, to demand that its legitimacy or "naturality" be acknowledged, often in the same vocabulary, using the same categories by which it was medically disqualified'.[46] Deviancy returns from abjection by deploying just those terms that relegated it there in the first place. A dominant discourse cannot prevent 'abuse' of its resources. Even a text that aspires to contain a subordinate perspective must first bring it into visibility; even to misrepresent, one must present. And once that has happened, there can be no guarantee that the subordinate will stay safely in its prescribed place. Readers do not have to respect closures – we do not, for instance, have to accept that the independent women characters in Shakespearean comedies find their proper destinies in the marriage deals at the ends of those plays. We can insist on our sense that the middle of such a text arouses expectations that exceed the closure.

Conversely, a text that aspires to dissidence cannot control meaning either. It is bound to slide into disabling nuances that it fails to anticipate, and it cannot prevent the drawing of reactionary inferences by readers who want to do that. (Among other things, this might serve as a case against ultra-leftism, by which I mean the complacency of finding everyone else to be ideologically suspect.) There can be no security in textuality: no scriptor can control the reading of his or her text. And when, in any instance, either incorporation or resistance turns out to be the more successful, that is not in the nature of things. It is because of *their relative strengths in that situation*. So it is not quite as Jonathan Goldberg has recently put it, turning the entrapment model inside out, that 'dominant discourses allow their own subversion precisely because hegemonic control is an impossible dream, a self-deluding fantasy'.[47] Either outcome depends on the specific balance of historical forces. Essex's rebellion failed because he could not muster adequate support on the day. It is the same with competence. Williams remarks that the development of writing reinforced cultural divisions, but also that 'there was no way to teach a man to read the Bible ... which did not also enable him to read the radical press'. Keith Thomas observes that 'the uneven social distribution of literacy skills greatly widened the gulf between the classes'; but he illustrates also the fear that 'if the poor learned to read and write they would become seditious, atheistical, and discontented with their humble position'.[48] Both may occur, in varying degrees; it was, and is, all to play for.

It is to circumvent the entrapment model that I have generally used the term *dissident* rather than *subversive*, since the latter may seem to imply achievement – that something *was subverted* – and hence (since mostly the government did not fall, patriarchy did not crumble) that containment must have occurred. 'Dissidence' I take to imply refusal of an aspect of the dominant, without prejudging an outcome. This may sound like a weaker claim, but I believe it is actually stronger insofar as it posits a field necessarily open to continuing contest, in which at some conjunctures the dominant will lose ground while at others the subordinate will scarcely maintain its position. As Jonathan Dollimore has said, dissidence may provoke brutal repression, and that shows not that it was all a ruse of power to consolidate itself, but that 'the challenge really *was* unsettling'.[49]

The implications of these arguments for literary criticism are substantial, for it follows that formal textual analysis cannot determine whether a text is subversive or contained. The historical conditions in which it is being deployed are decisive. 'Nothing can be intrinsically or essentially subversive in the sense that prior to the event subversiveness can be more than potential; in other words it cannot be guaranteed a priori, independent of articulation, context and reception,' Dollimore observes.[50] Nor, independently of context, can anything be said to be safely contained. This prospect scandalizes literary criticism, because it means that meaning is not adequately deducible from the text-on-the-page. The text is always a site of cultural contest, but it is never a self-sufficient site.

It is a key proposition of cultural materialism that the specific historical conditions in which institutions and formations organize and are organized by textualities must be addressed. That is what Raymond Williams was showing us for thirty years. The entrapment model is suspiciously convenient for literary criticism, because it means that little would be gained by investigating the specific historical effectivity of texts. And, indeed, Don Wayne very shrewdly suggests that the success of prominent New Historicists may derive in large part from their skills in close reading – admittedly of a far wider range of texts – which satisfy entirely traditional criteria of performativity in academic criticism.[51] Cultural materialism calls for modes of knowledge that literary criticism scarcely possesses, or even knows how to discover – modes, indeed, that hitherto have been cultivated distinctively within that alien other of essentialist humanism, Marxism. These knowledges are in part the provinces of history and other social sciences – and, of course, they bring in their train questions of historiography and epistemology that require theory more complex than the tidy poststructuralist formula that everything, after all, is a text (or that everything is theatre). This prospect is valuable in direct proportion to its difficulty for, as Foucault maintains, the boundaries of disciplines effect a policing of discourses, and their erosion may, in itself, help to 'detach the power of truth from the forms of hegemony (social, economic and cultural) within which it operates at the present time' in order to constitute 'a new politics of truth'.[52]

Shakespearean plays are themselves powerful stories. They contribute to the perpetual contest of stories that constitutes culture: its representations, and our critical accounts of them, reinforce or challenge prevailing notions of what the world is like, of how it might be. 'The detailed and substantial *performance of a known model* of "people like this, relations like this", is in fact the real achievement of most serious novels and plays,' Raymond Williams observes;[53] by appealing to the reader's sense of how the world *is*, the text affirms the validity of the model it invokes. Among other things, *Othello* invites *recognition* that this is how people are, how the world goes. That is why the criteria of plausibility are political. This effect is not countered, as essentialist–humanists have long supposed, by literary quality; the more persuasive the writing, the greater its potential for political intervention.

The quintessential traditional critical activity was always interpretive, getting the text to make sense. Hence the speculation about character motivation, image patterns, thematic integration, structure: the task always was *to help the text into coherence*. And the discovery of coherence was taken as the demonstration of quality. However, such practice may feed into a reactionary politics. The easiest way to make *Othello* plausible in Britain is to rely on the lurking racism, sexism and superstition in British culture. Why does Othello, who has considerable experience of people, fall so conveniently for Iago's stories? We can make his gullibility plausible by suggesting that black people are generally of a rather simple disposition. To explain why Desdemona elopes with Othello and then becomes so submissive, we might appeal to a supposedly fundamental silliness and passivity of women. Baffled in the attempt to find motive for Iago's malignancy, we can resort to the devil, or the consequence of scepticism towards conventional morality, or homosexuality. Such interpretations might be plausible; might 'work', as theatre people say; but only because they activate regressive aspects of our cultural formation.

Actually, coherence is a chimera, as my earlier arguments should suggest. No story can contain all the possibilities it brings into play; coherence is always selection. And the range of feasible readings depends not only on the text but on the conceptual framework within which we address it. Literary criticism tells its own stories. It is, in effect, a subculture, asserting its own distinctive criteria of plausibility. Education has taken as its brief the socialization of students into these criteria, while masking this project as the achievement by talented individuals (for it is in the programme that most should fail) of a just and true reading of texts that are just and true. A cultural materialist practice will review the institutions that retell the Shakespeare stories, and will attempt also a self-consciousness about its own situation within those institutions. We need not just to produce different readings but to shift the criteria of plausibility.

From Alan Sinfield, *Faultlines: Cultural Materialism and the Politics of Dissident Reading* (Oxford, 1992), pp. 29–51.

NOTES

[In this essay, Alan Sinfield demonstrates that Othello comes to recognize Iago's story of his own barbarism because, in the racist context of Venetian society, Iago is more 'plausible' than Othello is himself. Sinfield, one of the founding cultural materialists, relates the deceptive plausibility of Iago to the plausibility affected by *Othello* – or, in fact, by any literary text or ideological production. Resistant readings refuse to help texts make sense or cohere. Instead, they look for faultlines, the conflicts and contradictions that any order produces within itself. Some faultlines in *Othello*, for example, have to do with early modern ideas of gender relations, matchmaking and marriage. In Sinfield's reading, *Othello* is thus the occasion for a manifesto on the critical practice of cultural materialism. This essay was originally published as a chapter in Sinfield's book *Faultlines*. In that volume, it is followed by another chapter also dealing with *Othello*. There, Sinfield contests another form of false plausibility – consistency of character. Ed.]

1. *Othello* is quoted from the New Arden edition, ed. M. R. Ridley (London: Methuen, 1962). An earlier version of parts of this paper, entitled 'Othello and the Politics of Character' was published in Manuel Barbeito (ed.), *In Mortal Shakespeare: Radical Readings* (Santiago: Universidade de Santiago de Compostela, 1989).

2. Stephen Greenblatt, *Renaissance Self-Fashioning* (Chicago: University of Chicago Press, 1980), p. 245; and also pp. 234–9, and Greenblatt, 'Psychoanalysis and Renaissance Culture', in Patricia Parker and David Quint (eds.), *Literary Theory/Renaissance Texts* (Baltimore: Johns Hopkins University Press, 1986), p. 218. On stories in *Othello*, see further Jonathan Goldberg, 'Shakespearean Inscriptions: The Voicing of Power', in Patricia Parker and Geoffrey Hartman (eds.), *Shakespeare and the Question of Theory* (New York: Methuen, 1985), pp. 131–2.

3. Ania Loomba, *Gender, Race, Renaissance Drama* (Manchester University Press, 1989), p. 48. See also Doris Adler, 'The Rhetoric of *Black* and *White* in *Othello*', *Shakespeare Quarterly*, 25 (1974), 248–57.

4. Louis Althusser, 'Ideological State Apparatuses', in Althusser, *Lenin and Philosophy and Other Essays*, trans. Ben Brewster (London: New Left Books, 1971), pp. 160–5.

5. Peter Stallybrass, 'Patriarchal Territories: The Body Enclosed', in Margaret W. Ferguson, Maureen Quilligan, and Nancy J. Vickers (eds.), *Rewriting*

the Renaissance (Chicago: University of Chicago Press, 1986), p. 139. Greenblatt makes a comparable point about Jews in Marlowe's *Jew of Malta*, though in *Othello* he stresses Iago's 'ceaseless narrative invention': see *Renaissance Self-Fashioning*, pp. 208, 235. On Blacks in Shakespearean England, see Loomba, *Gender, Race, Renaissance Drama*, pp. 42–52; Ruth Cowhig, 'Blacks in English Renaissance Drama and the Role of Shakespeare's *Othello*', in David Dabydeen (ed.), *The Black Presence in English Literature* (Manchester: Manchester University Press, 1985).

6. Althusser, *Lenin and Philosophy*, pp. 123–8. For further elaboration of the theory presented here, see Alan Sinfield, *Literature, Politics and Culture in Postwar Britain* (Oxford: Basil Blackwell; Berkeley: University of California Press, 1989), ch. 3.

7. Colin Sumner, *Reading Ideologies* (London and New York: Academic Press, 1979), p. 288.

8. Anthony Giddens, *Central Problems in Social Theory* (London: Macmillan, 1979), pp. 69–71, 77–8. Giddens's development of *langue* and *parole* is anticipated in Michel Foucault, *The Order of Things* (London: Tavistock, 1970), p. 380.

9. Stephen Orgel, 'Nobody's Perfect: Or Why Did the English Stage Take Boys for Women?', *South Atlantic Quarterly*, 88 (1989), 7–29, pp. 8–10. Jonathan Goldberg writes of the Duke's scripting in *Measure for Measure* in his *James I and the Politics of Literature* (Baltimore: Johns Hopkins University Press, 1983), pp. 230–9. See also Steven Mullaney, *The Place of the Stage* (Chicago: University of Chicago Press, 1988), pp. 107–10.

10. On attitudes to Turks, see Simon Shepherd, *Marlowe and the Politics of Elizabethan Theatre* (New York: St Martin's Press, 1986), pp. 142–9. The later part of Othello's career, in fact, has been devoted entirely to state violence – as Martin Orkin has suggested, he is sent to Cyprus to secure it for the colonial power: see Orkin, *Shakespeare against Apartheid* (Craighall, South Africa: Ad. Donker, 1987), pp. 88–96.

11. Karl Marx and Friedrich Engels, *The German Ideology* (London: Lawrence & Wishart, 1965), p. 61. See further Althusser, *Lenin and Philosophy*, pp. 139–42; Pierre Bourdieu, 'Cultural Reproduction and Social Reproduction', in Richard Brown (ed.), *Knowledge, Education and Cultural Change* (London: Tavistock, 1973).

12. See Lynda E. Boose, 'The Family in Shakespearean Studies; or – Studies in the Family of Shakespeareans; or – the Politics of Politics', *Renaissance Quarterly*, 40 (1987), 707–42; Carol Thomas Neely, 'Constructing the Subject: Feminist Practice and the New Renaissance Discourses', *English Literary Renaissance*, 18 (1988), 5–18.

13. Kathleen McLuskie, 'The Patriarchal Bard: Feminist Criticism and Shakespeare', in Jonathan Dollimore and Alan Sinfield (eds.), *Political*

Shakespeare (Manchester: Manchester University Press; Ithaca, N.Y.: Cornell University Press, 1985), p. 97. For a reply to her critics by Kathleen McLuskie, see her *Renaissance Dramatists* (Hemel Hempstead: Harvester Wheatsheaf, 1989), pp. 224–9; and for further comment, Jonathan Dollimore, 'Shakespeare, Cultural Materialism, Feminism and Marxist Humanism', *New Literary History*, 21 (1990), 471–93.

14. Carolyn Ruth Swift Lenz, Gayle Greene and Carol Thomas Neely (eds.), *The Woman's Part* (Urbana: University of Illinois Press, 1980), p. 5.

15. McLuskie, 'Patriarchal Bard', p. 92.

16. McLuskie, p. 92; Boose, 'Family in Shakespearean Studies', pp. 734, 726, 724. See also Ann Thompson, ' "The warrant of womanhood": Shakespeare and Feminist Criticism', in Graham Holderness (ed.), *The Shakespeare Myth* (Manchester: Manchester University Press, 1988); Judith Newton, 'History as Usual?: Feminism and the New Historicism', *Cultural Critique*, 9 (1988), 87–121.

17. Richard Ohmann, *English in America* (New York: Oxford University Press, 1976), p. 313. See V. N. Voloshinov, *Marxism and the Philosophy of Language*, trans. Ladislav Matejka and I. R. Titunik (New York and London: Seminar Press, 1973), pp. 17–24, 83–98.

18. Antonio Gramsci, *Selections from the Prison Notebooks*, ed. and trans. Quintin Hoare and Geoffrey Nowell-Smith (London: Lawrence & Wishart, 1971), p. 324.

19. Judith Butler, *Gender Trouble* (London: Routledge, 1990), pp. 6, 15, 142–3, 147. See Celia Kitzinger, *The Social Construction of Lesbianism* (London: Sage, 1987). Diana Fuss asks: 'Is politics based on identity, or is identity based on politics?' (*Essentially Speaking* [London: Routledge, 1989], p. 100, and see ch. 6).

20. Neely, 'Constructing the Subject', p. 7.

21. J. Hillis Miller, 'Presidential Address, 1986: The Triumph of Theory, the Resistance to Reading, and the Question of the Material Base', *PMLA* 102 (1987), 281–91, pp. 290–1. Cf., e.g., Raymond Williams, 'Base and Superstructure in Marxist Cultural Theory', *New Left Review*, 82 (1973), 3–16; reprinted in Williams, *Problems in Materialism and Culture* (London: Verso, 1980; New York: Schocken Books, 1981). James Holstun, 'Ranting at the New Historicism', *English Literary Renaissance*, 19 (1989), 189–225, makes more effort than most to address European/Marxist work.

22. Peter Nicholls, 'State of the Art: Old Problems and the New Historicism', *Journal of American Studies*, 23 (1989), 423–34, pp. 428, 429.

23. Don E. Wayne, 'New Historicism', in Martin Coyle, Peter Garside, Malcolm Kelsall and John Peck (eds.), *Encyclopedia of Literature and Criticism* (London: Routledge, 1990), p. 795. I am grateful to

Professor Wayne for showing this essay to me in typescript. Further on this topic, see Jean E. Howard and Marion F. O'Connor, 'Introduction', Don E. Wayne, 'Power, Politics and the Shakespearean Text: Recent Criticism in England and the United States', and Walter Cohen, 'Political Criticism of Shakespeare', all in Jean E. Howard and Marion F. O'Connor (eds.), *Shakespeare Reproduced* (London: Methuen, 1987); Louis Montrose, 'Professing the Renaissance: The Poetics and Politics of Culture', in H. Aram Veeser (ed.), *The New Historicism* (New York: Routledge, 1989), pp. 20–4; Alan Liu, 'The Power of Formalism: The New Historicism', *English Literary History*, 56 (1989), 721–77.

24. Greenblatt, *Renaissance Self-Fashioning*, pp. 120, 209–14. For further instantiation, see pp. 173–4.

25. Carolyn Porter, 'Are We Being Historical Yet?', *South Atlantic Quarterly*, 87 (1988), 743–86; see also Porter, 'History and Literature: "After the New Criticism"', *New Literary History*, 21 (1990), 253–72.

26. Stephen J. Greenblatt, *Learning to Curse: Essays in Early Modern Culture* (London: Routledge, 1990), pp. 164–6.

27. Shakespeare, *Macbeth*, ed. Kenneth Muir, 9th ed. (London: Methuen 1962), 1.4.12–13.

28. William Shakespeare, *King Henry V*, ed. J. H. Walter (London: Methuen, 1954), act 5, Chorus, 29–35.

29. Raymond Williams, *Culture* (Glasgow: Fontana, 1981), p. 201.

30. Porter, 'Are We Being Historical Yet?', p. 774. For important recent discussions of the scope for movement in the early modern state, see Richard Cust and Ann Hughes (eds.), *Conflict in Early Stuart England* (London: Longmans, 1989), esp. Johann Sommerville, 'Ideology, Property and the Constitution'.

31. I am not happy that race and sexuality tend to feature in distinct parts of this chapter; in this respect, my wish to clarify certain theoretical arguments has produced some simplification. Of course, race and sexuality are intertwined, in *Othello* as elsewhere. See Loomba, *Gender, Race, Renaissance Drama*, pp. 48–62; Karen Newman, ' "And wash the Ethiop white": Femininity and the Monstrous in *Othello*', in Howard and O'Connor (eds.), *Shakespeare Reproduced*; Jonathan Dollimore, *Sexual Dissidence* (Oxford: Oxford University Press, 1991), part 4.

32. I set out this argument in Alan Sinfield, *Literature in Protestant England, 1560–1660* (London: Croom Helm, 1983), ch. 4. See also Juliet Dusinberre, *Shakespeare and the Nature of Women* (London: Macmillan, 1976); Simon Shepherd, *Amazons and Warrior Women* (Brighton: Harvester, 1981), pp. 53–6, 107–18; Catherine Belsey, *The Subject of Tragedy* (London: Methuen, 1985), ch. 7; Dympna Callaghan, *Woman and Gender in Renaissance Tragedy* (Atlantic Highlands,

N.J.: Humanities Press, 1989), ch. 2 et passim; McLuskie, *Renaissance Dramatists*, pp. 31–9, 50–5 et passim.

33. *Certain Sermons or Homilies* (London: Society for Promoting Religious Knowledge, 1899), p. 534.

34. Sir Philip Sidney, *Arcadia*, ed. Maurice Evans (Harmondsworth: Penguin Books, 1977), p. 501.

35. Robert Burton, *The Anatomy of Melancholy*, ed. Holbrook Jackson (London: Dent, 1932), 3:52–3.

36. *Certain Sermons*, p. 589.

37. Henry Smith, *Works*, with a memoir by Thomas Fuller (Edinburgh: 1886), 1:32, 19.

38. Gerrard Winstanley, *Works*, ed. G. H. Sabine (Ithaca, N.Y.: Cornell University Press, 1941), p. 599.

39. William Perkins, *Christian Economy* (1609), in *The Works of William Perkins*, ed. Ian Breward (Abingdon: Sutton Courtenay Press, 1970), pp. 418–19.

40. Lawrence Stone, *The Family, Sex and Marriage* (London: Weidenfeld & Nicolson, 1977), p. 137. See also ibid., pp. 151–9, 178–91, 195–302; Charles and Katherine George, *The Protestant Mind of the English Reformation* (Princeton: Princeton University Press, 1961), pp. 257–94; Christopher Hill, *Society and Puritanism in Pre-Revolutionary England* (London: Panther, 1969), pp. 429–67; Louis Adrian Montrose, ' "Shaping Fantasies": Figurations of Gender and Power in Elizabethan Culture', in Stephen Greenblatt (ed.), *Representing the English Renaissance* (Berkeley: University of California Press, 1988), pp. 37–40; Lisa Jardine, *Still Harping on Daughters* (Brighton: Harvester, 1983), ch. 3; Leonard Tennenhouse, *Power on Display* (London: Methuen, 1986), pp. 17–30, 147–54; Patrick Collinson, *The Birthpangs of Protestant England* (London: Macmillan, 1988), ch. 3.

41. Callaghan, *Woman and Gender*, p. 21; also pp. 19–22, 101–5. On women's scope for negotiation, see also Ann Rosalind Jones, *The Currency of Eros: Women's Love Lyric in Europe, 1540–1620* (Bloomington: Indiana University Press, 1990), pp. 1–10.

42. Montrose, ' "Shaping Fantasies" ', p. 37. For the thought that the men in *Othello* are preoccupied with their masculinity but ineffectual, see Carol Thomas Neely, *Broken Nuptials in Shakespeare's Plays* (New Haven: Yale University Press, 1985), pp. 119–22.

43. John Clarke, Stuart Hall, Tony Jefferson, and Brian Roberts, 'Subcultures, Cultures and Class', in Stuart Hall and Tony Jefferson (eds.), *Resistance through Rituals* (London: Hutchinson; Birmingham: Centre for Contemporary Cultural Studies, 1976), p. 12. The final

phrase is quoted from E. P. Thompson's essay 'The Peculiarities of the English'.

44. Giddens, *Central Problems*, p. 6. See further Raymond Williams, *Marxism and Literature* (Oxford: Oxford University Press, 1977), pp. 108–27; Fredric Jameson, 'Reification and Utopia in Mass Culture', *Social Text*, 1 (1979), 144–8; Colin Gordon, 'Afterword', in Michel Foucault, *Power/Knowledge* (Brighton: Harvester, 1980).

45. Michel Foucault, *The History of Sexuality: Volume 1*, trans. Robert Hurley (New York: Random House, Vintage Books, 1980), pp. 95–6. Also, as Jonathan Culler has remarked, Foucault's exposure of the ubiquity of regulatory practices may itself be experienced as liberatory: Culler, *Framing the Sign* (Oxford: Blackwell, 1988), pp. 66–7.

46. Foucault, *History of Sexuality*, p. 101. See Jonathan Dollimore and Alan Sinfield, 'Culture and Textuality: Debating Cultural Materialism', *Textual Practice*, 4:1 (Spring 1990), 91–100, p. 95; and Jonathan Dollimore, 'Sexuality, Subjectivity and Transgression: The Jacobean Connection', *Renaissance Drama*, n.s., 17 (1986), 53–82.

47. Jonathan Goldberg, 'Speculations: *Macbeth* and Source', in Howard and O'Connor, *Shakespeare Reproduced*, pp. 244, 247. See also Jonathan Goldberg, *Writing Matter: From the Hands of the English Renaissance* (Stanford: Stanford University Press, 1990), esp. pp. 41–55.

48. Williams, *Culture*, pp. 94, 110; Keith Thomas, 'The Meaning of Literacy in Early Modern England', in Gerd Baumann (ed.), *The Written Word: Literacy in Transition* (Oxford: Clarendon Press, 1986), pp. 116, 118.

49. Dollimore, 'Shakespeare, Cultural Materialism, Feminism and Marxist Humanism', p. 482. See also Holstun, 'Ranting at the New Historicism'.

50. Dollimore and Sinfield, *Political Shakespeare*, p. 13; discussed in Dollimore and Sinfield, 'Culture and Textuality'. See also Alan Liu's argument that we need to consider not only subjects and representation, but action: Liu, 'Power of Formalism', pp. 734–5.

51. Wayne, 'New Historicism', in Coyle, Garside, Kelsall and Peck (eds.), *Encyclopedia*, pp. 801–2. See also Culler, *Framing*, p. 37; Porter, 'History and Literature', pp. 253–6.

52. 'The Political Function of the Intellectual', trans. Colin Gordon, *Radical Philosophy* 17 (1977), 12–15, p. 14; see Eve Tavor Bannet, *Structuralism and the Logic of Dissent* (London: Macmillan, 1989), pp. 170–83.

53. Raymond Williams, *Marxism and Literature* (Oxford: Oxford University Press, 1977), p. 209.

3

Charivari and the Comedy of Abjection in *Othello*

MICHAEL D. BRISTOL

The abusive language, the noisy clamour under Brabantio's window, and the menace of violence of the opening scene of *Othello* link the improvisations of Iago with the codes of a carnivalesque disturbance or charivari organized in protest over the marriage of the play's central characters. Charivari does not figure as an isolated episode here, however, nor has it been completed when the initial onstage commotion ends.[1] Despite the sympathy that Othello and Desdemona seem intended to arouse in the audience, the play as a whole is organized around the abjection and violent punishment of its central figures. If certain history plays can be read as rites of 'uncrowning' then this play might be read as a rite of 'un-marrying'.[2] In staging the play as a ceremony of broken nuptials, Iago assumes the function of a popular festive ringleader whose task is the unmaking of a transgressive marriage.[3]

As the action of *Othello* unfolds, the audience is constrained to witness a protracted and diabolical parody of courtship leading to a final, grotesquely distorted consummation in the marriage bed. To stage this action as the carnivalesque thrashing of the play's central characters is, of course, a risky choice for a director to make, since it can easily transform the complex equilibrium of the play from tragedy to *opera buffo*. Although the play is grouped with the tragedies in The First Folio and has always been viewed as properly belonging to this genre, commentators have for a long time recognized the precarious balance of this play at the very boundaries of farce.[4] *Othello* is a text that evidently lends itself very well to parody, burlesque and caricature.[5] Alteration of the play's formal characteristics, however, would not be the most serious problem encountered in contemplating a carnivalized performance. Since the basis for the charivari is an interracial marriage, many of the strongest effects of this ritual practice would be realized here through use of derisory and stereotypical images of 'The Moor'.

It is important to remember that Othello does not have to be a black African for this story to work itself out. Racial difference is not absolutely required to motivate any of the fundamental plot moves here. The feelings expressed by the various characters that prompt each of the turns in the action could just as well be tied to some other difference between the two romantic protagonists, and in fact in the concrete unfolding of the story the difference in age seems as important if not more important than the fact of Othello's blackness.[6] The image of racial otherness is thus supplementary to the primary narrative interest here. At the time of the play's earliest performances, the supplementary character of Othello's blackness would be apparent in the white actor's use of black-face makeup to represent the conventionalized form of 'The Moor'. In the initial context of its reception, it seems unlikely that the play's appeal to invidious stereotypes would have troubled the conscience of anyone in the audience. Since what we now call racial prejudice did not fall outside prevailing social norms in Shakespeare's society, no one in the early audience would have felt sympathy for Othello simply on the grounds that he was the victim of a racist society.[7] It is far more probable that 'The Moor' would have been seen as comically monstrous. Under these conditions the aspects of charivari and of the comical abjection of the protagonists would have been entirely visible to an audience for whom a racist sensibility was entirely normal.[8]

At the end of the sixteenth century racism was not yet organized as a large-scale system of oppressive social and economic arrangements, but it certainly existed in the form of a distinctive and widely shared *affekt-complex*. Racism in this early, prototypical, form entails a specific physical repugnance for the skin colour and other typical features of black Africans. This sensibility is not yet generalized into an abstract or pseudoscientific doctrine of racial inferiority, and for this reason it is relatively difficult to conceive of a principled objection to this 'common-sensical' attitude. The physical aversion of the English towards the racial other was rationalized through an elaborate mythology, supported in part by scriptural authority and reinforced by a body of popular narrative.[9] Within this context, the image of the racial other is immediately available as a way of encoding deformity or the monstrous.

For Shakespeare and for his audience the sensibilities of racial difference were for all practical purposes abstract and virtually disembodied, since the mythology of African racial inferiority was not yet a fully implemented social practice within the social landscape of early modern Europe. Even at this early stage, however, it had already occurred to some people that the racial other was providentially foreordained for the role of the slave, an idea that was to be fully achieved in the eighteenth- and nineteenth-century institutions of plantation slavery and in such successor institutions as segregation and apartheid. The large-scale forms of institutional racism that continue to be a chronic and intractable problem in modern societies are, of course, already latent within the abstract racial mythologies of the sixteenth century, since these mythologies enter into the construction of the social and sexual imaginary both of the dominant and of the popular culture. In more recent contexts of reception the farcical and carnivalesque potentiality of the play is usually not allowed to manifest itself openly. To foreground the elements of charivari and comic abjection would disclose in threatening and unacceptable ways the text's ominous relationship to the historical formation of racism as a massive social fact in contemporary Europe, and in the successor cultures of North and South America as well as in parts of the African homeland itself. Against this background the text of *Othello* has to be construed as a highly significant document in the historical constitution both of racist sensibility and of racist political ideology.

Othello is a text that severely tests the willingness of an audience to suspend its disbelief, although the problem is not necessarily that the situation can degenerate into farce. For many commentators it is not the potentially ludicrous character of the action, but the exacerbated pathos of the ending that has provoked discomfort amounting to revulsion with this play. Horace Howard Furness found the play horrible, and wished Shakespeare had never written it.[10] A more direct form of protest is described in an anecdote recounted by Stendhal: 'L'année dernière (août 1822), le soldat qui était en faction dans l'intérieur du théâtre de Baltimore, voyant Othello qui, au cinquième acte de la tragédie de ce nom, allait tuer Desdemona, s'écria: "Il ne sera jamais dit qu'en ma présence un maudit nègre aura tué une femme blanche." Au même moment le soldat tire son coup de fusil, et casse un bras a l'acteur qui faisait Othello. Il ne se passe pas d'années san que les journaux ne rapportent des faits semblables'.[11]

The moral that Stendhal wants to draw from the story of the soldier in Baltimore is that only someone who is extremely ignorant or stupid – that is, an American – fails to distinguish an actual murder from a dramatic representation of one. In the perhaps more definitive variant of the anecdote, the performance takes place in a barn, and the unlucky actor playing Othello is not merely wounded but killed outright. In this version the soldier's behaviour is less a matter of the 'perfect illusion' described by Stendhal, but rather a militant defence of white women, notwithstanding the fictional status of Desdemona's 'murder'. Although the tale about the misguided soldier and the luckless actor in Baltimore may in all likelihood be itself a fiction, the *fantasy* of rescuing Desdemona from the clutches of a murderous black man has probably occurred more than once to various spectators in the history of the play's many performances.[12] Such a wish to prevent the catastrophe, to rewrite the play by disrupting its performance, has its basis in the equivocal ontological and social status of theatre as an institutionalized form of representation. The tension and uneasiness provoked by the ambiguous 'reality' of every theatrical performance is, however, greatly heightened in the case of *Othello*.[13]

In his ruminations on the ontological status of the representations that confront an audience across the proscenium, Stanley Cavell identifies *Othello* as the exemplary instance of acute theatrical discomfort, amounting to an outright refusal of the mise-en-scène: 'What is the state of mind in which we find the events in a theater neither credible nor incredible? The usual joke is about the Southern yokel who rushes to the stage to save Desdemona from the black man. What is the joke?'[14] Cavell's willingness to take this joke seriously suggests that the impulse to rescue Desdemona is not some sort of fantastical aberration, but is in fact a response common to a great many [male?] viewers. Something real is at stake for the audience of *Othello*, even though the actual performance of the play depends on universal acceptance of its status as a fiction:

> At the opening of the play it is fully true that I neither believe nor disbelieve. But I am something, perplexed, anxious. ... Much later, the warrior asks his wife if she has said her prayers. Do I believe he will go through with it? I know he will; it is a certainty fixed forever; but I hope against hope he will come to his senses; I appeal to him,

in silent shouts. Then he puts his hands on her throat. The question is: What, if anything, do I do? I do nothing; that is a certainty fixed forever. And it has its consequences. *Why* do I do nothing? Because they are only pretending? ... Othello is not pretending.[15]

Does Cavell want to suggest that the Southern yokel is somehow doing the right thing, and that performances of *Othello* should henceforth be disrupted? Such disruption is not actually recommended here, but Cavell is willing to take such a possibility seriously in order to point out that such a violation of theatrical etiquette has substantive moral content. But if this is true, then behaving properly in a theatre also has a moral content vis-à-vis the action represented. Cavell does not push the argument to the point of suggesting that suspension of disbelief and acquiescence in the social conventions of performance amounts to complicity in a murder. To the contrary, the disruption of the mise-en-scène would really be a trivial gesture, since the murder will take place no matter what anyone does at any given theatrical performance. For, as Cavell puts it, 'Quiet the house, pick up the thread again, and Othello will reappear, as near and as deaf to us as ever. The transcendental and the empirical crossing; possibilities shudder from it'.[16] Cavell wants to make himself and his readers accountable for their response as moral agents to what the play discloses, and therefore he must insist on the element of consent and affirmation theatre demands from the members of an audience.

Given the painful nature of the story, the history of both the interpretation and the performance of *Othello* have been characterized by a search for anaesthetic explanations that allow the show to go on. These consoling interpretations, and the institutional suspension of disbelief that is the condition of the possibility of any performance, usually work to prevent disruptions of the play in performance. Nevertheless, the history of anguished responses to this play signals a chronic unwillingness amounting at times to outright refusal to participate in the performance of a play as the ritual or quasi-ritual affirmation of certain social practices. *Othello* occupies a problematic situation at the boundary between ritually sanctioned reality and theatrically consensual fiction. Does the play simply depict an inverted ritual of courtship and marriage, or does its performance before an audience that accepts its status as a fiction also invite complicity in a social ritual of comic abjection, humiliation and victimization? What does it mean, to borrow a usage from French, to 'assist' at a performance of this text? At a time when the large-scale social consequences of racist sensibilities had not yet become visible it may well have been easy to accept the formal codes of charivari as the expression of legitimate social norms. In later contexts of reception it is not so easy to accept *Othello in the form of a derisory ritual of racial persecution*, because the social experience of racial difference has become such a massive scandal.

Ritual and theatre have a long history of strained and sometimes openly hostile relations. This conflict between authentic hieratic ceremonies and the meretricious performances of actors is, however, deeply equivocal. The manifest antagonism between the liturgical forms of religion and the dramatic spectacles of the theatre are continually haunted by the trace of a hidden complicity. The integrity of religious practice depends to a considerable extent, therefore, on the control of access to redemptive media and to places of sanctity within a given community. Such integrity is, of course, of decisive importance for maintaining the collective life of the believers.

For Emile Durkheim, every rite, both in its aspect of ceremonial formality and in the conventional transgression that accompanies it, is a process by which a community reproduces modes of consciousness and social interaction that maintain its solidarity over time.[17] Durkheim argues that ritual depends on a fundamental misrecognition. A community reaffirms its own well-established social hierarchies, experienced by the believers as a manifestation of the sacred. The divine presences evoked in ritual may in fact be non-existent, but contact with the sacred is not, for that reason, some kind of delusionary fantasy, since the communal life so richly experienced in ritual has a concrete and sensuous actuality that does support and sustain the members of the community.[18] Ritual misrecognition always has some element of objective cogency, no matter how fantastical its overt manifestations may be and no matter how fallacious the interpretations of the participants. Moreover, the 'anomie' that appears at the time of the festival is a functional undifferentiation that strengthens the resolution and closure that concludes the rite. Misrecognition is not, therefore, some sort of mistake, but the absolutely necessary condition for the possibility of social continuity. Those responsible for the management of liturgical practice must always ensure that ritual, despite its spectacular accoutrements, is never linked openly to theatre. The ontological claims on which ritual depends are not always easy to sustain, for the very good reason that the practical exigencies of any liturgy are not very different from those of a theatrical performance. The distinction between a priest's vestments and an actor's costume is never an easy one to maintain, and this is especially so in a historical setting like Elizabethan and Jacobean England, where some theatrical costumes were in fact expropriated vestments transferred from the altar to the stage.

Contamination of religious authority by illicit contact with theatre was a condition that occasioned chronic anxiety during the early modern period, and this anxiety has been examined in a number of recent studies.[19] Stephen Greenblatt's important essay on 'Shakespeare and the Exorcists', for example, shows that the scandal of exorcism is precisely its character as a theatre that dissembles its own theatricality.[20] The evacuation of religious significance from exorcism, the chastisement of its practitioners, and the instruction of the public in the correct allocation of charismatic and juridical authority are all accomplished by means of a thoroughgoing theatricalization of exorcism. This is done in part by the exposure of various theatrical techniques and special effects used by the exorcists on an unsuspecting audience, and in part by the restaging of the exorcists' performances in a juridical setting. As Greenblatt shows, however, the use of theatre as the primary instrument for this evacuation of a vitiated or inauthentic ritual is extremely dangerous. By asserting openly its capacity for dissimulation, theatre addresses the element of misrecognition necessary to any liturgical enactment of the sacred. Theatre thus has the capacity to theorize all redemptive media and even to make visible the links between ritual, repression and social contradiction. The strategy of evacuation through the use of a theatrical pedagogy, though carefully focused on specific inauthentic practices, is paradoxically self-condemnatory in the way it foregrounds the element of collective misrecognition on which charismatic and juridical authority depends.

Despite its capacity to theorize ritual practices, theatre is not simply the logical 'opposite' of liturgy. There are important isomorphisms between these two symbolic protocols. Ritual and theatre are based on formalities, on conventional social etiquette, and on the use of selected artefacts or symbols within a well-defined spatial frame.[21] In addition, theatre resembles ritual in that it requires its own particular form of 'misrecognition' in the form of a temporary and contractual suspension of disbelief. This is, however, a knowledgeable misrecognition that contrasts radically with the unselfconscious and unreflective misrecognition necessary for ritual.[22] Knowledgeable misrecognition is, however, a paradoxical condition, one that can inspire precisely those feelings of acute discomfort experienced, for example, at performances of *Othello*.

The apparent dilemma between a classic sociology of religion that interprets ritual as a necessary though wholly unselfconscious misrecognition and a classic sociology of theatrical reception that interprets performance in light of a contractual misrecognition may be resolved in part by an appeal to Mikhail Bakhtin's category of the carnivalesque. Carnival is an ensemble of practices that seems to be both 'full' of positive social content, like a ritual, and 'empty' of any substantive social meaning, like a theatrical performance. This theory can help to make sense of the apparently paradoxical notion of a knowledgeable misrecognition that seems to be the condition of the possibility of a theatrical performance. One of the salient features of carnival is its capacity to open up an alternative space for social action.[23] Within the spatio-temporal boundaries of a carnivalesque event, the individual subject is authorized to renegotiate identity and to redefine social position vis-à-vis others. In Bakhtin's reading of Carnival, the social effervescence and the energy generated by a radical popular will to otherness is not simply recaptured for the purposes of the official culture. In its capacity for excess and derangement, carnival empowers the popular element to voice its opposition to the imperatives of official culture.

The theory of Carnival distinguishes between the affirmative character of ritual consciousness as such, and the negative and corrosive force of popular festive form. This distinction corresponds to the distinction between 'official culture' – the legitimated stories and interpretations of social hierarchy reproduced in the ideological apparatus – and 'popular culture' – the alternative values and interpretations of the social life-world sedimented in the symbolic practices of various excluded or partially excluded groups. Carnival analyses and dismantles the official order of things, not in a spirit of pure negation, but rather as the expression of an alternative understanding of the social world as an ensemble of material practices.[24] To be sure, this alternative understanding may be profoundly conservative in its thematic content and in its evaluation of various social practices. However, such a conservatism by no means implies a blanket endorsement of all decisions taken by individuals and groups with access to mechanisms of political power, or an indiscriminate willingness to submit to authority. In fact, the knowledge sedimented in the artefacts and the symbolic vocabularies of carnival is a reaffirmation of practical consciousness that may be significantly at odds with the ideologies officially sanctioned by ruling elites.[25] This practical consciousness is best thought of as the outlook of social agents sufficiently knowledgeable to 'get on' within the constraints of economic and institutional reality.[26] Such knowledgeability is not always equivalent to the self-understanding of a particular social agent, but is instead sedimented within certain institutional practices, including but not limited to the conventions of theatre and of theatre going.

Bakhtin's view of Carnival is in some sense a development of what appears to be the contrasting position articulated in Durkheim's sociology of religion. It is important to realize, however, that Bakhtin's anthropology preserves the central insight of Durkheim's sociology of religion and of the view that both official ritual and its popular cognates, as moments of greatly intensified social life, tend powerfully towards the reaffirmation of a deeply felt way-of-being-together-in-the-world.[27] The notion of the carnivalesque, however, adds to the sociology of religion an element that helps to account for the possibility of social change, and for the presence of differentiated interests that have to participate in the negotiation of that change. The carnivalesque then would be a mode of authentic cognition, a kind of para-scientific and pre-theoretical understanding of social forms that would disclose whatever is hidden by ritual misrecognition.

The following analysis sketches out a hypothesis that would interpret *Othello* as a carnivalesque text in the Bakhtinian sense. Carnival is operative here as something considerably more than a novel decor for the mise-en-scène, or an alternative thematics for interpretation. The play is read here as the carnivalesque derangement of marriage as a social institution and of the contradictory role of heterosexual desire within that institution. As a serio-comic or carnivalesque masquerade, the play makes visible the normative horizons against which sexual partners must be selected, and the latent social violence that marriage attempts to prevent, often unsuccessfully, from becoming manifest. More specifically, I want to draw attention to the play as an adaptation of the social custom, common throughout early modern Europe, of charivari.[28] This was a practice of noisy festive abuse in which a community enacted its objection to inappropriate marriages and more generally exercised a communal surveillance of sexuality. As Natalie Davis has pointed out, this 'community' actually consists of young men, typically unmarried, who represent a social principle of male solidarity that is in some respects deeply hostile to precisely that form of institutionally sanctioned sexuality whose standards they are empowered to oversee.[29]

The relationship of marriage is established through forms of collective representation, ceremonial and public enactments that articulate the private ethos of conjugal existence and mark out the communal responsibilities of the couple to implement and sustain socially approved 'relations of reproduction'. In the early modern period the ceremonial forms of marriage were accompanied (and opposed) by parodic doubling of the wedding feast in the forms of charivari.[30] This parodic doubling was organized by a carnivalesque wardrobe corresponding to a triad of dramatic agents – the clown (representing the bridegroom), the transvestite (representing the bride) and the 'scourge of marriage', often assigned a suit of black (representing the community of unattached males or 'young men').[31] Iago is neither unattached nor young, but part of his success with his various dupes is his ability to present himself as 'one of the boys'. Iago's misogyny is expressed as the married man's *ressentiment* against marriage, against wives in general and against his own wife in particular. But this *ressentiment* is only one form of the more diffuse and pervasive misogyny typically expressed in the charivari. And of course Iago's more sinister function is his ability to encourage a kind of complicity within the audience. In a performance, he makes his perspective the perspective of the text and thus solicits from the audience a participatory endorsement of the action.

The three primary 'characters' in charivari each have a normative function in the allocation of marriage partners and in the regulation of sexual behaviour. These three figures parody the three persons of the wedding ceremony – groom, bride and priest. It is the last of these three figures who confers both social and sacred authority on the marriage. The ensemble as a whole, however, is a travesty of the wedding ceremony itself. The counter-festive vocabulary of charivari provides the community with a system of critical resources through which marriage as a social arrangement and as a private form of sexuality may be either negated or reaffirmed.

Charivari features the three primary figures mentioned earlier, that is a bride, a groom and a ringleader who may in some instances assist the partners in outwitting parental opposition, but who may also function as a nemesis of erotic desire itself and attempt to disrupt and to destroy the intended bond. In the actual practice of charivari, the married couple themselves are forced to submit to public ridicule and sometimes to violent punishment.[32] In its milder forms, a charivari allows the husband and wife to be represented by parodic doubles who are then symbolically thrashed by the ringleader and his followers. This triad of social agents is common to many of Shakespeare's tragedies of erotic life, and it even appears in the comedies. Hamlet stages 'The Murder of Gonzago' partly as a public rebuke to the unseemly marriage of Claudius and Gertrude.[33] This is later escalated to a fantasy of the general abolition of the institution of monogamy, 'I say we will have no more marriages'. Hamlet's situation expresses the powerful ambivalence of the unattached male towards marriage as the institutional format in which heterosexual desire and its satisfaction are legitimated. His objection to the aberrant and offensive union of mother and uncle is predicated on the idealization of marriage, and in this case on the specific marriage of mother and father. This idealization is, however, accompanied by the fantasy of a general dissolution of the institution of monogamy back into a dispensation of erotic promiscuity and the free circulation of sexual partners. A similar agenda, motivated by a similar ambivalence, is pursued by Don John, in *Much Ado About Nothing*, and by Iachimo, in *Cymbeline*.

The argument I hope to sketch out here requires that readers or viewers of *Othello* efface their response to the existence of Othello, Desdemona and Iago as individual subjects endowed with personalities and with some mode of autonomous interiorized life. The reason for such selective or willful ignorance of some of the most compelling features of this text is to make visible the determinate theatrical surfaces. To the extent that the surface coding of this play is openly manifested, the analysis presented here will do violence to the existence of the characters in depth. Instead of striving to understand the grandeur and the sublime dignity of the play's hero and heroine, this argument seeks to 'stop at the surface' in order to focus attention on the carnivalesque scenario or charivari that governs the dramatic action.

In order to grasp the primary characters of *Othello* at this level of representation it is necessary to withdraw from the position of empathy for the characters as subjects constituted in the way we are constituted, and to seek out an appropriate mode of counter-identification. I believe that the withdrawal of empathy and of identification from the play's main characters is difficult, not least because the experience of individual subjectivity as we have come to know it *is* objectively operative in the text. It has been suggested, in fact, that the pathos of individual subjectivity was actually invented by Shakespeare, or that this experience appears for the first time in the history of Western representation in his plays. A variant of this position would be the view suggested by Brecht and elaborated by Catherine Belsey that a specific array of subject positions characteristic of bourgeois culture was created and elaborated in that great sociocultural laboratory known as Elizabethan Drama.[34] Whether this view is accurate or not, however, there is the more immediate difficulty that we desire, as readers and viewers, to reflect on and to identify with the complex pathos of individual subjectivity as it is represented in Shakespeare's oeuvre. This is especially so, perhaps, for professional readers and viewers, who are likely to have strong interests in the experience of the speaking/writing subject and in the problematic of autonomy and expressive unity. The constellation of interests and goal-values most characteristic of the institutional processing of literary texts has given rise to an extremely rich critical discourse on the question of the subject; it is precisely the power and the vitality of this discourse that makes the withdrawal of empathy from the characters so difficult. Nevertheless, for these characters to exist as Othello, Desdemona and Iago, they have to use the carnivalesque 'wardrobe' that is inscribed within this text, and this wardrobe assigns them the roles of clown, transvestite and 'scourge of marriage' in a charivari.

The clown is a type of public figure who embodies the 'right to be other', as Bakhtin would have it, since the clown always and everywhere rejects the categories made available in routine institutional life.[35] The clown is therefore both criminal and monster, although such alien and malevolent aspects are more often than not disguised. Etymologically 'clown' is related to 'colonus' – a farmer or settler, someone not from Rome but from the agricultural hinterland. As a rustic or hayseed the clown's relationship to social reality is best expressed through such contemporary idioms as 'He's out of it!', or 'He doesn't know where it's at!' In the drama of the early modern period a clown is often by convention a kind of country bumpkin, but he is also a 'professional outsider' of extremely flexible social provenance. Bakhtin has stressed the emancipatory capacity of the clown function, arguing that the clown mask embodies the 'right to be other' or *refus d'identité*. However, there is a pathos of clowning as well, and the clown mask may represent everything that is socially and sexually maladroit, credulous, easily victimized. And just as there is a certain satisfaction in observing an assertive clown get the better of his superiors, so is there also satisfaction in seeing an inept clown abused and stripped of his dignity. This abuse or 'thrashing' of the doltish outsider provides the audience with a comedy of abjection, a social genre in which the experience of exclusion and impotence can be displaced onto an even more helpless caste within society.

To think of Othello as a kind of blackface clown is perhaps distasteful, although the role must have been written not for a black actor, but with the idea of black make-up or a false-face of some kind. Othello is a Moor, but only in quotation marks, and his blackness is not even skin deep but rather a transitory and superficial theatrical integument. Othello's Moorish origins are the mark of his exclusion; as a cultural stranger he is, of course, 'out of it' in the most compelling and literal sense. As a foreigner he is unable to grasp and to make effective use of other Venetian codes of social and sexual conduct. He is thus a grotesque embodiment of the bridegroom – an exotic, monstrous and funny substitute who transgresses the norms associated with the idea of a husband.

To link Othello to the theatrical function of a clown is not necessarily to be committed to an interpretation of his character as a fool. Othello's folly, like Othello's nobility and personal grandeur, are specific interpretations of the character's motivation and of his competence to actualize those motives. The argument here, however, is that the role of Othello is already formatted in terms of the abject-clown function and that any interpretation of the character's 'nature' therefore has to be achieved within that format. The eloquence of Othello's language and the magnanimity of his character may in fact intensify the grotesque element here. His poetic self-articulation is not so much the *expression* of a self-possessed subject but is instead a form of discursive indecorum that strains against the social meanings objectified in Othello's counter-festive *persona*. Stephen Greenblatt identifies the joke here as one of the 'master plots of comedy', in which a beautiful young woman outwits an 'old and outlandish' husband.[36] Greenblatt reminds us here that Othello is functionally equivalent to the gull or butt of an abusive comic action, but he passes over the most salient feature of Othello's outlandishness, which is actualized in the blackface make-up essential to the depiction of this character. To present Othello in blackface, as opposed to presenting him just as a black man, would confront the audience with a comic spectacle of abjection rather than with the grand opera of misdirected passion. Such a comedy of abjection has not found much welcome in the history of the play's reception.

The original audience of this play in Jacobean England may have had relatively little inhibition in its expression of invidious racial sentiments, and so might have seen the derisory implications of the situation more easily. During the nineteenth century, when institutional racism was naturalized by recourse to a 'scientific' discourse on racial difference, the problem of Othello's outlandishness and the unsympathetic laughter it might evoke is 'solved' by making him a Caucasoid Moor, instead of a 'Veritable Negro'.[37] Without such a fine discrimination, a performance of *Othello* would have been not so much tragic as simply unbearable, part farce and part lynch mob. In the present social climate, when racism, though still very widespread, has been officially anathematized, the possibility of a blackface Othello would still be an embarrassment and a scandal, though presumably for a different set of reasons. Either way, the element of burlesque inscribed in this text is clearly too destabilizing to escape repression.

If Othello can be recognized as an abject clown in a charivari, then the scenario of such a charivari would require a transvestite to play the part of the wife. In the context of popular culture in the early modern period, female disguise and female impersonation were common to charivari and to a variety of other festive observances.[38] This practice was, among other things, the expression of a widespread 'fear' of women as both the embodiment of and the provocation to social transgression. Within the pervasive misogyny of the early modern period, women and their desires seemed to project the threat of a radical social undifferentiation.[39] The young men and boys who appeared in female dress at the time of Carnival seem to have been engaged in 'putting women in their place' through an exaggerated pantomime of everything feminine. And yet this very practice required the emphatic foregrounding of the artifice required for any stable coding of gender difference. Was this festive transvestism legitimated by means of a general misrecognition of the social constitution of gender? Or did the participants understand at some level that the association of social badness with women was nothing more than a patriarchal social fiction that could only be sustained in and through continuous ritual affirmation?

Female impersonation is, of course, one of the distinctive and extremely salient features of Elizabethan and Jacobean dramaturgy, and yet surprisingly little is known of how this mode of representation actually worked.[40] The practice of using boy actors to play the parts of women is a derivative of the more diffuse social practice of female impersonation in the popular festive milieu. Were the boy actors in Shakespeare's company engaging in a conventional form of ridicule of the feminine? Or were they engaged in a general parody of the artifice of gender coding itself? A transvestite presents the category of woman in quotation marks, and reveals that both 'man' and 'woman' are socially produced categories. In the drama of Shakespeare and his contemporaries, gender is at times an extremely mobile and shifting phenomenon without any solid anchor in sexual identity. To a considerable degree gender is a 'flag of convenience' prompted by contingent social circumstances, and at times gender identity is negotiated with considerable grace and dexterity. The convention of the actor 'boying' the woman's part is thus doubly parodic, a campy put down of femininity and, at another level, a way to theorize the social misrecognition on which all gender allocations depend.

Desdemona's 'femininity' is bracketed by the theatrical 'boying' of her/his part. This renders her/his sexuality as a kind of sustained gestural equivocation and this corresponds to the exaggerated and equivocal rhetorical aspect of Desdemona's self-presentation. As Desdemona puts it, 'I saw Othello's visage in his mind'; in other words, her initial attraction to him was not provoked by his physical appearance. The play thus stipulates that Desdemona herself accepts the social prohibition against miscegenation as the normative horizon within which she must act. On the face of it she cannot be physically attracted to Othello, and critics have usually celebrated this as the sign of her ability to transcend the limited horizons of her acculturation. These interpretations thus accept the premise of Othello as physically undesirable and insinuate that Desdemona's faith is predicated on her blindness to the highly visible 'monstrosity' of her 'husband'. In other words, her love is a misrecognition of her husband's manifestly undesirable qualities. Or is it a misrecognition of her own socially prohibited desire? Stanley Cavell interprets her lines as meaning that she saw his appearance in the way that he saw it, that she is able to enter into and to share Othello's self-acceptance and self-possession.[41] On this view Desdemona is a kind of ide- alization of the social category of 'wife', who can adopt the husband's own narrative fiction of self as her own imaginary object. Desdemona is thus both a fantasy of a sexually desirable woman and a fantasy of absolute sexual compliance. This figure of unconditional erotic submission is the obverse of the rebellious woman, or shrew, but, as the play shows us, this is also a socially prohibited *métier* for a woman. In fact, as Stephen Greenblatt has shown in his very influ- ential essay, the idea that Desdemona might feel an ardent sexual desire for him makes Othello perceive Iago's insinuations of infidelity as plausible and even probable.[42] The masculine fantasy projected in the figure of Desdemona cannot recognize itself as the object of another's desire.

Like all of Shakespeare's woman characters, Desdemona is an impossible sexual object, a female artefact created by a male imagination and objectified in a boy actor's body. This is, in its own way, just as artificial and as grotesque a theatrical manifestation as the blackface Othello who stands in for the category of the husband. What is distinctive about Desdemona is the way she embodies the category of an 'ideal wife' in its full contradictoriness. She has been described as chaste or even as still a virgin and also as sexually aggressive, even though very little unambiguous textual support for either of these readings actually exists.[43] Her elopement, with a Moor no less, signals more unequivocally than a properly arranged marriage ever could that the biblical injunction to leave mother and father has been fulfilled. It is probably even harder to accept the idea of Desdemona as part of a comedy of abjection than it is to accept Othello in such a context. It is, however, only in such a theatrical context that the hyperbolic and exacerbated misrecognition on which marriage is founded can be theorized.

At the level of surface representation then, the play enacts a marriage between two complementary symbols of the erotic grotesque. This is a marriage between what is conventionally thought to be hideous and repellent with what is most beautiful and desirable. The incongruity of this match is objectified in the theatrical hyper-embodiment of the primary categories of man and woman or husband and wife. It is not known to what extent Elizabethan and Jacobean theatre practice deliberately foregrounded its own artifice. However, the symbolic practice of grotesque hyper-embodiment was well known in popular festive forms such as charivari. The theatrical coding of gender in the early modern period is thus still contaminated by the residue of these forms of social representation.

The marriage of grotesque opposites is no more a private affair or erotic dyad than a real marriage. Marriage in the early modern period, among many important social classes, was primarily a dynastic or economic alliance negotiated by a third party who represented the complex of social sanctions in which the heterosexual couple was inscribed.[44] The elopement of Desdemona and Othello, as well as their reliance on Cassio as a broker or clandestine go-between, already signals their deliberate intention to evade and thwart the will of family. To the extent that readers or viewers are conditioned by the normative horizons that interpret heterosexual love as mutual sexual initiative and the transcendence of all social obstacles, this elopement will be read as a romantic confirmation of the spiritual and disinterested character of their love.[45] However, it can also be construed as a flagrant sexual and social blunder. Private heterosexual felicity of the kind sought by Othello and Desdemona attracts the evil eye of erotic nemesis.[46]

The figure of erotic nemesis and the necessary third party to this union is Othello's faithful lieutenant, Iago. It is Iago's task to show both his Captain and his audience just how defenceless the heterosexual couple is against the resources of sexual surveillance. The romantic lovers, represented here through a series of grotesque distortions, do not enjoy an erotic autonomy, though such erotic autonomy is a misrecognition of the socially inscribed character of 'private' sexuality. Iago's abusive and derisory characterizations of the couple, together with his debasement of their sexuality are a type of social commentary on the nature of erotic romance. The notion of mutual and autonomous self-selection of partners is impugned as a kind of mutual delusion that can only appear under the sign of monstrosity. In other words the romantic couple can only 'know' that their union is based on mutual love *and on nothing else* when they have 'transcended' or violated the social codes and prohibitions that determine the allocation of sexual partners.

Iago is a Bakhtinian 'agelast', that is, one who does not laugh. He is, of course, very witty, but his aim is always to provoke a degrading laughter at the follies of others rather than to enjoy the social experience of laughter *with* others. He is a demythologizer whose function is to reduce all expressivity to the minimalism of the quid pro quo. The process represented here is the reduction of quality to quantity, a radical undifferentiation of persons, predicated on a strictly mechanistic, universalized calculus of desire. Characters identified with this persona appear throughout Shakespeare's oeuvre, usually in the guise of a nemesis of hypocrisy and dissimulation. Hamlet's 'I know not seems' and Don John's 'it cannot be denied I am a plain dealing villain' are important variants of a social/ cognitive process that proclaims itself to be a critique of equivocation and the will to deception. It is ironic, of course, that these claims of honesty and plain dealing are so often made in the interests of malicious dissimulation. What appears to be consistent, however, in all the variants of this character-type, is the disavowal of erotic attachment and the contemptuous manipulation of the erotic imagination.

The supposedly 'unmotivated' malice enacted by this figure is puzzling, I believe, only when read individualistically. Is Iago envious of the pleasure Othello enjoys with Desdemona, or is he jealous of Othello's sexual enjoyment of Emilia? Of course, both of these ideas are purely conjectural hypotheses that have no apparent bearing on Iago's actions. In any case, there is no sustained commitment to either of these ideas, as numerous commentators have pointed out. Nevertheless, there is an important clue to understanding Iago as a social agent in these transitory ruminations. Iago seems to understand that the complex of envy and jealousy is not an aberration within the socially distributed erotic economy, but is rather the fundamental precondition of desire itself. Erotic desire is not founded in a qualitative economy or in a rational market, but rather in a mimetic and histrionic dispensation that Iago projects as the envy-jealousy system.[47] In this system men are the social agents, and women the objects of exchange. Iago's actions are thus socially motivated by a diffuse and pervasive misogyny that slides between fantasies of the complete abjection of all women and fantasies of an exclusively masculine world.

Iago's success in achieving these fantasies is made manifest in the unbearably hideous tableau of the play's final scene. If the play as a whole is to be read as a ritual of unmarrying, then this ending is the monstrous equivalent of a sexual consummation. What makes the play unendurable would be the suspicion that this climax expresses all too accurately an element present in the structure of every marriage. This is an exemplary action in which the ideal of companionate marriage as a socially sanctioned erotic union is dissolved back into the chronic violence of the envy-jealousy system. Iago theorizes erotic desire, and thus marriage, primarily by a technique of emptying out Othello's character, so that nothing is left at the end except the pathetic theatrical integument, the madly deluded and murderous blackface clown. Desdemona, the perfect wife, remains perfectly submissive to the end. And Iago, with his theoretical or pedagogical tasks completed, accepts in silence his allocation to the function of sacrificial victim and is sent off to face unnamed 'brave punishments'.

Finita la commedia. What does it mean to accept the mise-en-scène of this play? And what does it mean to *know* that we wish it could be otherwise? To the extent that we want to see a man and a woman defying social conventions in order to fulfill mutual erotic initiatives, the play will appear as a thwarted comedy and our response will be dominated by its pathos. But the play also shows us what such mutual erotic initiatives look like from the outside, as a comedy of abjection or charivari. The best commentators on this play have recognized the degree to which it prompts a desire to prevent the impending debacle and the sense in which it is itself a kind of theatrical punishment for the observers.[48] This helpless and agonized refusal of the mise-en-scène here should suggest something about the corrosive effect on socially inscribed rituals of a radical or 'cruel' theatricality.

The idea of theatrical cruelty is linked to the radical aesthetics of Antonin Artaud. However, the English term 'cruelty' fails to capture an important inflection that runs through all of Artaud's discussions of theatre. The concept is derived from words that mean 'raw' or 'un-processed'. In French '*cruauté*' expresses with even greater candour this relationship with 'le cru' and its opposition to 'le cuit'. Cruelty here has the sense of something uncooked, or something prior to the process of a conventional social transformation or adoption into the category of the meaningful.[49] *Othello*, perhaps more than any other Shakespeare play, raises fundamental questions about the institutional position and the aesthetic character of Shakespearean dramaturgy. Is Shakespeare raw – or is he cooked? Is it possible that our present institutional protocol for interpreting his work is a way of 'cooking' the 'raw' material to make it more palatable, more fit for consumption?

The history of the reception of *Othello* is the history of attempts to articulate ideologically correct, that is, palatable interpretations. By screening off the comedy of abjection it is possible to engage more affirmatively with the play's romantic liebestod. Within these strategies, critics may find an abundance of meanings for the tragic dimension of the play. In this orientation the semantic fullness of the text is suggested as a kind of aesthetic compensation for the cruelty of its final scenes. Rosalie Colie, for example, summarizes her interpretation with an account of the play's edifying power: 'In criticizing the artificiality he at the same time exploits in his play, Shakespeare manages in *Othello* to reassess and to reanimate the moral system and the psychological truths at the core of the literary love-tradition, to reveal its problematics and to reaffirm in a fresh and momentous context the beauty of its impossible ideals.'[50] This is recognizably the language of the ritual misrecognition of what the play as a comedy of abjection is capable of theorizing. The fullness of the play, of course, is what makes it possible for viewers and readers to participate, however unwillingly, in the charivari, or ritual victimization of the imaginary heterosexual couple here represented. Such consensual participation is morally disquieting in the way it appears to solicit at least passive consent to violence against women and against outsiders, but at least we are not howling with unsympathetic laughter at their suffering and humiliation.

Colie's description of the play's semantic fullness is based in part on her concept of 'un-metaphoring' – that is, the literalization of a metaphorical relationship or conventional figuration. This is a moderate version of the notion of theatrical cruelty or the unmaking of convention that does not radically threaten existing social norms. In other words, the fate of Desdemona and Othello, or Romeo and Juliet, is a cautionary fable about what happens if a system of conventional figurations of desire is taken literally. But the more powerful 'un-metaphoring' of this play is related not to its fullness as a tragedy, but to its emptiness as a comedy of abjection. The violent interposing of the charivari here would indeed make visible the *political* choice between an aestheticized ritual affirmation and a genuine refusal of the sexual mise-en-scène or relations of reproduction in which this text is inscribed.

From *Renaissance Drama*, n.s. 21 (1990), 3–21.

NOTES

[In order to recognize the comedy and grotesquery in Othello, Iago and Desdemona – that is, to be able to 'withdraw empathy from them' – Michael D. Bristol turns to Marxist theorist Mikhail Bakhtin's notion of the carnivalesque. Bristol discovers that the characters of *Othello* correspond to the stock types of the charivari: the clown, the transvestite and the scourge of marriage. As a charivari, the play invites the audience to attend the public shaming of a married couple. Bakhtin wrote most of his works in Russia in the 1930s, but he was not much known in the West before the 1960s. This essay shows why, since then, he has been highly influential. Ed.]

1. Francois Laroque, 'An Archaeology of the Dramatic Text: *Othello* and Popular Traditions', *Cahiers Élisabéthains*, 32 (1987), 13–35. See also T. G. A. Nelson and Charles Haines, 'Othello's Unconsummated Marriage', *Essays in Criticism*, 33 (1981), 5–7.

2. Carol Neely, *Broken Nuptials in Shakespeare's Plays* (New Haven: Yale University Press, 1985).

3. Michael Neill, 'Unproper Beds: Race, Adultery and the Hideous in *Othello*', *Shakespeare Quarterly*, 40 (1989), 383–413.

4. Thomas Rymer, *A Short View of Tragedy*, in *Shakespeare: The Critical Heritage*, 6 vols, ed. Brian Vickers (London: Routledge and Kegan Paul, 1974), 2, 27. See also Susan Snyder, *The Comic Matrix of Shakespeare's Tragedies* (Princeton: Princeton University Press, 1979), pp. 70–4.

5. Lawrence Levine, *Highbrow/Lowbrow* (Cambridge, Mass.: Harvard University Press, 1988), pp. 14–20; Neill, 'Unproper Beds', 391–3.

6. Janet Stavropoulos, 'Love and Age in *Othello*', *Shakespeare Studies*, 19 (1987), 125–41.

7. G. K. Hunter, 'Elizabethans and Foreigners', *Shakespeare Survey*, 17 (1964), 37–52; and '*Othello* and Colour Prejudice', *Proceedings of the British Academy*, 53 (1967), 139–63. See also Eldred Jones, *Othello's Countrymen: The African in English Renaissance Drama* (Oxford: Oxford University Press, 1965); Martin Orkin, '*Othello* and the "Plain Face" of Racism', *Shakespeare Quarterly*, 38 (1987), 166–88.

8. Karen Newman, ' "And Wash the Ethiop White": Femininity and the Monstrous in *Othello*', in *Shakespeare Reproduced: The Text in History and Ideology*, ed. Jean Howard and Marion O'Connor (London: Methuen, 1987), pp. 143–61.

9. Winthrop Jordan, *White Over Black* (Chapel Hill: University of North Carolina Press, 1968); Elliot H. Tokson, *The Popular Image of the Black Man in English Drama 1550–1688* (Boston: G. K. Hall, 1982).

10. *The Letters of Horace Furness*, ed. Horace Howard Furness, 2 vols. (Boston: Houghton Mifflin, 1922), 149, 156.

11. Stendhal, *Racine et Shakespeare*, ed. Pierre Martino, *Oeuvres Complètes*, 37 vols, 18 (Paris: Edouard Champion, 1925): 'Last year (August of 1822), the soldier standing guard at the interior of the theatre in Baltimore, seeing Othello who, in the fifth act of the tragedy of that name, was going to kill Desdemona, cried out "It will never be said that in my presence a damned black would kill a white woman". At that moment the soldier fired his gun, and broke the arm of the actor who played Othello'. [Author's translation.]

12. A concrete example of the enactment of such a fantasy might be the rescue of Elsie Stoneman by the Ku Klux Klan in D. W. Griffith's *Birth of a Nation*. See Michael Rogin, 'The Sword Became a Flashing Vision', *Representations*, 9 (1985), p. 161ff.

13. Stephen Greenblatt, 'Martial Law in the Land of Cokaigne', in *Shakespearean Negotiations: The Circulation of Social Energy in Renaissance England* (Berkeley: University of California Press, 1988), pp. 133–4.

14. Stanley Cavell, *Disowning Knowledge in Six Plays of Shakespeare* (Cambridge, Mass.: Cambridge University Press, 1987), p. 98ff.

15. Cavell, *Disowning Knowledge*, p. 100.

16. Ibid., p. 101.

17. Emile Durkheim, *The Elementary Forms of Religious Life*, trans. J. Swain (New York: The Free Press, 1967), pp. 39, 57, 463–74.

18. Anthony Giddens, *The Constitution of Society: Outline of the Theory of Structuration* (Cambridge, Mass.: The Polity Press, 1986), pp. 169–74. See also Giddens, *Durkheim* (London: Fontana Press, 1978), and Dominick La Capra, *Emile Durkheim: Sociologist and Philosopher* (Chicago: University of Chicago Press, 1985).

19. Jonas Barish, *The Antitheatrical Prejudice* (Berkeley: University of California Press, 1981); O. B. Hardison, *Christian Rite and Christian Drama in the Middle Ages: Essays in the Origin and Early History of Modern Drama* (Baltimore: Johns Hopkins University Press, 1965); Stephen Mullaney, *The Place of the Stage: License, Play and Power in Renaissance England* (Chicago: University of Chicago Press, 1988); Richard Schechner, *Performance Theory* [revised and expanded edition] (New York: Routledge, 1988); Victor Turner, *From Ritual to Theatre: The Human Seriousness of Play* (New York: Performing Arts Journal Publications, 1982).

20. Stephen Greenblatt, 'Shakespeare and the Exorcists', in *Shakespearean Negotiations: The Circulation of Social Energy in Renaissance England* (Berkeley: University of California Press, 1988), pp. 94–128.

21. Erving Goffman, *Frame Analysis: An Essay on the Organization of Experience* (Cambridge: Harvard University Press, 1974).

22. Greenblatt, 'Exorcists', p. 106.

23. Mikhail Bakhtin, *Rabelais and his World*, trans. Hélène Iswolsky (Cambridge, Mass.: MIT Press, 1968), pp. 145–96, *passim*; see also his *The Dialogic Imagination*, trans. Caryl Emerson and Michael Holquist (Austin: University of Texas Press, 1983), pp. 167–224; and Claude Gaignebet, *Le Carnaval· Essai de mythologie populaire* (Paris: Payot, 1974).

24. See the discussion of 'The Texts of Carnival' in my *Carnival and Theater: Plebeian Culture and the Structure of Authority in Renaissance England* (London: Methuen, 1985), pp. 59–111.

25. See, for example, Emmanuel Le Roy Ladurie, *Carnival in Romans*, trans. Mary Feeney (New York: G. Braziller, 1979).

26. Giddens, *The Constitution of Society*, pp. 3–4, *passim*.

27. Bristol, *Carnival and Theater*, pp. 26–59.

28. Jacques Le Goff and Jean-Claude Schmitt (eds.), *Le Charivari: Actes de la table ronde organisée à Paris 9, 25–27 Avril 1977 par l'École des*

Hautes Études en Sciences Sociales et le Centre National de la Récherche Scientifique (Paris: Mouton, 1977); E. P. Thompson, 'Rough Music: Le Charivari Anglais', *Annales: Économies, Sociétes, Civilizations*, 27 (1972), 285–312; Henri Rey-Flaud, *Le Charivari: Les rituels fondamentaux de la sexualité* (Paris: Payot, 1985); David Underdown, *Revel, Riot, and Rebellion: Popular Politics and Culture in England 1603–1660* (Oxford: Clarendon Press, 1985), pp. 99–103.

29. Natalie Davis, 'The Reasons of Misrule: Youth Groups and Charivaris in Sixteenth-Century France', *Past and Present*, 50 (1981), 49–75. On the topic of 'male solidarity' see Eve Kosofsky Sedgwick, *Between Men: English Literature and Homosocial Desire* (New York: Columbia University Press, 1985).

30. See Violet Alford, 'Rough Music or Charivari', *Folklore*, 70 (1959), 505–18; Nicole Belmont, 'Fonction de la dérision et symbolisme du bruit dans le charivari'; Natalie Z. Davis, 'Charivari, honneur et communauté à Lyon et à Genève au XVIIe siècle'; Martine Grinberg, 'Charivaris au Moyen age et à la Renaissance. Condamnation des rémariages ou rites d'inversion du temps?', all in LeGoff and Schmitt (eds.), *Le Charivari*. See also Michael D. Bristol, 'Wedding Feast and Charivari', in *Carnival and Theater*, pp. 162–79.

31. For the importance of 'youth groups' and of unmarried men see Davis, 'The Reasons of Misrule'.

32. Martin Ingram, 'Le Charivari dans l'Angleterre du XVIe et du XVIIe siècle. Aperçu historique'; Robert Muchembled, 'Des conduites de bruit au spectacle des processions. Mutations mentales en déclin des fêtes populaires dans le Nord de la France', both in LeGoff and Schmitt (eds.), *Le Charivari*.

33. Davis, 'The Reasons of Misrule', p. 75.

34. Catherine Belsey, *The Subject of Tragedy* (London: Methuen, 1985); Bertolt Brecht, *The Messingkauf Dialogues*, trans. John Willett (London: Methuen, 1965).

35. Bakhtin, *Dialogic Imagination*, pp. 158–67.

36. Stephen Greenblatt, *Renaissance Self-Fashioning: From More to Shakespeare* (Chicago: University of Chicago Press, 1981), p. 234.

37. Newman, ' "And Wash the Ethiop white" ', p. 144.

38. Natalie Z. Davis, ' "Women on Top": Symbolic Sexual Inversion and Political Disorder in Early Modern Europe', in *The Reversible World: Symbolic Inversion in Art and Society*, ed. Barbara Babcock (Ithaca: Cornell University Press), pp. 147–90.

39. Linda Woodbridge, *Women and the English Renaissance: Literature and the Nature of Womankind, 1540–1620* (Urbana: University of Illinois Press, 1984).

40. Phyllis Rackin, 'Androgyny, Mimesis, and the Marriage of the Boy Heroine on the English Renaissance Stage', *PMLA*, 102 (1987), 29–42.

41. Cavell, *Disowning Knowledge*, p. 129ff.

42. Greenblatt, *Renaissance Self-Fashioning*, pp. 237–52.

43. Arguments for a chaste or virginal Desdemona are found in Nelson and Haines, 'Othello's Unconsummated Marriage', pp. 1–18, as well as in Pierre Janton, 'Othello's Weak Function', *Cahiers Élisabéthains*, 34 (1988), 79–82. The idea of a sexually aggressive Desdemona is to be found in Greenblatt, *Renaissance Self-Fashioning*, p. 237ff., and in Stephen Booth, 'The Best *Othello* I ever saw', *Shakespeare Quarterly*, 40 (1989), 332–6.

44. On the 'triangular' character of erotic desire, see René Girard, *Deceit, Desire, and the Novel*, trans. Yvonne Freccero (Baltimore: Johns Hopkins University Press, 1965), pp. 1–52.

45. Niklas Luhmann, *Love as Passion: The Codification of Intimacy*, trans. Jeremy L. Gaines and Doris Jones (Cambridge, Mass.: Harvard University Press, 1986).

46. Paul Dumouchel and Jean Pierre Dupuy, *L'Enfer des choses: René Girard et la logique de l'économie* (Paris: Éditions de Seuil, 1979). See also Tobin Siebers, *The Mirror of Medusa* (Berkeley: University of California Press, 1983).

47. Jean-Christophe Agnew, *Worlds Apart: The Market and the Theater in Anglo-American Thought*, 1550–1750 (Cambridge: Cambridge University Press, 1986), pp. 6–7, *passim*.

48. In addition to Cavell and Greenblatt, see, for example, Kenneth Burke, '*Othello*: An Essay to Illustrate a Method', *The Hudson Review*, 4 (1951), 165–203; Carol Thomas Neely, 'Women and Men in *Othello*. "What should such a fool / Do with so Good a Woman?"' in *The Woman's Part: Feminist Criticism of Shakespeare*, ed. Carolyn S. Lenz, Gayle Greene and Carol Thomas Neely (Urbana: University of Illinois Press, 1980), pp. 211–39; Patricia Parker, 'Shakespeare and rhetoric: "dilation" and "delation" in *Othello*', in *Shakespeare and the Question of Theory*, ed. Patricia Parker and Geoffrey Hartman (London: Methuen, 1985); Edward Snow, 'Sexual Anxiety and the Male Order of Things in *Othello*', *English Literary Renaissance*, 10 (1980), 384–412; Peter Stallybrass, 'Patriarchal Territories: The Body Enclosed', in *Rewriting the Renaissance: The Discourses of Sexual Difference in Early Modern Europe*, ed. Margaret W. Ferguson, Maureen Quilligan and Nancy Vickers (Chicago: University of Chicago Press, 1986).

49. Antonin Artaud, *The Theater and its Double*, trans. by Mary Caroline Richards (New York: Grove Press, 1958), p. 42, *passim*.

50. Rosalie Colie, *Shakespeare's Living Art* (Princeton: Princeton University Press, 1974), p. 167. For other recuperative readings within quite different normative horizons see, for example, Karen Newman, ' "And Wash the Ethiop white" ', pp. 143–61; C. L. Barber and Richard P. Wheeler, *The Whole Journey: Shakespeare's Power of Development* (Berkeley: University of California Press, 1986), pp. 272–81; Robert Heilman, *Magic in the Web* (Lexington: University of Kentucky Press, 1956); Norman Holland, *The Shakespearean Imagination: A Critical Introduction* (Bloomington: University of Indiana Press, 1964), pp. 197–216; Arthur Kirsch, *Shakespeare and the Experience of Love* (Cambridge: Cambridge University Press, 1981), pp. 10–39.

4

Impertinent Trifling: Desdemona's Handkerchief

HARRY BERGER, JR.

– that's but a trifle here –
– we make trifles of terrors –

Too much attention has been paid to the symbolic meanings of the famous handkerchief and too little to such considerations as its putative size (is it as big as a flag or as small as a facial tissue?) and the odd circumstances of its appearance and removal. Just when Othello's rage has reached a first climax, Desdemona enters to tell him he is keeping his dinner and dinner guests waiting (3.3.283–5).[1] 'I am to blame', he replies, and her next questions – 'Why is your speech so faint? are you not well?' (ll. 286–7) – tell us to hear something more in his reply than an apology for delaying dinner. 'I am to blame' is at the same time a logical response to the thought that concludes the soliloquy he has just uttered: 'If she be false O, then heaven mocks itself, / I'll not believe it' (ll. 282–3). 'Haply', he is to blame, 'for I am black, / And have not those soft parts of conversation / That chamberers have'; therefore 'She's gone' (ll. 267–71). Seeing Desdemona approach, he veers away from that dread conclusion and, in effect, blames himself for believing it possible. But perhaps he is to blame for having aroused her desire in the first place. The idea that 'this forked plague is fated to us' (l. 280) – 'us' males, husbands and especially 'great ones' (l. 277), not to mention great ones who are black, who don't have extended manners, who are somewhat 'declin'd' in years (l. 269) – this idea, manured by

Iago, allows Othello to share the blame with Desdemona and leads him to answer her questions by hinting at his imaginary horns:

> Othello   I have a pain upon my forehead, here.
> Desdemona Faith, that's with watching, 'twill away again;
>   Let me but bind your head, within this hour
>   It will be well again.
> Othello   Your napkin is too little:
>   Let it alone, come, I'll go in with you.
> Desdemona I am very sorry that you are not well.
>   (ll. 288–93)

The crucial object makes its appearance modestly and anonymously as a 'napkin', and that is what Emilia also calls it before she enlarges on its significance and Iago's interest in it, after which she teasingly offers it to Iago as 'that same handkerchief' (l. 309). Thus almost as soon as it appears, we learn that it has already been the topic of much conversation and observation, fetishized by Othello as a token of Desdemona's love and fidelity, and loved by her for this reason. To learn this is to realize that, in the moment of Desdemona's producing and then losing the handkerchief, an extraordinary event has taken place. Of course, Othello's 'Let *it* alone' is teasingly laconic, but whether 'it' denotes his forehead or the napkin, the result of his command is that Desdemona drops the napkin, and this tells us how she heard the statement. Yet he had 'conjur'd her she should ever keep it', and 'she reserves it evermore about her' (ll. 298–9). This precious object could hardly go unrecognized, and it would be perverse to stage the episode in a manner that concealed the handkerchief from Othello (for example, by having Desdemona wad it up in her hand). She, at any rate, knows what she is dropping. To represent Othello as recognizing it makes him perceive what she offers to bind his head with. If she registers that recognition, she must hear him countermand his general conjuration in ordering her to drop the handkerchief before he escorts her offstage.

When Othello points to the pain on his forehead and Desdemona says 'that's with watching', she obviously refers to his staying up too late, working too hard, and so on; yet listening to the phrase with Othello's ears may give it a different ring, for it comes after a stretch of dialogue between him and Iago in which much has been made of perceiving, observing, seeing, scanning and noting (ll. 245–56); 'watching' may, like standing the watch, mean protecting against trouble, and it may also mean looking for trouble. Desdemona's

' 'twill away again' then has the force of a shallow consolation, like his 'I'll not believe it'; and (still listening with his ears) her repeating the sentiment in the next line's 'within this hour / It will be well again' sounds suspiciously dismissive: perhaps her offer to 'bind' his head is an offer to hide his horns and seel up his eyes – and with the very handkerchief that signifies the power of the gift that binds her to him in loving obligation. If she has abused and soiled the gift, if she is doing so now with this brazen gesture, it makes sense for him to protect himself by refusing the offer. He will not let her touch him with it, and his command is so phrased as to persuade her he wants her to drop the fetish and leave it behind. But doesn't he notice that she drops the precious keepsake? Only a little later in the same scene, he explodes when Iago, who has not left the stage and still has the handkerchief, all but gives him the 'ocular proof' he demanded (l. 366), telling him that 'today' he saw 'Cassio wipe his beard' with it (ll. 445–6). Presumably Iago does not know that Othello has seen the handkerchief several minutes earlier – Emilia neglects to tell him when or under what conditions she found the handkerchief. But doesn't Othello remember? It is evidently useful to him to disremember in order to set up the possibility of Desdemona's losing it. For on the one hand she does not deserve to keep it if she has violated what it represents; if on the other hand she loses it in spite of his conjuration, she violates what it represents. Thus by helping Desdemona lose the handkerchief and by disremembering the episode, Othello facilitates the production of the ocular proof that will give him vantage to exclaim on her.

If Desdemona normally keeps the handkerchief 'evermore about her', why doesn't she pick it up before going offstage? Emilia tells Iago she 'let it drop by negligence' (l. 315), and at 3.4.19 Desdemona wonders, 'Where should I lose that handkerchief, Emilia?' What could cause such unexpected negligence and forgetfulness? What motivates Desdemona's act of disremembrance? The gesture that interprets Othello's 'Let it alone' as a command to let go of the handkerchief signals a double rejection. In his rejection of her offer to soothe him, she hears the message that she does not deserve and should not have the handkerchief. Dropping it may be read simultaneously as an act of obedience and as a contestatory gesture rejecting his rejection – he doesn't deserve the love and fidelity her possession of the handkerchief symbolizes. Dropping the handkerchief enables her to be in the position of losing it, and losing it, she knows, would be 'enough / To put him to ill thinking' if he were capable of jealousy, which of course he isn't (ll. 23–4). So (one is tempted to say), knowing this, she loses it. And later having elicited from him all the signs of jealousy, she ignores the signs and firmly denies that she has lost the handkerchief (ll. 81–4). Her stubbornness in this exchange is closely and strangely linked to the maddening stubbornness with which she changes the subject from the handkerchief to Cassio. In spite of her devotion to and concern for Othello, her sense of injured merit keeps her from acknowledging his jealousy while pursuing a course of rhetorical action that aggravates it.

Othello and Desdemona work closely together to lose the handkerchief and to disremember its loss. In the dissociated agency of deep emplotment, the playing-through of disowned desires and apprehensions, they cooperate with Iago by losing the handkerchief in order to make the kind of trouble for themselves, for each other, that both are motivated to make. 'Give me the ocular proof', Othello commands Iago (3.3.366), but not until after he has helped provide a likely candidate for that function. Desdemona's dropping the handkerchief is already ocular proof: if she is unfaithful she should not have the handkerchief; if she does not have it, she is unfaithful. For Desdemona his rejection of her offer to soothe him with the handkerchief is already ocular proof that he has rejected her, and losing the handkerchief puts her in a good position to test the force and meaning of his rejection.

The fruits of disremembrance are harvested in 3.4. Desdemona initiates the action by sending the Clown in search of Cassio, then pauses to wonder about the handkerchief and to assure Emilia that Othello is incapable of jealousy. Seeing Othello approach, she says, 'I will not leave him now till Cassio / Be called to him' (ll. 28–9).[2] Othello barges in with a series of broad hints about her lechery that hark back in tone to Iago's quips and his comments on hand-paddling in 2.1. To Othello's angry variations on the topic of her moist and liberal hand, she responds at first with reserve, then more tartly, and finally, as if to put an end to this nonsense and get back to *her* topic of choice,

> Desdemona   I cannot speak of this; come, come, your promise.
> Othello   What promise, chuck?
> Desdemona   I have sent to bid Cassio come speak with you.
>
> (ll. 44–6)

I find it hard to imagine that Desdemona – the Desdemona who engaged in what Ridley disapprovingly calls 'cheap backchat' with

Iago and in innocently flirtatious palm-paddling with Cassio (2.1.167), the Desdemona who displayed acquaintance with humoural theory just before Othello's entrance in 3.4 – grasps the meaning of Othello's little disquisition on her hot hand (ll. 32–43) with a jot less clarity than the editors who gloss his adjectives: 'The palm, if hot and moist, was taken to be an indication of "hot" desires'; '*liberal*] free, and so "too free" and so "loose" '.[3] She knows whereof she 'cannot speak', or will not speak. It is she, after all, and not Emilia who first brings up the possibility of 'ill thinking' and jealousy, but only to rule it out in advance. Immediately after she does so, Othello enters displaying all the signs of ill thinking and jealousy. Far from appearing ingenuously unaware of the jealousy with which he confronts her from this point on, she shows rather that she refuses to acknowledge it – refuses to acknowledge that he has any cause, therefore any right, to be jealous, refuses to acknowledge even the possibility of behaviour on her part which could be misinterpreted. As Rymer huffily and astutely observes, '*Othello*'s Jealousie, that had rag'd so loudly and had been so uneasie to himself, must have reach'd her knowledge. ... And yet she must still be impertinent in her suit for *Cassio*'.[4] After 3.4 her refusal to acknowledge his jealousy modulates into a desire to rise above it – or, to put it more precisely, a desire to show herself rising above it. Yet if we take simple interlocutory logic into account and premise that her ability to ignore or rise above Othello's jealousy depends on his expressing it, her behaviour from 3.4 on leads to an interesting conclusion: Desdemona secures that ability by pushing the button that lights up his angry-husband display; she acts in a manner calculated to evoke from him the signs of ill thinking that denote the passion she won't acknowledge.

The battle between them is joined when Othello, armed (as he thinks) with his ocular proof, prepares to establish the guilt that will justify the sentence of death he has already passed on Desdemona (3.3.483–5). His preparation – in effect, the argument for the prosecution – consists in conferring the broadest possible significance on her betrayal, which he interprets as misuse of the generous gift of power he has bestowed on her, the apotropaic power to ward off the contamination of their coupling by moderating the sexuality she arouses. This gift, this alienated power, together with the sexuality he both desires and fears, makes Desdemona her captain's captain and her general's general. It is to insure against the risk involved in alienating power – the risk (let us say it now) of

castration – that Othello reifies gift and power together in the second gift of the handkerchief. Thus he tries to reclaim some of the
control he has alienated by making Desdemona responsible for the
power she has and potentially guilty for its misuse. In its structure
this tactic resembles Portia's bestowal of the ring on Bassanio after
she admits, 'Myself, and what is mine, to you and yours / Is now
converted' (*The Merchant of Venice*, 3.2.166–7). The compensatory
function of the ring is identical to that of the handkerchief:

> I give ... this ring,
> Which when you part from, lose, or give away,
> Let it presage the ruin of your love,
> And be my vantage to exclaim on you.
>   (ll. 171–4)

It is important to remember that the gift of the handkerchief is,
like Othello's courtship, introduced as part of the prehistory of the
play. Desdemona has been apprised of and embraced the general
tenor of the gift since before her arrival at Cyprus. Yet if we recall
this when Othello parries Desdemona's 'I have sent to bid Cassio
come speak with you' with his handkerchief attack, we may be
puzzled as to the status of the Egyptic narrative he tells. Is he now
filling in details omitted when he first gave her the handkerchief? His
meticulous exposition and her puzzled responses suggest this is the
case. It is idle to wonder whether he had such a narrative in mind
from the beginning, but the fantasy he unfolds is obviously para-
bolic, and the parable is consistent with the divided attitude towards
sexuality and blackness his language displays in 1.2 and 1.3. The
parable conveys, in Carol Neely's words, 'something of Othello's ...
imagined relations to ... the myth of African men's sexual excess',
that is, he makes the handkerchief symbolize first the wife's sexual
power over her husband and then the chastity that the husband
demands as an always-inadequate placeholder for the virginity she
lost when she subdued him to her love (3.4.53–61, 67–73).[5] The
burden of the parable is that if the exotic blackness of the romantic and heroic stranger gives way to the monstrous blackness of the
Barbary horse, it will be – it already is – her fault.

Desdemona's 'Is't possible?' (l. 66) punctuates the parable's
first thesis and her 'I'faith, is't true?' (l. 73) punctuates the second.
These puzzled responses are themselves puzzling. Given what we
have already heard from her, it is not clear that these questions
express the wide-eyed bewilderment of the naive auditor. They may

suggest that she realizes for the first time how serious he was when 'he conjur'd her she should ever keep it', and realizes also that the conjuration contained as an admonitory nucleus his 'vantage to exclaim on [her]'. I hear as much anger as perplexity in the placement and voicing of her questions: *Can he really be holding me responsible and setting me up this way? Is my noble Moor going mad? Is he actually going to make a Thing, threaten me with matchless 'perdition', over my losing the handkerchief?* 'Then would to God that I had never seen it!' (l. 75). The intensity of her recoil may be measured by setting it against the fetishistic attachment described by Emilia: 'she so loves the token, ... / That she reserves it evermore about her, / To kiss, and talk to' (3.3.297–300). What she cherished as a token of his love she now rejects as a token of his bad faith. The terms of his threat are themselves revealingly obfuscatory: the implied perdition she faces is that *he* will 'hold *her* loathly' and 'hunt / After new fancies' (3.4.60–1, my emphasis). But since the parable follows his harping on her moist hand, the threat has the hapless ring of the betrayed victim's desire for revenge: her losing the handkerchief or giving it away not only symbolizes but also actualizes both her failure to moderate his desire and her success in moderating another's.

I imagine Desdemona as capable of hearing this message in Othello's words and offended by his aggressive yet devious power plays as much as she is dismayed by his unstable behaviour and the groundless accusation he all but makes. For it is not fear and trembling alone that her three mendacious utterances convey:

> Desdemona It is not lost, but what an if it were? ...
> I say it is not lost.
> Othello Fetch't, let me see it
> Desdemona Why, so I can sir, but I will not now,
> This is a trick, to put me from my suit,
> I pray let Cassio be receiv'd again.
> (ll. 81, 83–6)

Her tone is at first defiant and truculent and then dismissive as she counter-attacks with her own weapon and continues to rub Cassio in Othello's face:

> Othello Fetch me that handkerchief, my mind misgives.
> Desdemona Come, come,
> You'll never meet a more sufficient man.

Othello	The handkerchief!
Desdemona	I pray, talk me of Cassio.
Othello	The handkerchief!
Desdemona	A man that all his time

Hath founded his good fortunes on your love,
Shar'd dangers with you, –

Othello	The handkerchief!
Desdemona	I'faith, you are to blame.

                                        (ll. 87–94)

Her concluding utterance echoes his 'I am to blame' and has the same indeterminate reference. He is to blame for what? His treatment of Cassio? His treatment of her? Her losing the handkerchief? She ducks away from Emilia's second question about jealousy and continues to make excuses for Othello later in the scene, attributing his 'puddled ... spirit' to state matters. 'Pray heaven', Emilia responds, that 'it be state-matters, as you think, / And no conception, nor no jealous toy / Concerning you', at which Desdemona exclaims, 'Alas the day, I never gave him cause!' (ll. 137–40, 153–6). That note of rueful but defiant self-exoneration underlies her interlocutory moves in 3.4: Othello is not the sort of man to be jealous (and if he were, it would be the result of humoural imbalance); if he *is* jealous, it must be because of the handkerchief's magic or its loss; perhaps, as Emilia helpfully suggests later, he is jealous because he is jealous (jealousy is a self-begotten monster [ll. 159–60]); at any rate, it has nothing to do with Desdemona. All she can do is implore heaven to 'keep that monster from Othello's mind' (l. 161). Othello can't – that is, he shouldn't – be jealous because she never gave him cause, and it would be unworthy of him to imagine something unworthy of her. Therefore she will ignore the signs of jealousy. Her way of ignoring them is to deny she lost the handkerchief in order to deny his interpretation of the loss. If the loss of the token signifies or actualizes the loser's infidelity, it signifies or actualizes falsely with respect to her, and she rejects its lie. If she has to lie in order to maintain the truth, Othello is to blame for that as well as for evading the Cassio problem, for making her badger him about it, and for mistreating the man who shared with him the dangers not only of war but also of courtship.

Desdemona's heated exchange with Othello displays an interest in keeping him angry, but angry on her terms, not his: she brushes past his demands for the handkerchief and irritates him by switching to a topic entirely unrelated to jealousy, a topic she has already seen him reluctant to deal with, the topic of Cassio. There is no indication in her language that she associates Cassio with Othello's display of jealousy, much less that she is angrily taunting him with the possibility that she has committed adultery. She frames the Cassio Project as an enterprise that has everything to do with gender – with the struggle of will between her and Othello – and nothing to do with sex. This strategy is consistent with (and reinforces) her refusal to acknowledge Othello's jealousy. Yet, as I have suggested, not only does the refusal seem perversely self-scotomizing, it accompanies behaviour that seems, even more perversely, to arouse and intensify the very object of that refusal, the jealousy that gives her vantage, if not to exclaim on Othello, then to dramatize her injured merit ('I never gave him cause', 'you are to blame', 'poor Barbary' [3.4.156 and 94; 4.3.33]). To view it from this standpoint is to throw the harshest light on her motivation – that is, if encouraging his unjustified jealousy is important to her own self-justification, what better way to do this than couple her persistence in denying his jealousy with her persistence in rubbing the salt of Cassio into its wound?

This is no doubt too harsh a light. It's enough to say that ignoring Othello's jealousy allows Desdemona to defend herself and even seize the offensive in 3.4. It gives her permission to bring up Cassio as often as she likes without for a moment having to entertain the not improbable possibility that Othello suspects a liaison between her and this most 'sufficient man' who helped bring them together. Yet the Cassio Project remains the instrument of her anger, and she is not unaware of its effect. 'I have spoken for you, all my best', she tells Cassio, 'And stood within the blank of his displeasure / For my free speech' (ll. 124–6). In 4.1 her persistence in this line produces the predictable climax of the collision course on which she and Othello have set themselves. Speaking to Lodovico in Othello's presence, she tells him of the 'unkind breach' between Othello and Cassio and predicts that Lodovico will 'make all well' (ll. 220–1). Othello, who is reading about Cassio's replacing him as governor, interjects, 'Are you sure of that?' Desdemona's 'My lord?' indicates that she is aware he is listening (ll. 222–3). Her next comment seems meant to be overheard by him. To Lodovico's inquiry about the breach, she replies that it is 'most unhappy' and that she 'would do much / To atone them, for the love [she] bear[s] to Cassio' (ll. 227–8). This piece of free speech draws 'Fire and brimstone!' from Othello (l. 229), and why shouldn't she expect that, since she is harping on what she knows displeases him, and her comment is itself a continuance of her effort to 'atone them'? Moreover, their exchanges are now being monitored by Lodovico and his attendants, which affects the way her response to Othello – another 'My lord?' (l. 229) – can be played and heard: not only *What did you say? I didn't hear you* but also *Say that again, so everyone can hear it.* By the end of the skirmish that follows, Lodovico has shifted from a bystander to Desdemona's partisan:

Othello	Fire and brimstone!
Desdemona	My lord?
Othello	Are you wise?
Desdemona	What, is he angry?
Lodovico	May be the letter mov'd him;
	For, as I think, they do command him home,
	Deputing Cassio in his government.
Desdemona	By my troth, I am glad on't.
Othello	Indeed!
Desdemona	My lord?
Othello	I am glad to see you mad.
Desdemona	How, sweet Othello?
Othello	Devil! [*Striking her.*]
Desdemona	I have not deserv'd this.
Lodovico	My lord, this would not be believ'd in Venice,
	Though I should swear I saw't: 'tis very much,
	Make her amends, she weeps.

(ll. 229–39)

Desdemona's second question has demonstrative or even exclamatory force because directed to Lodovico: 'What, is he angry?' equals *Look, he's angry.* Her reply to Lodovico's news is ambiguous: she is truly glad because they will return to Venice and leave the Cassio problem behind them; she is glad to hear Cassio will be not only reinstated but promoted; perhaps also, since she has just heard Lodovico speculate that the letter may have caused Othello's anger, *she* is glad to hear the news even if *he* isn't. Given this choice of targets, Othello's 'Indeed!' is relatively restrained, only a warmup, and Desdemona's third 'My lord?' challenges him to speak up and say what's on his mind. He does not directly meet the challenge but throws 'I am glad' back in her face and muffles his meaning, if not his aggression, enough to confuse several commentators and elicit another inquiry from Desdemona. 'How, sweet Othello?' is, again, ambiguous in its reach, and the work done by 'sweet' is affected by the scope of 'How?' Because Othello's utterance is more than an ejaculation or mutter, because it redirects attention from the letter to her, and because it is a cryptic non sequitur, I take Desdemona's question to be asking for a more explicit restatement: *What are you getting at? Why do you call me – or how am I – mad? Why are you talking and behaving this way? I see that you're angry, but why take it out on me?* Her words contain something like a challenge to him to come clean. She solicits accusation and he withholds it. But this is a drama she, more than he, is displaying for Lodovico's benefit. Thus although her 'sweet Othello' may be no more than a gesture of affection and concern, an attempt to soothe him (comparable to her earlier offer to bind his head with the handkerchief), it can't escape the aggressiveness of the context or the performative edge given it by the presence of onstage spectators. 'Sweet Othello' shows Lodovico her love and concern for her husband and asks him to join her in wondering why Othello is being so hostile: *See, I love him, why is he talking to me this way?* Even in terms of Desdemona's preferred interpretation of her 'for the love I bear to Cassio', she may be expected to know why he is talking to her thus. In her terms Othello clearly overreacts and enables Desdemona to show Lodovico the spectacle of an unjustly battered wife.

To return for a moment to Othello's 'I am glad to see you mad', the most satisfactory gloss on the utterance is the one proposed by Ridley, who links it to 'Are you wise?': ' "are you in your right wits?" (that is, thus openly to speak of love for Cassio). ... "I am glad to see that you have so manifestly taken leave of your senses, and betrayed yourself publicly" '.[6] But if this is what Othello insinuates, he refrains from saying so outright, and the gap between insinuated message and cryptic utterance is important because it is part of a withholding pattern: Othello never mentions Cassio by name to Desdemona until 5.2.48 and after 3.3.76 makes no pronominal reference to him in her presence. This is especially noticeable in the accusation scene, 4.2, during which, as Kenneth Muir points out, 'he does not give her a chance of defending herself by naming her supposed lover, her accuser, or the evidence against her'.[7] When he finally mentions Cassio in 5.2 (and mentions him together with the handkerchief), he does so on the mistaken assumption that Cassio has been killed. I conclude from this that he doesn't want to give her a chance to clear herself by confronting him together with Cassio. He has a use for his jealousy. But, as we have seen, Desdemona also has a use for it. Her insistence on mentioning Cassio in the martial context of her project has the same effect as – and reinforces – Othello's refusal to

mention Cassio in the venerean context. She departs from her withholding pattern only once, responding in a justifiable moment of
weakness to Othello's 'thou art false as hell' with 'To whom,
my lord? with whom? how am I false?' He avoids the questions
('O Desdemona, away! away! away!'), and she herself then obediently veers away through 'Am I the occasion of those tears, my lord?'
to the hypothesis that he may be unhappy because he suspects her
father had a hand in his recall to Venice – therefore, 'Lay not your
blame on me; if you have lost him, / Why, I have lost him too'
(4.2.40–8). After this exchange Othello and Desdemona collaborate
in redirecting blame from the third party, steering it back to her so
that he can continue belabouring her as if she is the sole offender and
she can continue protesting her honesty and injured merit.

This collaboration is founded and dependent on the losing of the
handkerchief, which in turn has its potential meanings preinscribed
by the terms of Othello's gift, terms he mystifyingly displaces or
injects into 'the web of it' as its 'magic'. Karen Newman observes
that this 'snowballing signifier ... first appears simply as a love token
given by Othello to Desdemona and therefore treasured by her', but
it would be more accurate to say that it first *disappears* as a love
token and that, at its appearance or disappearance, what it represents is not so simple. Newman herself remarks on its 'doubleness':
'when the handkerchief is first given, it represents her virtue and
their chaste love, but it later becomes a sign, indeed a proof, of her
unfaithfulness'.[8] Yet Emilia's 'he conjur'd her she should ever keep
it' places the representational emphasis less on *her* virtue and *their*
chaste love than on *his* desire to test her fidelity. Whatever the object
symbolizes must be something he entrusts to her safekeeping – this
something could include his reputation – and the point of the gift is
that it transfers accountability from him to her. Should she lose it,
she will bear the culpability of losing all that he has decided to make
it stand for.

The sense that Othello presented the handkerchief not only as a
gift but also as a threat or warning is of course reinforced in 3.4,
after it has become a sign of her unfaithfulness. Othello blusters that
the gift of chaste desire to be entrusted to and safeguarded by the
woman is the man's:

> ... while she kept it
> 'T would make her amiable, and subdue my father
> Entirely to her love: but if she lost it,

Or made a gift of it, my father's eye
Should hold her loathly, and his spirits should hunt
After new fancies.

(ll. 56–61)

Thus, if we have only Emilia's and Othello's comments to judge by, we must conclude that 'when the handkerchief is first given' the anticipation of betrayal is already woven into the web of the gift, the terms of which express an anxiety about, a potential proof of, Desdemona's unfaithfulness. The apotropaic function of the handkerchief may be suggested by recalling an earlier exchange:

> Brabantio Look to her, Moor, have a quick eye to see:
> She has deceiv'd her father, may do thee.
> Othello My life upon her faith: honest Iago,
> My Desdemona must I leave to thee.

(1.3.292–5)

The handkerchief transfers responsibility for his life to her faith. In 3.4, having – as he thinks – proved her unfaithful, he makes it represent the power (of prophetesses, mothers, wives, virgins) she has lost but also, coterminously, the power he has lost – has tried and failed to domesticate – because of her.

It is in this gestural drama more than in the reified web of the handkerchief that symbolic action resides. The action is not merely iconographic – not merely elicited from a description of the object ('a handkerchief, / Spotted with strawberries' [3.3.441–2]). It is agentive. That is, the handkerchief becomes the locus and medium of a complex motivational conflict between agents who displace or alienate their agency from themselves to it as to a scapegoat, a *pharmakon*, a fetish. The poison in Othello's gift is mystified as the magic in the web. The agency of subjects and discourses is detextualized both in and as the handkerchief. But the handkerchief itself is, as Emilia says, only 'a trifle' (5.2.229), the word picked up by Rymer in his notorious critique of 'the *Tragedy of the Handkerchief*' that is 'a Tragedy of this *Trifle*'.[9]

Othello and Desdemona are not alone in promoting the loss of the handkerchief. Someone else is complicit with them and, indeed, makes it possible for them to capitalize later on its loss. After they go offstage leaving the handkerchief behind them in 3.3, Emilia snaps it up, for at that point she does not view it as an unconsidered trifle:

> I am glad I have found this napkin;
> This was her first remembrance from the Moor,

> My wayward husband hath a hundred times
> Woo'd me to steal it, but she so loves the token,
> For he conjur'd her she should ever keep it,
> That she reserves it evermore about her,
> To kiss, and talk to; I'll ha' the work ta'en out,
> And give't Iago: what he'll do with it
> Heaven knows, not I,
> I nothing know, but for his fantasy.
>
> (ll. 294–303)

The final line here is the First Quarto variant; the Folio reads 'I nothing, but to please his fantasy'. The elided verb in the Folio version could be *do* or *wish*, but the influence of the preceding phrase suggests the Quarto's 'know'. Emilia disowns knowledge in a manner that recalls Brakenbury's 'I will not reason what is meant hereby, / Because I will be guiltless from the meaning' (*Richard III*, 1.4.93–4), but her 'because' is more indirect: *my husband is a little weird ('wayward') and is probably up to some mischief, but it's none of my business; he has odd fancies or whims, and my job is to humour him and keep him happy*. When she offers it to Iago, she wonders what he will do with the handkerchief he has 'been / So earnest to have me filch', and she has a moment of hesitation:

> Emilia If it be not for some purpose of import,
>   Give me 't again, poor lady, she'll run mad,
>   When she shall lack it.
> Iago   Be not you known on 't, I have use for it.
>
> (3.3.321–4)

'[P]oor lady, she'll run mad' sounds a note of pity verging on condescension, as if for a child who has been imposed upon by the Moor's strangely demanding act of donation; Desdemona will have to suffer the consequences not only of her negligence but also of the enthusiasm with which she embraces the odd conditions attendant on his gift. Momentarily distanced from Desdemona by her own acquiescence in Iago's 'fantasy', Emilia expresses the mixture of curiosity, sympathy and censure with which members of the serving class scrutinize the follies of their (often less worldly) betters.

Emilia, then, anticipates trouble but blinkers herself and throws in her lot with Iago. The dramatic crescendo of threats that concludes 3.3 enhances our sense of Desdemona's vulnerability and of Emilia's contribution to it. In 3.4 an onstage Emilia remains mum during the whole stretch of dialogue in which Othello spins out his history of the handkerchief and hectors Desdemona about its whereabouts. After he leaves, Desdemona expresses her unhappiness 'in the loss of it' and thus gives Emilia a chance to make her less unhappy by speaking up. Emilia's refusal is therefore all the more conspicuous: she responds with an evasively general witticism about men's mistreatment of women (ll. 100–3). This pattern of nondisclosure continues into the fourth act. At the beginning of 4.2, Emilia learns from Othello himself, as he questions her for evidence of Desdemona's infidelity, that he suspects Cassio. She stoutly defends Desdemona against his misguided suspicion in words that carry the true Desdemonan pitch: 'if she be not honest, chaste, and true, / There's no man happy' (ll. 17–18). Then she leaves the stage when Othello orders her to summon Desdemona, returns with her five lines later, is thereafter shortly and curtly dismissed again as if she were Desdemona's procuress (ll. 27–30), and returns some sixty lines later just in time – as the Quarto places her entrance – to hear Othello ranting about 'that cunning whore of Venice, / That married with Othello' and to give him another chance to call Emilia 'madam' before he exits (ll. 91–6). 'Alas', she exclaims, 'what does this gentleman conceive?' and, a moment later, 'what's the matter with my lord?' (ll. 97, 100). Has she forgotten the discussion that opened the scene? Critics comment on the dramatic irony and heightened suspense of Emilia's all but fingering Iago in this scene, yet her failure to mention the scene's opening discussion is equally damaging and of a different order of complicity. Her failure to put two and two together and recognize that the scoundrel she describes is Iago is strictly part of a negotiation between the play and its audience, a venerable mechanism for driving spectators/readers wild by conspicuously blocking and deferring anagnorisis until too late. But her silence about her conversation with Othello is part of Emilia's negotiations with Desdemona and Iago. This is the second time she fails to report something she has seen or heard, though here, as before, she is well positioned to know that her failure can increase Desdemona's jeopardy along with Othello's jealousy. These lapses are deeply problematic; they haunt the interchange between Emilia and Desdemona from the handkerchief episode on.

I hasten to add that none of this should be construed as reflecting adversely on Emilia's loyalty and devotion to Desdemona, any more than Desdemona's passive–aggressive reactions to Othello reflect adversely on her loyalty and devotion to him. It is just that Emilia's behaviour in the play is charted along, and straddles, two different trajectories, one dominated by Desdemona and the other by Iago. In the first she is a faithful attendant, in the second a close-mouthed watcher. The relation between these trajectories is textually underdetermined and therefore open. Like one of Philip McGuire's 'open silences', it solicits performative and contextual interpretation. It wants, in other words, to be motivated, and several motivational cues present themselves as candidates for inspection to anyone imagining or staging the speaker of Emilia's language.

First, in the context of socioliterary allusion, Emilia occupies a well-stencilled and recognizable position, that of the servant or attendant who innocently or corruptly helps betray her mistress in order to humour her lover. Examples are Pryene in the tale told by Phedon in *Faerie Queene* (Book 2, stanza 14) and Margaret in *Much Ado About Nothing*. According to *Much Ado*'s notoriously inconsistent stage directions, Margaret is not among the dramatis personae listed in the Quarto for the repudiation scene (4.1); the possibility that she might be present, watching but not exposing the slander of Hero, is not thereby foreclosed, but it is not thematized. Emilia's collusion with Iago over the handkerchief differs from the charade Don John and Borachio have Margaret innocently perform, because it involves Emilia in a voyeuristic exercise of the power of nondisclosure. Within the citational context, one of the motives imaginable for Emilia is a socially coded pleasure in watching one's betters misbehave and suffer, a pleasure Don John and Iago vigorously pursue in their self-appointed roles as performers of the villain's and victim/revenger's discourses.

Emilia's relationship to Iago provides a second context. Does she remain silent because she is afraid of Iago? Because she is interested in finding out what her weird husband is up to? Because in such matters a wife should obey her husband? – though her silence about the handkerchief is not something Iago explicitly enjoins; it appears to be Emilia's decision. In their interchange at 3.3.305–13, she offers the handkerchief as a gesture that seems partly an attempt to surprise and please him, partly a rebuke to his brusque and chiding manner. The gesture suggests that she finds his manner more a challenge than a threat. At 4.2.147–9 she rattles him by mocking his idle jealousy. Her discomposure at discovering his villainy in 5.2 suggests that she has previously humoured him as a kind of crank, a buffoon, that is, *a husband*, like herself an exemplary player in the Venetian game of marriage, a game that reflects and reproduces the cynical norms they both articulate as conventional wisdom.

This is the game depicted for Desdemona by Iago in 2.1 and by Emilia in 4.3. It is the game Desdemona refuses to play, and her anomalous marriage to Othello promises at first to flout its rules. After Othello finds a use for the game, Desdemona continues to represent herself as an exception and to buttress her claim by denying that their marriage could be jeopardized by suspicions for which there are obviously no grounds. I can imagine an Emilia who expects husbands to be jealous, who is intrigued by the possibility of Othello's conforming to the rule, and who may even be willing to prove her point to Desdemona by the silence that facilitates his conformity. In 3.4 Emilia disingenuously puts Desdemona to the test. Having watched Othello go on about the handkerchief, heard Desdemona defy him with her lies and talk of Cassio, and seen Othello storm offstage, Emilia asks, 'Is not this man jealous?' (l. 96). This is scarcely reducible to a request for information. It has the force of a rhetorical question soliciting Desdemona's assent; the force, perhaps, of a *Q.E.D.*, as if Emilia has just run off an experiment that proves Desdemona's marriage is no more impervious than hers to the slings and arrows of outrageous husbands. The demonstration is set up at the beginning of 3.4:

> Desdemona   Where should I lose that handkerchief, Emilia?
> Emilia   I know not, madam.
> Desdemona   Believe me, I had rather lose my purse
>   Full of crusadoes: and but my noble Moor
>   Is true of mind, and made of no such baseness
>   As jealous creatures are, it were enough
>   To put him to ill thinking.
> Emilia   Is he not jealous?
> Desdemona   Who, he? I think the sun where he was born
>   Drew all such humours from him.
> (ll. 19–27)

At the end of the demonstration, when Emilia archly repeats her question, Desdemona swerves from a direct answer and steers her perplexity towards the handkerchief:

> Emilia   Is not this man jealous?
> Desdemona   I ne'er saw this before:
>   Sure there's some wonder in this handkerchief,
>   I am most unhappy in the loss of it.
> (ll. 96–9)

Her refusal to enlighten Desdemona allows Emilia to put pressure on Desdemona to acknowledge both the truth about Othello and the larger truth that their marriage is not the exception Desdemona thinks it is – that it is as difficult, as precarious, as frangible as any other. Not even the divine Desdemona can avoid being victimized by the misogynist discourse that governs relations between men and women, wives and husbands, in and out of Venice.

Desdemona continues to resist this pressure. When she can no longer justify Othello's behaviour, she justifies her own. Indeed, after Othello has struck and bewhored her, she more insistently affirms her difference and uniqueness not only against his slander but also against Emilia's worldly norm. In 4.3 she appropriates the childlike and wounded bewilderment of poor Barbary to put questions to the Emilian voice of experience: *can there be women who abuse their husbands as grossly as Barbary and I were abused? would you do such a deed?* Unlike the run of women described by and including Emilia, she would never dream of cheating on her husband. And as if to dramatize her innocence by a show of unworldly ignorance, she goes so far as to claim not to believe 'there is any such woman' (l. 83). Thus where Iago wants to prove to himself that he can make Othello jealous, and where Emilia wants to prove to Desdemona that Othello is jealous, Desdemona seems intent on showing she can rise above his jealousy when she can no longer deny it.

Given the predicament Desdemona is placed in by her position at the juncture where 'in one line' the 'crafts' of Iago, Emilia and Othello 'directly meet' (*Hamlet*, 3.4.210), what can she do? For she *is* being unjustly victimized, and that needs to be emphasized in the face of the argument that she won't let Othello victimize her all by himself but will get herself victimized, make him do it, be his partner in crime. At one tender moment she all but acknowledges the anger behind her militantly nonviolent resistance when, after rationalizing his rage as a reaction to state matters, she says,

> beshrew me much, Emilia,
> I was (unhandsome warrior as I am)
> Arraigning his unkindness with my soul;
> But now I find I had suborn'd the witness,
> And he's indicted falsely.
> (3.4.148–52)

'Unhandsome warrior' is like a lifeline of self-accusation thrown from the 'O my fair warrior!' it remembers (2.1.182). But if this makes for tenderness of tone, the legalistic rhetoric that follows resonates more harshly. She concedes that she persuaded herself to misinterpret the behaviour she witnessed, but hers remains the prerogative of judgement, the power of indictment, and she derives that power from 'the authority of her merits' as the 'deserving woman' she knows herself to be (ll. 144–6). Those merits measure his unkindness, which is still the defendant and may still undergo a new trial in her 'soul's court of justice'.[10] She will give him another chance.

Desdemona is indeed a warrior, a trooper, who defends against the fate predicted by Iago in 2.1: it is possible to be a good wife and yet to avoid being reduced to a suckler of fools and chronicler of small beer. When the man she loves begins very soon, and unaccountably, to abuse her, she turns the other cheek. She makes excuses for him. She forgives him. Finally, when all else fails, she reduces herself to poor Barbary, who, forsaken by her mad lover, dies singing the Willow Song. From one line of this song – '*Let nobody blame him, his scorn I approve*' (4.3.51) – she takes the idea for her death scenario in 5.2: after reviving to announce that she is 'falsely, falsely murder'd' and 'A guiltless death I die', she answers Emilia's 'who has done this deed?' with 'Nobody, I myself, farewell: / Commend me to my kind lord, O, farewell' (ll. 118–26). Thus she bids 'her wrong stay, and her displeasure fly' (2.1.153). 'Let nobody blame him' solicits pity and praise for the innocent victim who has the charity to forgive. But at the same time, the phrase arraigns his unkindness by creating the presupposition that he *is* to blame and is *being* blamed by others, so that her charity only intensifies our sense of the wrong he did, and the instruction coded in her speech act is, *Let everyone blame him*. The same effect is serially produced in her final three utterances. The complex balance of the final gesture is testified to by the diverse and sensitive reactions of several critics. On the one hand, Desdemona 'effectively authorizes' Othello's view of the murder as a sacrifice, 'allowing him to have the last word'; 'her last breath is a protective lie'; she is thus 'fully in collusion with Othello's destruction of her', for 'if she did not actually kill herself, she unwittingly invited death through the nobility of a love that platonically (and foolishly) refused to register Othello's metamorphosis'.[11] On the other hand, in this emphasis on her ennobling if suicidal power lurks the suggestion that her final utterance disempowers, arraigns and indicts Othello: it was she who drove him to it and made him less than himself; if she dies helping him live his lie about her, it is to intensify his sense of her value and of his loss; if she represents herself as having invited 'death through the nobility of a love that ... refused', and so on, it is to prove to him that he couldn't have killed her without her complicity.

It must be obvious that this account of Desdemona has taken an odd but not unusual critical turn. In spite of my effort to portray Desdemona as a strong and admirable figure, a true member of the sisterhood that includes Rosalind, Helena, Portia and Hermione, my frequent reliance on free indirect discourse snidely exposes her utterances and motives to the citational rhetoric of moral disapproval. The message this procedure conveys is *let nobody blame her*. It is as if in my delight to find Desdemona complicit in her undoing and thus prove my point about the redistribution of complicities, I equate her complicity with moral culpability rather than discursive responsibility. Granted that free indirect discourse is a form of paraphrastic mimicry and thus easily lends itself to critique or parody of its object, it derives this power from its aptness as a technique for representing self-representation. One therefore ought to be able to deploy the technique without prejudice in (let us say) a non-Flaubertian manner to register the traces in language of the motivational and discursive pressures on the stories people tell themselves and others. I look for negotiations between those pressures and the pressure to maintain self-esteem – the cardinal value in the normative stories one is told to tell about oneself – in the linguistic signs of the activity I have elsewhere called 'practical unconsciousness', the materials for which are supplied by the network of discourses circulating through the speech community of the play.[12] Now it may be appropriate to aim free indirect discourse tendentiously towards the normative stories per se and towards the strategies of misrecognition they mobilize on their behalf, but that isn't the same as using paraphrastic mimicry against a particular storytelling subject, Desdemona, for example. Yet I don't think the foregoing account of her complicity is 'wrong'; it is one-sided; it gloats too much over its discovery of the extent to which she shares with Othello and Iago responsibility for what happens.

A less tendentious view of Desdemona might begin with the observation that her final words permit of a paraphrase that amounts to a refutation of her earlier claim, 'I never gave him cause': to say 'Nobody, I myself' is to acknowledge that she gave him cause. As a confessional gesture, this edges towards self-accusation. But if a glimmer of the sinner's discourse is discernible, it remains faint: 'falsely murder'd', she dies a 'guiltless death', not, however, as one who *was* victimized but as one who *got* victimized; she accepts responsibility, not culpability. Can the words signify that she accepts responsibility for *his* culpability? Isn't that what 'my kind lord' may suggest if one imagines it uttered with no trace of bitterness, sarcasm or reproach? This reading, however, doesn't neutralize the more tendentious interpretation unfolded earlier. She acknowledges that she gave him cause and even perhaps – pushing it towards the sinner's desire for punishment – that she deserves what she got. But her prosecution of the victim's discourse, culminating in her reduction of herself to poor Barbary, who, saintlike, forgives her tormentor, vibrates through her last words and solicits a different reading: he will discover too late what a jewel he has thrown away. Thus 'I gave him cause' struggles with *I never gave him cause*, and *I deserve what I got* struggles with *he'll deserve what he gets*; and in my reading of Desdemona, these combatants remain locked in mortal embrace.

From *Shakespeare Quarterly*, 47:3 (1996), 235–50.

NOTES

[Thomas Rymer, so dismissive of the 'ado' over a handkerchief in *Othello*, has been proved many times wrong in his assessment. Lynda E. Boose demonstrated how important the handkerchief is to the meanings of *Othello*, and so in his very different manner does Harry Berger, Jr. Berger shows how 'Othello and Desdemona work closely together to lose the handkerchief and to disremember its loss', just as, later, they 'collaborate in redirecting the blame from the third party [Cassio], steering it back to her'. This essay does not blame the victim on the gendered grounds that earlier, misogynist analyses did; instead, through close reading, it analyses Desdemona in as unsentimental and tough-minded a way as it does Othello. At the same time, Berger admits the jeopardies of his critical practice: 'It is as if in my delight to find Desdemona complicit in her undoing...I equate her complicity with moral culpability rather than discursive responsibility'. 'Close reading' has fallen somewhat out of fashion in some critical circles, largely because it was the chief strategy of the New Criticism. But it is not incompatible with theory, as this essay illustrates. In fact, all the new practices originate in close reading. Theory guides the questions which critics put closely to the text. Ed.]

1. Quotations from *Othello* follow the Arden text (ed. M. R. Ridley [London: Methuen, 1958]). Unless otherwise noted, quotations from other Shakespeare plays follow *The Riverside Shakespeare*, ed. G. Blakemore Evans (Boston: Houghton Mifflin, 1974).

2. I have here kept the Arden line count but replaced Ridley's First Quarto reading ('Let Cassio') with the Folio variant ('till Cassio'). The Folio is the basis of most modern editions.

3. Ridley (ed.), 2.1.109–66n, 3.4.32n, 3.4.34n.

4. Thomas Rymer, 'A Short View of Tragedy ... ' (London, 1693), reprinted in *Critical Essays of the Seventeenth Century*, ed. J. E. Spingarn, 3 vols. (Oxford: Clarendon Press, 1908), 2:208–55, especially p. 246.

5. Carol Thomas Neely, 'Circumscription and Unhousedness: *Othello* at the Crossroads', paper delivered at the 1992 meeting of the Shakespeare Association of America in Kansas City. I'm grateful to Professor Neely for sending me a copy of the paper. See also Neely's *Broken Nuptials in Shakespeare's Plays* (New Haven, CT, and London: Yale University Press, 1985), pp. 128–9. For a similar and equally stimulating interpretation, see Janet Adelman, *Suffocating Mothers: Fantasies of Maternal Origin in Shakespeare's Plays, 'Hamlet' to 'The Tempest'* (New York and London: Routledge, 1992), pp. 68–9. Adelman lays more emphasis on the parable's strange conjunction of maternal power with virginity as representing 'the impossible condition of male desire, the condition always already lost' (p. 69).

6. Ridley (ed.), 4.1.234n.

7. The New Penguin *Othello*, ed. Kenneth Muir (Harmondsworth: Penguin, 1968), p. 209.

8. Karen Newman, *Fashioning Femininity and English Renaissance Drama* (Chicago and London: University of Chicago Press, 1991), p. 91.

9. Rymer in Spingarn (ed.), 2:251 and 254.

10. The New Folger Library *Othello*, ed. Barbara A. Mowat and Paul Werstine (New York: Washington Square Press, 1993), 3.4.173n.

11. Emily C. Bartels, 'Making More of the Moor: Aaron, Othello and Renaissance Refashionings of Race', *Shakespeare Quarterly*, 41 (1990), 433–54, especially p. 454; Eamon Grennan, 'The Women's Voices in *Othello*: Speech, Song, Silence', *Shakespeare Quarterly*, 38 (1987), 275–92, especially p. 290; Adelman, p. 280 (Adelman's paraphrase of Kay Stockholder's argument in 'Form as Metaphor: *Othello* and Love-Death Romance', *Dalhousie Review*, 64 [1984–85], 736–47, especially pp. 744–5); James L. Calderwood, *The Properties of 'Othello'* (Amherst: University of Massachusetts Press, 1989), p. 36.

12. On practical unconsciousness, see my 'What Did the King Know and When Did He Know It? Shakespearean Discourses and Psychoanalysis', *South Atlantic Quarterly*, 88 (1989), 811–62, especially pp. 830–1.

5

Brothers of the State: *Othello*, Bureaucracy and Epistemological Crisis

ELIZABETH HANSON

The reading of *Othello* I offer here began as an attempt to consider a problem I encountered while engaged in a different project, one focused not on Shakespearean mimesis but on the discourses that surrounded the use of interrogatory torture in Elizabethan England.[1] Presenting an account of torture as an epistemological struggle in which the victim was imagined as a powerful self-enclosed subject whose inwardness both incited and frustrated the state's desire for knowledge, I was repeatedly asked by audiences and readers, in tones ranging from concern to prurience, about women as torture victims. A scene which coupled bodily domination with a will to know, it would seem, demanded a woman at its centre. What was more, many people could think of a female character, if not a woman, who was, if not tortured, then constructed as precisely the kind of epistemological problem which I claimed the torture victim posed: the possessor of a hidden truth discontinuous with any evidence that might stand for it. That female character was, of course, Desdemona.[2]

But the historical records tell us that with only two exceptions, Anne Askew, the radical Protestant lady-in-waiting to Catherine Parr, and Margaret Ward, a Catholic, the victims of interrogatory torture in Renaissance England were men. Women were interrogated in connection with suspected offences, imprisoned, whipped and

125

otherwise brutalized in attempts to control vagrancy, prostitution and witchcraft, but when it came to interrogatory torture, in which the infliction of pain backed a demand that the victim speak the secret truth he possessed, the body in question was male.[3] The most obvious explanation for women's escape from torture is that their more restricted sphere of activity gave them limited opportunity to become embroiled in treasonable activities. Indeed, insofar as many of the victims of torture were missionary priests, women were specifically precluded from the activity which the state sought to discover through torture. Such an explanation, however, tends to rationalize the resort to torture as a response to an objective threat, and thus leaves out of account the manner in which, in the discourses of torture, the subject's alleged treasonous activity comes to stand for the mystery of his mind, raising the possibility that the mind itself is the object of the torturers' anxiety. Thus we might profitably reframe the connection between the limitations of women's sphere and their escape from torture as a hypothesis: the function of women as tokens of exchange between men rather than as social agents, at least in the classes most directly involved in affairs of state, may have meant that it was difficult both for Elizabethan authority and those who resisted it to conceive of women as sites of a powerful, withheld, inner truth. In other words, the restriction of women's social activity meant that they were less likely than their male counterparts to become the locus for the phenomenon of mind.

The cases of two women who were victimized in the Catholic persecutions furnish a suggestive gloss on the implicit gendering of the subject position imputed to the victim in the discourse of torture. Robert Southwell's account of Margaret Ward, a woman who had been tortured and executed for having supplied an imprisoned priest with a rope, presents her as a martyr but insists on the anomaly of her situation: 'A maiden among a thousand, in whose frail sex shone a courage hard to parallel ... she had been flogged and hung up by the wrists, the tips of her toes only touching the ground so that she was now crippled and half-paralysed; but the tortures had only served to strengthen this most shining martyr for her last struggle'.[4] If Margaret Ward's performance as the stoic, self-enclosed torture victim makes her exceptional, a maiden among a thousand, the fate of Ann Bellamy, whose family sheltered Southwell and who betrayed him to the pursuivants, furnishes a reminder of the feminine norm. The eldest daughter of a Catholic gentleman, Bellamy was arrested during a crackdown against recusants in the winter of 1592.

In prison she was raped by the arch-rackmaster and priest-hunter Richard Topcliffe, and was found after three months' imprisonment, in the words of a Catholic reporter, 'in most dishonest disorder', that is, pregnant. Apparently on a promise from Topcliffe that none of her family would be harmed, she agreed to lure Southwell to their house, where he was arrested. Ann was then married off to Topcliffe's servant, according to Southwell's biographer 'in church and with the blessing of her parents', thereby providing her husband (a weaver's son) with a country-house.[5] In its horrific overlay of the state's discovering operations and the fulfillment of female sexual roles as bride, bearer of children and vehicle for the transmission of property, Ann Bellamy's story suggests a discursive connection between women's gendered position and the spilling of information; her rape and pregnancy construct her as a body which swells and opens without her volition, a means through which boundaries can be breached and things transmitted: land, blood – and secrets. Southwell himself, it should be noted, was relentlessly tortured before his execution but, according to contemporary Catholic reports, could never be made to betray himself or anyone else.[6]

If the story of Ann Bellamy seems to efface the possibility of the female subject as a site of epistemological resistance, *Othello* insists upon it. The recognition that Desdemona had eyes and chose Othello leads the men in the play to impute to her a capacity for secrecy, as in the outburst of thwarted patriarchal authority – 'trust not your daughters' minds / By what you see them act'[7] – and this epistemological anxiety is passed with Desdemona from her father to her husband. How then are we to understand the apparent discrepancy between the role women play (or don't play) in the discourse of torture and the position that Desdemona occupies in the closely related evidentiary discourse called *Othello*? What representational strategies may be at work here, both in the relationship between sex/gender issues and matters of state authority, and between theatrical and political or administrative discourses? And how does attention to these questions complicate our understanding of the kind of evidence the theatre of Renaissance England offers about the culture of the period?

At this juncture let me hasten to note that if *Othello* conjures up the spectre of an epistemologically resistant female subject, it just as thoroughly lays it. Othello's wife proves to have been wholly his own; it was his ancient who secretly kept his heart attending on himself. *Othello* validates the epistemological anxiety the inwardness of another arouses, an anxiety which from the beginning is linked with misogyny, but redirects it from women to a subordinate officer. In the process Desdemona is both literally and figuratively emptied of life, rendered as cold and unproblematic as her chastity, while, in what Thomas Rymer pointed out was a highly indecorous end for a tragic villain, Iago remains alive for questioning.[8] Moreover, it is here, where Iago retreats once and for all behind the door of truth, that the play explicitly intersects with the discourse of torture. Lodovico and Gratiano, acting on behalf of 'the Venetian state', give orders for Iago's torture three times in the last seventy lines of the play. Indeed, the play's final construction of Iago as an insoluble problem of knowledge bears a remarkable similarity to the process of discovery and enclosure that defined the victim in the Elizabethan torture chamber. Like the Jesuits, Edmund Campion and Thomas Cottam, who were brought to confess some secrets before lapsing into a final stoic silence, Iago 'part confess[es]', before admonishing his captors to 'Demand me nothing, what you know, you know, / From this time forth I never will speak word' (5.2.304–5) – the proclamation of impenetrability which prompts Gratiano's 'Torments will ope thy lips' (l. 306).[9] Moreover, Iago's secrets (again, like Campion's) have been opened metonymically in intercepted letters, and his unwitting collaborator, Emilia, has informed on him. But despite the state's possession of ample information there remains a sense of epistemological lack that focuses on the vexed issue of his motive; it will take 'cunning cruelty, / That can torment him much and hold him long' (ll. 334–5) before the Venetian state gains mastery over this villain.

This transfer of the male characters' epistemological frustration from the wife to the subordinate officer is emblematized in the final scene of *Othello*. Lodovico commands Iago (and with him the audience) to 'Look on the tragic loading of this bed, / This is thy work' (5.2.364–5). On the loaded bed is the detritus of the hidden scenes with which Iago has been tantalizing and enraging his male interlocuters throughout the play: the black ram and the white ewe, Desdemona 'topp'd', the scene that Iago insists it is impossible Othello or anyone else should see. What we are given here, however, is not the unveiling of a sexual secret but rather the spectacle of a chain of male 'supervision' focused on a loaded bed from which the possibility of sexual activity has been eliminated. The orders Lodovico issues at the close of the play make clear that this 'supervision' is not simple prurience but the operation of a social and political order in which men (and only men are left alive) act on the orders of, or step into the place of other men, their relations ultimately ratified by the distant authority of the Venetian state. Commanding first that the loaded bed be hid, then arranging for the proper succession of 'the fortunes of the Moor' (l. 367) to Desdemona's uncle, Gratiano, investing Cassio as Othello's successor, enjoining him to enforce the torture of Iago and finally dispatching himself back to Venice to report the tragedy, Lodovico overlays the loaded bed with state business. He thus induces us to shift our focus, and see, underlying the problematic of marital jealousy, the power relations that define the Venetian polity. The effect, then, is to deconstruct the scene of Desdemona topp'd, exposing it not as a truth, nor even as a lie, but as the effect of relations between men, relations which, when that scene is emptied out, will achieve a new configuration marked by frustration and violence, as Cassio, the new governor, enforces the torture of the ensign.

The significance of this displacement of Desdemona by Iago, of the loaded bed by the scene of torture, may become clearer if we consider the conclusion of another Shakespearean play contemporaneous with *Othello*. At the end of *Measure for Measure*, as the Duke's plot begins to come to light, Escalus, accusing 'Friar Lodowick' of slandering the Duke, orders, 'To th'rack with him! – We'll touse you / Joint by joint, but we will know his purpose'.[10] This event is forestalled, of course, by the discovery of the 'friar's' identity and, therefore, 'his purpose' in the struggle to drag him away to prison and torture – the discovery that authority already knows and controls this schemer's secret intent. With the re-establishment of the Duke's authority, the site of treachery shifts and first Angelo and then Lucio become the object of the state's threatened violence. The Duke sentences him and Lucio to be executed following their marriages only to remit all torments save marriage itself, a conclusion that is possible because both men are fully known to the Duke. But as Lucio shrewdly recognizes in his complaint that 'Marrying a punk, my lord, is pressing to death, / Whipping and hanging' (ll. 520–1), the Duke's cancellation of his execution is not an act of mercy but a translation of the state's power to torment the subject's body into more indirect subjugation through marriage that will inevitably entail cuckoldry. Nor is it just marriage to a punk that affords such prospects, as the insinuating intimacy of the comment with which the Duke hands Marianna to Angelo – 'I have confessed her and I know her virtue' (l. 524) – and his intended appropriation of the object of Angelo's desire – Isabella – suggests. In the 'comic' resolution of *Measure for Measure*, the state's torment of the subject's body is subsumed into marriage with its attendant threat of cuckoldry – a result which also confirms the Duke's epistemological mastery of subordinate men.

The ability of marriage both to obviate state violence and, it would seem, to produce the anxieties which in *Othello* will lead back to it makes clear that marriage in these plays is a temporary configuration within a larger field of unstable political relations. Both *Othello* and *Measure for Measure* present political worlds in which the sacralized centre of power has been superseded by a structure of delegated authority, in *Othello* because the action has absented itself from the centre, in *Measure for Measure* because the sacralized centre has absented itself from the polity. With the ambiguous exception of Duke Vincentio, the principal male characters in these plays are deputies, men acting on behalf of an authority that does not originate in them. Leonard Tennenhouse has argued that the vogue for disguised ruler plays in 1604–05 (of which *Measure for Measure* was an instance) constituted a 'remarkable moment' when, just after the succession of James, a succession determined not by the previous monarch's body but by the judgement of her Privy Councillors, playwrights were first able to imagine the state 'as a mechanism run by deputies or substitutes'.[11] To Tennenhouse this perception is truly 'momentary', for the plays he considers (which do not include *Othello*) end with the restoration of the sacralized ruler, the identification finally of authority's true origin. But *Othello*, and the threatening gloss it furnishes on *Measure for Measure*, suggests that Shakespeare's vision may have been more radical. Inhering *nowhere*, state authority in these plays realizes itself dialectically through its continual conferral onto agents from whom it is then recovered in the discovery that a link within the chain of command is in fact a treacherous Other on whom authority must wreak its vengeance. The potential ambiguity as to whether Othello or Iago would be this treacherous Other reveals the systemic rather than the moral nature of this treachery.

Marriage, the public attribution of a woman to a man, is a precarious alternative to torture in the working out of this dialectic because, as Eve Sedgwick has brilliantly demonstrated, a wife can serve as the material ground where hierarchical differences between men can be contested and established.[12] But the work that the wife is forced to perform in this system is multiple and contradictory.

A temporarily more successful strategy than torture, marriage not only fixes the positions of men, but also permits the anxiety that attends the replication of authority to be projected onto women and coded as gender difference, which is then equated with treachery. Indeed, the wife is inevitably imagined as a potential whore, that is, as an attribute not merely of her husband but of others in the chain of command (Othello extends this to 'the general camp / Pioners and all' [3.3.351–2]) because of the very exchangeability of the men between whom she mediates. Her imagined whoredom also holds out the possibility that subordinates can in fact be discovered, that there is an act that they can be caught in. What the wife promises are opportunities for knowledge, occasions for framing systemic ambiguities as secrets to be discovered.

In short, what I am suggesting here is that in its final substitution of the scene of torture for the loaded bed, and of the ensign for the wife as the object of epistemological frustration, *Othello* explicitly addresses the question I raised earlier, of the relationship between the construction of women in the period and the discourse of the epistemologically resistant subject played out in torture. In fact the play reveals this relationship to constitute a representational *econ-omy*, a system of exchange, or more precisely of exploitation, in which certain kinds of stories are told about women in order to avoid or to manage certain problems in the relationships between men. In the remainder of the paper I want to explore in detail how this economy works, and what the visibility of its operation in *Othello* tells us about the state that could so insistently generate those problems. Then, I will conclude by turning to the necessarily more speculative question this reading raises, of the relationship between the theatre and other domains of discourse and experience in the period.

* * *

A good place to begin an account of the play's representational economy is with a site of excess, Iago's notoriously too prolix motive-hunting, in which he claims that he hates Othello because he has preferred Cassio as his lieutenant, but also because 'it is thought abroad, that 'twixt my sheets / He's done my office' (1.3.384–6), or, as he puts it later, because 'the lustful Moor / Hath leap'd into my seat' (2.1.290–1), adding this time, 'I do love [Desdemona] too' (l. 286) and 'I fear Cassio with my nightcap too' (l. 302) – a fellow who, just to keep things reciprocal, he obscurely damns with a fair wife. Iago's enumerations of his grievances, in which the professional slight slides into a fantasy of universal cuckoldry, indicates an alarming slippage in the play between marital and military orders – a condition which the play underscores when Othello, hearing Desdemona speak of 'the love I bear to Cassio' (4.1.228), explodes 'Fire and brimstone' (l. 229), and Lodovico ascribes his anger to the letter from Venice 'deputing Cassio in his government' (l. 232).[13] What makes this slippage between cuckolding and military rotations so alarming is not merely the imaginative threat which military place changing poses to marital exclusivity, but also the way in which marital exclusivity exposes the exchangeability of men on which the military depends as a state of ontological free fall, a derivation of fixed status and therefore of identity. Iago's motives represent the consciousness of the career officer: he fears that he is always being replaced by (and believes that he can replace) the other men in the hierarchy.

It is a fear that the play itself helps to validate. If Iago professes himself a consummate actor, one of those 'Who, trimm'd in forms, and visages of duty, / Keep yet their hearts attending on themselves' (1.1.50–1), he in fact does his damage through the ease with which his own state of mind seems to communicate itself to others. It is Iago, after all, who first imagines himself a cuckold and notes 'I know not if't be true ... / Yet I, for mere suspicion in that kind, / Will do, as if for surety' (1.3.386–8), straightaway 'engender[ing]' the plot that will bring Othello to declare that 'to be once in doubt / Is once to be resolv'd' (3.3.183–4).[14] Iago's uncanny success in inducing Othello to replicate his suspicions has to do with the reflexive relation between such replication and the content of the suspicions themselves: the fear that another man is taking one's place. Thus the point here is not that Iago rather than Othello is the origin of these anxieties, but that they are by their very nature without any particular psychic proprietor. Even Cassio, with no prompting from Iago, frets about what will happen, 'I being absent, and my place supplied' (3.3.17). Changing places with another may be Iago's technique for subversion, but it is also the condition of service to the Venetian state, as Iago reveals in his representation of his secret difference which simultaneously proclaims his identity with his superior: 'in following [Othello] I follow but myself' (1.1.58).

Of course, the ability of men in the Venetian army to stand in for one another is complicated by Othello's racial difference, a difference that serves to enforce the discontinuity both between the men in the ranks and their supreme commander and between the commander and the Venetian oligarchy he serves.[15] But the Moor at the head of the Venetian forces is also the most telling sign of the dependence of the professional 'gradation' on exchangeability. Although the play signals the fact only obliquely, Othello is, of course, a mercenary, 'a knave of common hire' (1.1.125), like the gondolier who carries Desdemona to him, paid to defend the trade routes of a mercantilist city-state. As both a party to, and a function of Venetian commerce, he is its epitome, as Roderigo's description of him as an 'extravagant and wheeling stranger / Of here and everywhere' (1.1.136–7) attests. Othello's generalship reveals that the professional hierarchy he heads is constructed through a system of exchange that makes disparate things equivalent, a fact that differentiates that 'gradation' from patriarchy and oligarchy which are maintained naturally (as it were) by blood. This difference underlies Iago's complaints about Cassio's promotion, which oscillate between arguments based on exchange value and nostalgic attempts to assimilate professional advancement to traditional patriarchal transmissions of authority. 'I know my price', he tells Roderigo, 'I am worth no worse a place' (1.1.11), yet laments the 'old gradation' in which 'each second stood heir to the first' (ll. 37–8). But if these perceptions seem to contradict each other they are also mutually enabling. It is Iago's racist, misogynist attachment to 'natural' order, evident in his ability to reduce 'others' to predictable traits, as in 'these Moors are changable in their wills' (1.3.347–8) or 'She must have change' (l. 352), that permits him the Machiavel's perception that the hierarchy in which he operates is artificial and therefore that he need not remain where he has been 'placed'. Thus 'price' is not only a mechanism for making horizontal equivalences (noble Moor = Venetian general, Florentine 'arithemetician' = Venetian lieutenant) but also for making vertical ones, such as ensign = lieutenant.

If the mercenary foundation of Othello's position remains largely subtextual, hinted at only in Iago's and Roderigo's outbursts of nativist resentment, it is because it has been mystified through transactions occurring before the play begins. Unlike Shylock, for instance, who tells Bassanio, 'I will buy with you, sell with you, talk with you, walk with you, and so following; but I will not eat with you, drink with you nor pray with you',[16] Othello has permitted mercenary exchange to merge into assimilation, first through acceptance of Brabantio's love and invitations and then through marriage

with his daughter. The play suggests that there is a cultural imperative at work in this process (Jessica's marriage and Shylock's forced
conversion at the end of *The Merchant of Venice* confirm this), that
trading relationships must be reconstructed as tribal bonds if the former are to be brought securely under the state's control. Thus, when
Brabantio protests his daughter's marriage to his 'brothers of the
state' (1.3.96), the conflict is represented as one, not between patriarchal authority and the state's need for Othello's services (although
we must see that this is the issue), but between atavistic and enlightened versions of patriarchal authority, in other words, between constructions of Othello as an 'erring barbarian' and as a likely and
desirable son-in-law for a Venetian nobleman. (The scene's conflation of state and familial matters which requires that the Duke speak
of 'Desdemona, as he were her own natural father', puts Rymer, that
infallible barometer of ideological strain, beside himself.)[17] In
Othello's case monetary exchange does not so much establish equivalences between things different in kind, as beget other transactions
that purport to efface difference. Thus Othello's blackness, that
apparently unambiguous signifier of otherness, can come and go;
Roderigo, whom Iago instructs on the price of men, sees Othello as
'the thicklips' (1.1.67), while the Duke, seeking to bind Othello to
Venetian interests, finds him 'far more fair than black' (1.3.290). In
the world of Venice marriage does not merely mark a realm of private property, opposed but also conceptually vulnerable to military
place changing. It also works both to delimit and, at least in
Othello's case, to promise passage to a tribal 'inside', the significance
of which is indistinguishably social and epistemological: a zone
whose inhabitants not only possess power and distinction, but
know one another without a system of exchange or the reading
of signs.[18]

The capacity of Othello's marriage to promise access to this inside
zone of unmediated knowledge accounts for a peculiar implication
of both the Duke's idealized, and Brabantio's enraged accounts of
this relationship: that Desdemona is not primarily a body to be
advantageously disposed of or controlled, but a 'soul' or a 'mind' to
be known by her intimates. In the case of the Duke this construction
clearly serves his political purpose. The disembodied symmetry of a
courtship conducted through 'such fair question / As soul to soul
affordeth' (1.3.113–14) suppresses the scene of miscegenation that
Iago's account of 'an old black ram ... tupping [a] white ewe'

(1.1.88–9) luridly conjures up, effacing the racial and national difference that the marriage actually serves to mediate. But the fact that the defeated father follows the Duke in construing the locus of his daughter's revolt as her mind suggests that this essence, which he has discovered to his dismay is not seen even by him, is not so much a metaphor for the inside constituted by the Venetian oligarchy as a hypostatization of its loss. Desdemona's escape to 'the gross clasps of a lascivious Moor' (l. 126) means that what Iago styles 'half [Brabantio's] soul' (l. 87) has proved as contingently related to him as his money bags. Having made Desdemona a marker of the inside, patriarchal authority (an interest that includes Othello and the Duke as well as Brabantio) discovers she has taken it with her when she went. Desdemona's mind as an object of epistemological anxiety emerges (together with her body as the subject of pornographic representation) when she slips, as she must, from an essential to a contingent relationship to her tribe.

The contradiction between the transactions which actually construct the Venetian polity and the imaginary intimacy of the insiders registers constantly in the language of the play, furnishing the rhetorical resources for Iago's assault against 'Othello's occupation'. Consider, for example, the way in which, in this world where men have prices and the state is served by hirelings, money is repeatedly invoked as a detachable attribute of self, in Roderigo's purse which he has shared with Iago, in the 'bags' (1.1.80) that Iago suggests have been stolen along with Desdemona, in the 'purse / Full of crusadoes' (3.4.21–2) that Desdemona says she would rather have lost than her handkerchief, in the purse that is 'trash' compared to Iago's good name. In these instances, particularly the last two, the invocation of money is accompanied by disavowal, an assertion of its negative valuation compared to some more precious attribute, such as a daughter, a token from a lover, or a name. Iago's famous sententia makes the point explicitly:

> Good name in man and woman's dear, my lord;
> Is the immediate jewel of our souls:
> Who steals my purse, steals trash, 'tis something, nothing,
> 'Twas mine, 'tis his, and has been slave to thousands:
> But he that filches from me my good name
> Robs me of that which not enriches him,
> And makes me poor indeed.
>
> (3.3.159–65)

Iago does more than suggest to Othello that he is being deprived of his name; he uses attributes of the self, a name and a purse, to model different kinds of relationship, and in so doing presses on the contradictions of Othello's position. If one of the suggestions loaded into this burdened utterance is that Desdemona could circulate like a purse of money, it also insists to the 'extravagant and wheeling stranger of here and everywhere' that his wife, daughter of the Venetian oligarchy, called 'jewel' by her father as he reluctantly cedes her to her husband, represents the 'immediate'.

Iago's disquisition on the good name indicates the way in which the epistemological problem he presents to Othello, is in fact a problem of social position. In particular it suggests the significance which metonymy and synecdoche, which might be called the tropes of contingent and intrinsic relation, come to bear in a world where so much depends on the difference between mercenary exchange and communion 'soul to soul'.[19] The language of *Othello* is cluttered with objects and body parts – the name, Iago's heart, Brabantio's bags, Desdemona's hand and, especially, her handkerchief – which are offered, mostly by Iago but also by others, to stand for people and functions and, most importantly, for unseen essences such as Desdemona's honour and Iago's thoughts. The capacity of metonymy and synecdoche to do this last trick, to represent in a particularly concrete way the absent or the invisible, makes them figures of evidence as well as relationship. Their structure is that of the clue – of Iago's 'imputation and strong circumstances which lead directly to the door of truth' (3.3.412–13). If metonymy and synecdoche seem to do similar things however, there is also an implicit hierarchy of these tropes; synecdoche, particularly of the body, insofar as it delivers 'immediate' access to the thing it represents, seems to promise access to unseen essences – things whose nature is to elude mediation.

When compared with this powerful trope, metonymy comes to figure the substitution or displacement involved in any act of representation, the discontinuity between an attribute and its possessor rather than the possessor himself. Such invidious comparison underlies Iago's pronouncements on the difference between a purse and a name, as well as Desdemona's preference for the handkerchief over the purse full of crusadoes. But of course, properly speaking, there are no synecdoches here at all; these examples in fact reveal that the synecdochic status of the handkerchief or the name is constructed through the comparison with the purse. And what is constructed can be deconstructed, as Iago makes clear. The name may be the immediate jewel of our soul, while money, endlessly exchangeable, can hardly be said to belong to us at all; but each is subject to filching. The message is hard to miss; Desdemona may be a part of her husband, but having married him, she has already started to circulate. Othello's tribal relation to Venice becomes once more a trading one. Not surprisingly then, when Othello finds Desdemona 'gone', his racial difference, effaced by communion soul to soul with the daughter of the Venetian oligarchy, reappears in his name. 'My name', he laments, 'that was as fresh / As Dian's visage, is now begrim'd, and black / As mine own face' (3.3.392–4).

Like Othello in his relation to Venice, the most important representative objects invoked in Othello in fact show a propensity to move up and down a continuum of relationship defined by monetary metonymy at one end and corporeal synecdoche at the other – a movement produced by continual gestures of comparison. Thus the handkerchief, which in Desdemona's speech is the synecdochic term she opposes to her purse, is in Iago's fateful suggestion to Othello the metonymic term he juxtaposes to that most intimate of possessions, 'her honour ... an essence that's not seen' (4.1.16). And when Othello, having realized that the handkerchief can circulate, interrogates Desdemona about its whereabouts, he tries desperately to assimilate it to corporeal synecdoche. He instructs Desdemona to 'make it a darling, like your precious eye' (3.4.64) – an admonition which conflates his fantasy of connection to Desdemona and Venice with his compensatory strategy of vigilant looking – and informs her that 'it was dyed in mummy, which the skilful / Conserve of maiden hearts' (ll. 72–3). Literally imbued with the body's hidden substances, the handkerchief promises to deliver unseen essences into the possession of an other; it was, after all, the gift of a 'charmer' who 'could almost read / The thoughts of people' (ll. 55–6). But 'almost' is, of course, the key word here, signalling an irreducible difference of 'thoughts' from the body which can, with skill, be conserved and merged with an object which another can possess.[20] In the handkerchief, corporeal synecdoche collapses into metonymy; the body itself proves merely incidental to the psychic interiority it is called upon to signify. The result is epistemological breakdown, a welter of ownerless body parts, dubious circumstantial and confessional 'proofs' and metaphysical essences that he invokes as he himself goes to pieces: 'Pish! Noses, ears and lips. Is't possible? – Confess – Handkerchief? – O devil!' (4.1.42–3).

As Desdemona's innocent participation in producing the hand-kerchief's ambivalence would indicate, the capacity of objects to embody both epistemological hope and futility, to offer and with-hold access to a possessor, is the effect not of a particular character's thinking but of the world of the play. But, as Peter Stallybrass has noted, it is a feature of *Othello* that Iago is made to function as the origin of meanings that in fact arise from the play's larger dis-course.[21] As we see Iago supplementing and organizing tropological instabilities, deploying them to devastating effect, the contradictions endemic to the Venetian state are reified as his intent. But the point here is not merely that Iago is a scapegoat, a lower class man made to speak the thoughts about Desdemona that other members of the Venetian polity must disallow, but rather that in using him this way, the play makes his intent, rather than Desdemona's honour, the legit-imate object of scrutiny. Thus Iago's construction of Desdemona's honour as a problem of evidence is inextricable from his grafting of her subjecthood to his own – a task he accomplishes by spinning out the metonymic / synecdochic web. When Desdemona's handkerchief, a trifling possession but dyed in conserve of maiden's hearts, comes to occupy the maddening boundary marked by 'almost', it joins Iago's heart which he has already situated there, its inaccessibility to all but himself proclaimed in the same moment he imagines that it could be worn on a sleeve like a token or a sign. The epistemologi-cal implications of this manoeuvre, in which the same object is made to furnish hope and frustration, emerge full force when Othello demands 'By heaven I'll know thy thought', and Iago replies, 'You cannot, if my heart were in your hand, / Nor shall not, while 'tis in my custody' (3.3.166–8). The heart, a mere body part, could never yield access to thought – and yet it might were it to leave Iago's custody.

In the simultaneous promise and frustration of access to unseen essences that Iago loads onto his heart and Desdemona's handker-chief we encounter the same impasse that is produced by the resort to torture, in which the attempt to make the body yield the soul's truth only confirms that truth's inaccessibility – the impasse which translates questions of loyalty into fierce encounters with the auton-omy of the subject.[22] Desdemona, constructed as a soul to be known and body which circulates, is sacrificed to this dilemma. But Iago goes beyond insinuating that he and Desdemona pose analogous problems for the would-be discoverer, mapping the slippage between intimate and contingent relation onto the social categories of wife and subordinate officer. In Iago's insinuations, Desdemona stands for an essence that Iago himself will deliver. Woman's honour, Iago insists, is the ultimate object of epistemological desire; behind the door of truth lies Desdemona topp'd. But he immediately displaces this scene with one that undermines, even as it purports to enforce, the feminine location of truth: Iago topp'd, lying with Cassio, who, he reports, would in his sleep 'kiss me hard / As if he pluck'd up kisses by the roots' (3.3.428–9). Here Iago is supposed to be a stand-in for Desdemona, the scene 'denot[ing] a foregone conclusion' (l. 434) rather than revealing truth's inner sanctum. And yet it also signifies the intimacy of men, Cassio's looseness of soul with his bedfellow representing the looseness that Iago also claims to be guilty of at this moment, as 'prick'd to't by foolish honesty and love' (l. 418) he spills the story to Othello. Constructed through a chain of representational displacements, the scene nevertheless proclaims the bond between men in the professional hierarchy as the site of unmediated knowledge, of access to soul. It is this promise which Iago holds out when in the exchange of vows with which this scene concludes, he offers up 'his wit, hand, heart' to Othello and declares, 'I am your own forever' (l. 486).

Iago's deployment of homoerotic scenes at these crucial moments indicates that his *modus operandi* is not simply the voicing of the crassest ideological and epistemological assumptions of his social world, but the supplanting of the visions those assumptions produce with the ones they are intended to repress, visions of the work male heterosexual desire and its concomitant misogyny actually perform. Thus if Iago's ostensible message is that Desdemona is sleeping with Cassio, what he pictures for Othello is the effect of that fantasy, the reframing of the chain of command as an unconscious, upwelling chain of confession. The tableaux of male intimacy Iago offers reframe the professional gradation, in which exchangeability is the first rule of identity, as a *gender* category whose homogeneity affords perfect knowledge, and in whose name Othello murders Desdemona 'else she'll betray more men' (5.2.6). This fellowship, formed through the exchange of Desdemona, but also more importantly, through her subsequent elimination, is not the same as the Venetian oligarchy, an inside always haunted by an implicit outside, but a potentially boundless utopia of masculine immediacy. Iago's remodelling of homosocial bonds as homoerotic scenes promises an intimacy beyond that afforded by the sharing of women. Thus, once Othello has resolved to kill Desdemona and Iago has made himself his general's 'own forever', Othello encounters Desdemona (who represented him so splendidly to the Senate) as a blank, 'fair paper made to write "whore" upon' (4.2.73), but not, apparently, a page on which he can read the word. Instead, she is a surface 'whiter ... than snow / And smooth as monumental alabaster' (5.2.4–5) which he declines to mark.

The fantasy of male intimacy which Iago promulgates to Othello, a fantasy which I have been suggesting is based on the governmental order within which men operate, is, of course, a deadly delusion. Desdemona will have scarcely been stifled before Iago is revealed to be 'a demi-devil' whose reasons for 'ensnar[ing Othello's] soul and body' (5.2.302–3) will forever elude ordinary moral natures. But the revelation of Iago's enmity cannot be styled a discovery of the truth in any simple sense; for the perfect knowledge he offers Othello and the utter unintelligibility he finally achieves for himself are alike in promising escape from the epistemological regime in which women make men known to each other, constituting 'property' and making it susceptible to transfer. Iago ultimately embodies both a sameness and a difference so absolute that it defeats mediation and can only be imagined as pure metaphysical essence. Thus he ends as the impenetrable subject under torture, sharing with the Elizabethan Jesuits a capacity to defeat the epistemological regime that constructs him.

In the case of *Othello*, however, this regime cannot be seen simply as the ferocious will to know of the state brought to bear on the secret heart of the subject. What produces Iago is normal administrative activity of the kind we see Lodovico engaging in as he commands that the loaded bed be hid, arranges for the succession of 'the fortunes of the Moor' to Desdemona's uncle, Gratiano, installs Cassio in Othello's post, exhorting him to torture Iago, and dispatches himself back to Venice to relate the events in Cyprus to the senate. A crisis has occurred but what we see here is maintenance, accomplished through men stepping into each other's places, connecting the margin of the Venetian state to its centre, ensuring that its laws are enforced. If Iago is figured at this moment as a pure excess of evil, 'more fell than anguish, hunger, or the sea' (l. 363), all he has done is to suggest to Othello that something like this scene would happen, that Othello would lose his occupation and Cassio step into his place. Iago is, we might say, the unconscious of the proto-bureaucratic state, not an ambitious state servant so much as an embodiment of the truth the state and its agents must repress: that its foundation is a radical absence of identity, and, therefore, that it is impossible to know the men who operate on its behalf.

***

I have been arguing that *Othello* presents us with a representational economy, a system of exchange between stories about wives and stories about men in the chain of command. But the end result of the play's exchanges is the dismantling of this economy, the declaration finally that the two kinds of stories are after all separate and incommensurate in much the same way as are Ann Bellamy's story and Robert Southwell's. The awesome self-enclosure (whether heroic or demonic) of the male subject bears no similarity to the pathos (whether degrading or ennobling) of women's subjugation in marriage. The point of this comparison is, of course, that the outcome in *Othello* is ideologically inflected, that the play produces meanings which are already the meanings of its culture. And yet, *Othello* arrives at this outcome not simply by presenting these meanings, but by setting up an alternative possibility, showing its audience how a woman might be constructed as an epistemologically resistant subject – while at the same time declaring this construction (however plausible) to be merely a pernicious story. One effect of this procedure is to mark the place Iago finally occupies as *reality*, conferring on the epistemologically impenetrable subordinate officer a kind of preeminent truth. The meaning of this effect is partly ideological – the play asks us to believe in this formation – but also possibly metatheatrical – the play asks us to distinguish the boundaries of theatrical representation, to see the play finally not as a mimesis of reality but as a negotiation with it, which installs Iago finally in a perversely privileged position.

There is, to my knowledge, no scene of interrogatory state torture in the drama of this period, despite the plenitude of stabbings, dismemberments, eye gougings, boilings and other atrocities for which the Renaissance English theatre is famous. The scene of Iago's torment, after all, takes place after the play has ended, in the same off-stage domain where the black ram tups the white ewe.[23] Like the spectacle of execution, torture apparently could not be played at, its motions divorced from the power they proclaim, its deadly force mocked through representation.[24] It is a restriction *Othello* calls attention to, for if the play presses the limits of decorum in its notorious final display of the loaded bed, it literally draws the theatrical line at torture. However, the rack, that potent symbol of the state's compulsion to wring truth from the subject, does appear on stage in another play of the same year, Chapman's *Bussy d'Ambois* (1604), when the jealous husband Montsurry uses it to interrogate his adulterous wife Tamyra. The incongruous overlay of state violence and domestic crisis which characterizes this unique instance of stage torture emblematizes the interpenetration of marital and state affairs on which *Othello* insists. But the semiotic disturbance which the introduction of the rack into the scene of marital crisis produces signals that whatever we are looking at here, it is not simply mimesis, either of domestic strife or of state power. The incongruity of the scene brings to our attention what cannot or will not be shown, making visible the constraints which operate on theatrical representation, constraints which may be as explicit as censorship or as implicit as generic convention or decorum. We see, in other words, the displacements, repressions and analogies on which representation depends.

I want to conclude by raising the possibility that the representational economy which *Othello* presents us with, in which the marriage bed is made the locus of epistemological anxiety only to be displaced by the fully masculinized, unrepresentable scene of state torture, suggests that the play tells us less about the cultural anxieties that women provoked than might at first appear, and more about the ways in which stories about women could be used to explore other more inchoate anxieties, about masculine subjection and masculine will, particularly as these are configured in state apparatuses. The play is saturated with gender ideology but it is an ideology that finally makes women embody not the impenetrable mysteries of mind or otherness but epistemological access, the surface of representation, fair paper to write on.

From *The Elizabethan Theatre XIV: Papers given at ... the University of Waterloo*, ed. A. L. Magnusson and C. E. McGee (Ontario, 1996), pp. 27–48.

NOTES

[Elizabeth Hanson's 'Brothers of the State' stages the relationship between a work of criticism and its readers. Having written on the interrogatory torture of traitors in Elizabethan England, she was 'repeatedly asked', she says, 'about women as torture victims'. In the first instance, she had been interested in the topic of interrogation because it raises issues of the mystery of the mind, the individual conceived as possessed of a 'powerful, withheld, inner truth'.

The question posed by her readers goes to the issue of whether in the early modern period it was possible for women to be conceived as possessed of a similar subjectivity. Hanson concludes that *Othello* does indeed demonstrate 'how a woman might be constructed as an epistemologically resistant subject' but continues that this is finally an indirection. Its most profound anxieties are not about women, gender relations and marriage, she says, but about men, their subjections and their wills, and the apparatuses of the state. Ed.]

1. See 'Torture and Truth in Renaissance England', *Representations*, 34 (1991), 53–84.

2. The connection between the kinds of interrogation involved in Renaissance torture and Othello's construction of Desdemona as an object of epistemological anxiety is explicitly made in Patricia Parker's '*Othello* and *Hamlet*: Dilation, Spying and the "Secret Place" of Woman', *Representations*, 44 (1993), 60–95. Unfortunately I did not read this essay until after my own was substantially written. Parker's argument, that the play conflates a rhetoric of discovery honed in contexts such as espionage and torture with a language of secrecy that marks anatomical literature about the female genitals, illuminates the connection I also want to explore between the treatment of Desdemona and the discovering operations of the Elizabethan State. Our readings diverge, however, insofar as Parker's analysis presupposes a more or less stably feminine gendering of the object of epistemological anxiety in *Othello* while I am concerned to demonstrate the contingency of this gendering, both in this play and on the Renaissance stage generally.

3. The case of witchcraft is a complicated and complicating one. In connection with the prosecution of witchcraft women were sometimes interrogated under circumstances that verged on torture, particularly in the cases connected with Matthew Hopkins' campaign in 1645–47. Even there, however, physical coercion tended to involve practices such as sleep deprivation rather than direct infliction of acute pain. See Keith Thomas, *Religion and the Decline of Magic* (Harmondsworth, Middlesex: 1971). More importantly, while witchcraft itself was construed as an epistemological problem generating debates about what properly constituted evidence of the crime and whether the crime could in fact occur, the prosecution of witchcraft does not seem to have made the witch *as subject* the focus of epistemological concern. For one thing, the witch's body, which supposedly bore a mark which if pricked felt no pain, proffered evidence of her crime that the witch herself had no power to hide. For another, the nature of the crime itself, which increasingly was construed as the pact with the devil, meant that the witch was merely a vehicle through which a greater power acted rather than the origin of the evil she did. Even where witchcraft was dealt with as a problem of knowledge the witch does not seem to have been made the possessor of secret truths. John Cotta, for example, connects the evidentiary problems posed by witchcraft to a true understanding of the crime itself which he claims

is actually a Satanically induced delusion, citing the case of a witch who thought she was flying through the air but all the while could be seen to be lying in her bed (*The Trial of Witchcraft* [London: 1616], p. 20). If this account locates witchcraft in the mind, witchcraft nevertheless does not constitute a secret which the witch could withhold, because she does not, in fact, know the truth. See Barbara Shapiro, *Probability and Certainty in Seventeenth-Century England* (Princeton: 1983), pp. 194–226 for an excellent discussion of the epistemological construction of witchcraft in the context of changes in religious, legal and scientific notions of proof and truth in the period.

4. Quoted in Christopher Devlin, *Life of Robert Southwell* (London: 1967), p. 175. See also Richard Challoner, *Complete Modern British Martyrology* (London: 1836), p. 113. Anne Askew's record of her torture is also illuminating in this regard. At issue throughout are doctrine and authority: she is rebuked for violating Paul's prohibition on women preaching ('I answered hym', she replies, 'that I knewe Paules meanynge so well as he ... and asked hym, how manye women he had seane, go into the pulpett and preache') and is questioned as to whether 'if the host should fall, and beast ded eate it, whether the beast ded receyve God or no' to which she responds by inviting the bishop to answer his own question. At this point the bishop protests that 'it was against the ordre of scoles, that he whych asked the questyon, shuld answere it. I tolde hym', she goes on, 'I was but a woman, & knewe not the course of scoles'. Gender is an explicit concern on both sides, linked to Askew's ability to control and resist her interrogation. But what is interesting about her account for my purposes is the absence of the discourse of secrecy and discovery that is so marked a feature of the later Jesuit interrogations. She is racked for information about Protestant courtiers and her torture is prolonged because 'she laye still and ded not crye' but what she calls attention to is simply her resistance to their force, not a conscience whose privacy she defends. See *The Examination of Anne Askew* (1546) and *The Lattre Examination of Anne Askew* (1547). These texts are available, transcribed and edited by John Bale in the Parker Society's *Select Works of John Bale*, ed. Henry Christmas (Oxford: 1849). *The Examinations* are also reproduced in John Foxe, *Acts and Monuments of these latter and perilous days* (1563), ed. George Townsend, 8 vols. (1838; rpt. 1965), Vol. 5.

5. My source for this story is Devlin, *Life*, pp. 256, 274–90. Devlin's sources are mostly reports of news obtained by Catholic informants and dispatched in letters by Henry Garnet and Richard Verstegan to Jesuit authorities. Devlin offers no account either of Ann's motives in betraying Southwell or of her parents' in consenting to her marriage, implying that both seemed to follow inevitably from her rape and pregnancy.

6. Southwell's cousin, Robert Cecil, who was present at some of the interrogations, is said in a contemporary Catholic report to have remarked that '... we have a new torture which it is not possible for a man to bear.

And yet I have seen Robert Southwell hanging by it, still as a tree-trunk, and no one able to drag one word from his mouth'. Apparently from a letter written by Henry Garnet, May 1, 1595 (cited in Devlin, p. 288).

7. Arden edition, ed. M. R. Ridley (London: 1958), 1.1.170–1. All further citations are to this edition.

8. Thomas Rymer, *A Short View of Tragedy* (1693; rpt. Menston, Yorkshire: 1970), p. 144.

9. See Hanson, 'Torture and Truth', pp. 74–5.

10. Arden edition, ed. J. W. Lever (London: 1965), 5.1.309–10. All further references are to this edition.

11. 'Representing Power: *Measure for Measure* in its Time', in *The Power of Forms in the English Renaissance*, ed. Stephen Greenblatt (Norman, Oklahoma: 1982), p. 141. On the engineering of James's succession, see Paul Johnson, *Elizabeth: A Study in Power and Intellect* (London: 1964), pp. 438–9.

12. Eve Kosofsky Sedgwick, *Between Men· English Literature and Male Homosocial Desire* (New York: 1985).

13. On the slippage between marital and military orders see Julia Genster, 'Lieutenancy, Standing In, and *Othello*', *ELH*, 57 (1990), pp. 785–809. Genster's article provides an interesting account of Elizabethan military reform and its literature in which military regulations of the period attempted to constitute 'a civil government structure within the army' (p. 790), a point clearly relevant to the parallel I want to draw between the worlds of *Othello* and the organizational dynamics of the early modern state.

14. William Empson makes the point that 'Iago is dragging Othello into his state of mind', in *The Structure of Complex Words* (London: 1951), p. 246.

15. Lewis Lewkenor, who Shakespeare possibly read, asserts that 'the Captaine Generall of [the Venetian] Armie … is always a straunger' in order to prevent political ambitions arising in the military. See *Commonwealth and Government of Venice* (1599), sig. S2v, cited in David C. McPherson, *Shakespeare, Jonson and the Myth of Venice* (Newark: 1990), p. 73.

16. *The Merchant of Venice*, Arden edition, ed. John Russell Brown (London: 1955), 1.3.30–4.

17. Rymer's complaint interestingly then shifts ground. He asserts that if such a marriage were to meet with acceptance in the House of Lords, 'the blackamoor must have changed his skin' (*Short View of Tragedy*,

p. 103). Removing the racial issue apparently makes it easier for him to imagine the state dealing in family matters.

18. In noting that Othello's marriage takes the outsider into a social 'inside', I follow Peter Stallybrass's invaluable essay, 'Patriarchal Territories: The Body Enclosed', in *Rewriting the Renaissance: Discourses of Sexual Difference in Early Modern Europe*, ed. Margaret W. Ferguson, Maureen Quilligan and Nancy J. Vickers (Chicago: 1986), pp. 123–44. My reading is slightly different, however, in asserting the epistemological as well as the social significance of this inside, and in linking it to the organization of the state as well as the structure of society. One implication of Stallybrass's approach which my own reading shares, and which deserves special mention, is that however attractive Desdemona may be as a character, however much she seems to voice an understanding of relationship that is a salvific alternative to Othello's madness, she is nevertheless a function of a complex ideology that produces her powerful position as a subject only and inevitably to close it down.

19. *Othello* has furnished rich material for critics seeking to connect rhetorical tropes to social and epistemological issues. See Patricia Parker, 'Shakespeare and Rhetoric: Dilation and Delation in *Othello*', in *Shakespeare and the Question of Theory*, ed. Patricia Parker and Geoffrey Hartman (New York and London: 1985), pp. 54–74 and Joel B. Altman, 'Preposterous Conclusions: Eros, *Enargeia*, and the Composition of *Othello*', *Representations*, 18 (1987), 129–57.

20. Desdemona's wondering response to Othello's account of the handkerchief's exotic origins ('Is't possible?' [l. 66] – 'I' faith, is't true?' [l. 73]) suggests that what we see here is a reprise of their courtship, that exchange which so fits the Duke's model of 'request and such fair question as soul to soul affordeth', that Othello can placidly claim, 'This only is the witchcraft I have us'd' (1.3.169). But the magical powers Othello attributes to the handkerchief to 'subdue' another to one's love also serve to confirm Brabantio's association of witchcraft with his foreign son-in-law. The idealized version of Othello's relationship to Desdemona thus becomes the ground on which his difference, and hence the impossibility of his communion soul to soul with a 'supersubtle Venetian', appears.

21. 'Patriarchal Territories', p. 139.

22. The parallel between the problem Iago sets up and the one recorded in the discourse of torture holds at the tropological as well as the conceptual level. Cardinal Allen, for instance, describing the torture of Edmund Campion, declared that 'if they had torn him in ten thousand pieces or stilled him to the quintessence, in that holy breast they should never have found any piece of those fained treasons' (*A Briefe Historie of the Glorious Martyrdome*, p. 13). If Allen's ostensible point is that Campion was not guilty, his words also suggest a fantasy of making the

body yield the soul's truth ('still[ing] him to the quintessence') which must collapse into the discovery that such truth can not be found in the flesh. The remark Catholics attributed to one of Campion's torturers, that one 'might sooner pluck his heart out of his bosom than rack a word out of his mouth that he made conscience of uttering', similarly seems to harbor a version of Iago's taunt about knowing his thoughts: 'You cannot if my heart were in your hand' (3.3.167). Cf. Simpson, p. 391.

23. Katharine Eisaman Maus, in 'Horns of a Dilemma: Jealousy, Gender and Spectatorship in English Drama', *ELH*, 54 (1987), 561–83, provides a valuable discussion of the relation between offstage sex scenes and the epistemological problems that *Othello* and other plays about jealousy in the period raise.

24. On the apparent taboo against representing torture and execution on the Renaissance stage see James Shapiro, ' "Tragedies naturally performed": Kyd's Representation of Violence', *Staging the Renaissance*, ed. David Scott Kastan and Peter Stallybrass (London and New York: 1991), pp. 99–113. The fascination exerted by the boundary between state violence and theatrical representation is suggested by other Jacobean tragedies (Webster's *The White Devil* [1612], Tourneur's *The Atheist's Tragedy* [1611]) which conclude by gesturing towards state violence that is not going to happen on stage. *The Atheist's Tragedy* is a particularly interesting example, putting ironic pressure on the taboo by bringing the scene of execution on stage at its conclusion, only grotesquely to preempt it by having the executioner dash out his own brains by mistake.

6

Othello on Trial

EMILY C. BARTELS

'*I am no Othello; Othello is a lie*'.[1]

One of the most remarkable moments on the early modern stage comes as Othello, 'the Moor of Venice', tells the story of his life before the Venetian court.[2] Remarkable because he stands before the Duke accused by an irate senator, Brabantio, of bewitching, seducing and eloping with a white woman, the senator's daughter, Desdemona. Yet Othello nonetheless takes charge of his own trial: he at once directs the court to 'send for the lady' (1.3.115), to hear her side of the story, and, in the interim, supplies all the necessary testimony himself. What's more, in that testimony, as Othello attempts to explain his integration into white society, he, in fact, comes out as Moor. He displays the 'story of [his] life' (1.3.129) as the centre of his story of courtship and underscores his resonantly non-European experiences – his contact with cannibals, Anthropophagi, headless Blemines, deadly breaches, hills whose heads touch heaven, slavery, and so on – as if to be a Moor were an asset and not (as Iago and friends would have it) a liability.

Indeed, all along Othello expects his service to the state easily to 'out-tongue' Brabantio's complaints (1.2.19). In justifying his elopement, Othello puts the fact that he 'love[s] the gentle Desdemona' (1.2.25) forward in his own defence, as if all that is under question is *how*, and not *that*, he, a black Moor, won the white Desdemona. 'That I have ta'en away this old man's daughter', he admits to the court, 'It is most true; true I have married her; / The very head and front of my offending / Hath this extent, no more' (1.3.78–81). 'This extent, no more' – suggesting that 'this extent', the fact of the marriage, is not itself a problem but the safe starting ground for the self-defence that follows, a spelling out, a 'round unvarnish'd tale', of his 'whole course of love' (1.3.90–1). And no one at court objects. The Duke imagines that his own daughter might respond like Desdemona, Brabantio withdraws his complaint, Othello resumes his place as general, and the dramatic action heads off to Cyprus, where Desdemona will replace Othello as the accused, at least for a while.

Yet while Othello exudes a winning confidence, critics have been sceptical of his footing in Venice. Recent race-oriented work assumes that the Venetian court could only have a love/hate relation to the Moor, who, though he is vital to the state's military defences, is also – unfortunately in Venice's eyes – black.[3] It is only because the Duke needs Othello to lead the Venetian forces against the Turks that the court lets the charges of witchcraft go and tolerates the miscegenous marriage (as well as the presence of the Moor). Otherwise, Othello's association with a white woman would do him (and probably her) in immediately.[4] For the most part, what has compelled these readings has been a desire to recover the histories of peoples that European colonialism silenced. Though it was the West and not the North Africans – in Hakluyt's terms, 'Negroes' and not 'Moors' – who would become the targets of New World slavery, critics have taken an interest in Shakespeare's representation of the Moor to get some take on how the 'black man' figured in a society that would, a century later, commit blacks to an unthinkable subjugation.[5]

Ironically, however, the starting point for these interrogations has implicitly been Venice. Whatever heritage Othello brings from non-European domains and however he presents his case, he is first a subject circumscribed by Venice, whose attitudes define and determine his place. Either Othello is 'a cultural stranger, … "out of it" in the most compelling and literal sense', 'unable to grasp and make effective use of … Venetian codes of social and sexual conduct', or he is 'a colonised subject existing on the terms of white Venetian society', 'trying to internalise its ideology'.[6] Or he is a split subject, aware of a 'pre-colonial' past but caught in a Venetian present, and torn between 'asserting his non-European glamour and denying his blackness'.[7] Even then, he already is, or will be, a 'colonial' subject, whose evocations of the past can only signal the start – in the 'pre-colonial' moment before it starts – of a colonialist trajectory, defined and imposed by Europe.

To define Othello thus, however, is to put serious constraints on the positions he, as speaking subject, can hold. If a colonialist Venice is the starting point of cultural identity, then the Moor must necessarily be 'out of it', however much he might attempt, or Venice force him, to internalize Venetian ideology. Say what he will, 'the weakness of the precariously cultured alien, of the "stranger" beneath', will poke through his 'frontal security'.[8] Hence, if he speaks (as he seems to speak at court) with bold self-confidence and self-possession, we will hear – indeed, must hear – in his words a false or hollow ring. His stories will sound like Europe's, his past like a prelude to Europe's future. Before we begin, then, we will already know what we are presumably looking at the play to find out – what it means, in the era before colonization and New World slavery took hold, to be 'the Moor of Venice'. And what it means, if we start with Venice as the focal point, is a Moor who is always, necessarily, out of place, however much he might try to be in.

The play is obviously interested in what happens as a Moor becomes integrated or integrates himself into European society, through marital and military avenues – and, significantly, at a moment when that society is engaged in an imperialist competition against the Turks.[9] From the start, that integration is delimited by a seething anti-Moor discourse, which Iago, Roderigo and Brabantio voice on the sidelines to force (they hope) the Moor's disintegration. Othello's presence is called into being as these currents collide – as the news of his elopement is overshadowed by Brabantio's attempts to disrupt the marriage and discredit Othello at court, which in turn are overshadowed by the Duke's desire to send Othello into service.

Still, while these dynamics clearly *surround* Othello, they do not ultimately *circumscribe* him. For significantly, the play assigns Othello a distinctive dramatic discourse that is separate from, though emerging within, the discourse of Venice. However far he falls into Iago's or Venice's fictions, from the start of the play to its end, Othello continues nonetheless to tell his own stories, to give voice to an uncircumscribed non-European identity and presence – once (in the speech with which I started) when he presents his 'round, unvarnish'd tale', again when he details the history of his mother's handkerchief for Desdemona, and finally when he recounts his tragedy at the end of the play. Although these stories, with their characterizing exoticism, may be read as the co-opted representations of a culturally dispossessed stranger, they, importantly also, need not be. The uncertainties within them open up the possibility that Othello may be instead a self-possessing subject who has as much power to circumscribe Venice as Venice has to circumscribe him.

I want to focus here on the first of those stories, Othello's opening testimony, which pivots on a telling of his life story and which consequently provides the critical background for our understanding of the Moor. For to understand the Moor as something more than the subject of colonial domination that Europe would impose, to see the breadth and flexibility that come, before colonialism, with his part, we must start not with Othello's circumscription but rather with his script.

To start with, and find the Moor within, Othello's script is, however, no easy matter. One of the most intriguing, and vexing, aspects of Othello's characterization is how little we finally know about him – about his nationality, religion, origins, residency, and so on. Othello himself is little help, boasting to Iago, ' 'tis yet to know' from what 'men of royal siege' he 'fetch[es] [his] life and being' (1.2.19, 21–2). And even when he outlines the story of his life, he provides a generic catalogue of clichéd wonders that pop up in descriptions of a number of non-European worlds. At Brabantio's invitation, he narrates:

> I spoke of most disastrous chances;
> Of moving accidents by flood and field,
> Of hair-breadth scapes i' th' imminent deadly breach,
> Of being taken by the insolent foe
> And sold to slavery, of my redemption thence
> And portance in my [travel's] history;
> Wherein of antres vast and deserts idle,
> Rough quarries, rocks, [and] hills whose [heads] touch
>   heaven,
> It was my hint to speak – such was my process –
> And of the Cannibals that each [other] eat,
> The Anthropophagi, and men whose heads
> [Do grow] beneath their shoulders.
>
> (1.3.134–45)

Renaissance spectators would hear in Othello's testimony echoes of representations not only of Africa (of, for instance, John Pory's translation of John Leo Africanus' *History and Description of Africa* [1600]) but also the New World (of, say, John Florio's translation of Michel de Montaigne's essay on 'the Caniballes' [1603], which addresses the peoples of Brazil).[10]

It is no wonder, then, that critics have declared Othello's 'claim to identity' 'tenuous and derivative', and have represented him as

'a character in a semi-fictional creation of colonialist travel narratives', whose 'only access' to his origins comes through 'the exotic
ascriptions of European colonial discourses'.[11] It is no wonder that
Mustapha Sa'eed in Tayeb Salih's postcolonial revision of *Othello,
Season of Migration to the North*, declares Othello 'a lie'. The
glimpse we get from Othello of his pre-Venetian past evokes a familiar European version of the non-European and sounds, to us at least,
like a colonialist 'lie' – one which Europe feeds to him before he,
wittingly or unwittingly, feeds it back to Europe, to secure his standing there.

   And yet, the story Othello tells is so obviously a fiction, that to
imagine that Shakespeare puts these words in Othello's mouth as
something Othello, or we, are supposed to buy as colonialism's truth
is to miss the crucial irony of the moment. For not only do these
exotic references not belong exclusively *to* any particular discourse;
they do not belong *within* any. In iteration after iteration, such catalogues of wonders appear notably out of synch within their parent
texts. In travel narratives such as Richard Eden's account of Africa
(included first in Eden's *Decades of the New Worlde* [1555] and
again in Hakluyt's *Principal Navigations* [1589]), they disrupt the
stream of eyewitness reporting and the claims to realism that tend to
guide the whole, appearing as fictional rather than semi-fictional,
and, as is sometimes explicit, textually rather than actually based.[12]

   In Pory, the situation is even more complex, and more pointedly
relevant to Othello, because the inscription of Africa as exotic
involves a play of competing voices, of a European and a Moor. Even
before colonization and postcolonialism became the crux of critical
movements, critics stressed the parallels between Othello and the
author of *The History and Description*, Al-Hassan Ibn-Mohammed
Al-Wezâz Al-Fâsi (or, in Pory, John Leo Africanus), a Europeanized
Moor who had travelled extensively in Africa, had been captured and claimed as a colonial subject under Pope Leo IX, and
had become known in Europe for his account of Africa.[13] As Pory
introduces John Leo, he imagines an Africa filled with '*manie
thousands of imminent dangers*' and '*marvel*[s]' that Leo survived:

> For *how many desolate cold mountaines, and huge, drie, and barren
> deserts passed he? How often was he in hazard to have beene cap-
> tived, or to have had his throte cut by the prowling* Arabians, *and
> wilde* Mores? *And how hardly manie times escaped he the Lyons
> greedie mouth, and the devouring jawes of the Crocodile?*
>   (I:6)[14]

Though the references are partly oblique, here is the exotic material for the life history Othello will present, with its 'disastrous chances' and 'hair-breadth scapes i' th' imminent deadly breach', its 'antres vast and deserts idle', its reference to slavery, and its images of devourers, the 'Cannibals that each other eat' and the 'greedy ear' of Desdemona who 'devour[s]' Othello's 'discourse' (1.3.149–50).

Yet, as critics have not yet adequately stressed, however much Othello resembles John Leo, his life story evokes not the words of John Leo but rather of John Pory.[15] And while the exotic vision Pory offers becomes part of Othello's narrative, it is noticeably *not* part of Leo's. For although Pory's promo leads us to expect from the *History* a sensationalized and personalized account of its author's travels, the translated text reads instead like a descriptive survey. In providing a description (or what, in his original title, translates as a 'geographicall historie') of Africa, Leo draws as much from others' eyewitness accounts and other authoritative texts, such as the chronicles of Ibn Khaldun and Ibna Rachu, as he does from his own experiences – so much so that the history has been repeatedly distinguished for its 'reliability', remaining (if Pory's biographer, William Powell, is right) 'the standard source of information about Africa in English until early in the nineteenth century'.[16] Even now, critics treat the *History* as a source of 'facts' about Africa that Renaissance (though not necessarily modern) audiences would have believed.[17]

And with good reason. Throughout the *History*, John Leo, as subjective traveller and observer, is notably distant and detached. Pory praises Leo for being '*so diligent a traveller; that there was no kingdome, province, signorie, or citie; or scarcelie any towne, village, mountaine, valley, river, or forrest which he left unvisited*' (I:6–7). But although Leo is an eyewitness to much of the terrain he surveys, his 'I' emerges primarily within his narrative as validation of some fact, something he 'knows' or 'saw' or 'procured to be at large declared unto me by most credible and substantiall persons, which were themselves eie-witnesses of the same' (III:971–2).[18] Even when he records being asked by certain African communities to intervene as 'judge' in their civil disputes, he makes clear that he is of use because he is a stranger, an outsider – and presumably objective – observer.[19] On the few occasions where he lapses into personal or sensational anecdote, those moments appear as digression, distinct from the main business of the book.[20] For example, after recording at some length his encounter with some Arabians (who, under the guise of saving Leo from a snowstorm, trick him, strip him and steal his horse), Leo declares himself 'determined to have written more co[n]cerning those [sorts of] things' (I:174). Yet he moves immediately back to facts ('The lande of Negros is extremely hot'), explaining: 'if I should commit to writing all things woorthie of memorie, a whole yeare were not sufficient for me' (I:174). At the end of the history, he insists that he has 'committed to writing' 'whatsoever I sawe woorthy the observation' (III:971). And by the end, we realize that the *'manie thousands of imminent dangers'* which Pory advertised as central to Leo's story are incidental to it, at best.

Moreover, Pory himself amplifies the *History*'s impersonal, encyclopedic edge by literally and figuratively mapping out the terrain (mostly south of the equator) 'which John Leo hath left undescribed' (I:24). Pory supplements Leo's text with a sizeable collection of his own documents and information on those regions, garnered from 'sundry ancient and late writers' (I:24), including, for starters: a 'generall description of all Africa' (covering almost one hundred pages in the modern edition) (I:12); a 'briefe relation concerning the *government of ... [Africa's] greatest princes*' (III:973); a *'discourse of the ... Religions professed in Africa'* (III:1001); a 'relation touching the state of *Christian Religion in the dominions of* Prete Ianni' (III:1030); and a description 'of the fortresses and colonies *maintained by the Spaniards and Portugals upon* the maine of Africa' (III:1064).

As Pory's career would play out, he would become the sort of chronicler that Richard Hakluyt (who considered Pory his successor and who encouraged Pory to translate Leo) had come to be. In addition to the *History*, the first of his major projects, Pory collaborated with Hakluyt on the last volume of the *Principal Navigations* (1600), probably published a collection of Abraham Ortelius's maps (1602), and, during several years' residence in Virginia, produced newsletters which historians have described as a starting point for the 'evolution of the newspaper in the United States'.[21] Pory has been characterized as a 'ready wit, accommodating himself to a variety of different occasions in an effort to make himself profitable to and for the commonwealth'.[22] Still, his framing of Leo's *History* suggests an urge to tell a story of Africa that Africans themselves would validate. Where Hakluyt prefaces the *Principal Navigations* with a sort of imperialist call-to-arms, a warning to England to get its global act together before the world was owned by Spain, Pory imagines Africans 'justly' saying to John Leo: *'thy books have ... led us the right way home; that we might at length acknowledge both*

who and where we are' (9). That Pory's intended readership is not
African but English and that Pory (who had never been to Africa)
speaks for Africans, as one who knows 'who and where' they
are, should, of course, give us pause. But the greater – because less
obvious – problem this veneer of objectivity poses to Pory's credibility is the contradictory vision it gives us of the Moor and his story,
which, Pory ultimately leads us to believe, is and is not Africa's. For
the Leo Pory praises here is not the Leo who was continually *'in
hazard'*, but a Leo who describes Africa *'judicially'* (8), a Leo whose
story complements and collapses into the depersonalized accounts
with which Pory surrounds it. Contextualized as it is by this authoritative supplementation, Pory's sensationalized promo thus seems
strangely out of place.

What makes the sensationalized account even more vexed is that
it emerges at a moment when Pory is simultaneously defending and
condemning Leo for being a Moor, a term which in Pory almost
always means Moslem. Expecting (if not also feeding) anti-Moslem
bias, at the start of his introduction Pory assures his readers that they
will find Leo, *'albeit by birth a* More, *and by religion for many
yeeres a* Mahumetan', nonetheless *'not altogither unfit to undertake
such an enterprise'* as writing a description of Africa, *'nor unwoor-
thy to be regarded'* (1:4). Part of what Pory uses to make Leo's birth
and religion less troubling is the claim that they, in fact, save him
from Africa's many hazards. Had Leo *'not at the first beene a* More
and a Mahumetan *in religion, and most skilfull in the languages and
customes of the* Arabians *and* Africans' (as well as travelling in
caravans or under the protection of *'great princes'*), Pory speculates,
*'I marvell much how ever he should have escaped so manie thou-
sands of imminent dangers'* (I:6). Yet Pory also makes clear that
Leo's Moorish background is finally not enough, at least not enough
to stop Pory from marvelling still *'how ever he escaped'*, *'how many
desolate cold mountaines, and huge, drie, and barren deserts passed
he'*, *'how often was he in hazard to have beene captived, or to have
had his throte cut'*, and so on. What is enough to save Leo and his
text is rather his conversion, which Pory represents as central to the
Moor's and Africa's stories. It was *'amidst all these his busie and
dangerous travels'*, as Pory tells it, that:

> it pleased the divine providence, for the discovery and manifestation
> of Gods woonderfull works, and of his dreadfull and just judgements
> performed in Africa (which before the time of John Leo, were either

> *utterly concealed, or unperfectly and fabulously reported both by*
> *ancient and late writers) to deliver this author of ours, and this present*
> *Geographicall Historie, into the hands of certaine* Italian *Pirates ...*
> [who] *presented him and his Booke unto* Pope Leo the tenth.
>
> (I:7)

While on the one hand Pory fills Africa with dangers to let Leo off
the hook for being a Moor, on the other he recycles those dangers
to emphasize Leo's – and the history's – need for God's deliverance.

No matter to the Anglican Pory that Leo converted to
Catholicism. No matter that the *History* covers the years before that
conversion and makes no mention of it. Pory himself draws attention to the event with a headnote identifying the place where '*the*
Author of this Historie was taken by Italian pirates, and carried
thence to Rome' (III:734). No matter that Leo finds 'excellent men'
among Africa's 'Christians, Jewes, and Mahumetans' alike (III:858),
sees in Moslem temples the image of Europe's churches (II:421),
understands Messa as both the Christian site where Jonah was cast
from a whale as well the site of a Moslem temple from which the
'prophet, of whom [the] great Mahumet foretold, should proceed'
(II:249). No matter, that is, that in Leo Christian and Moslem sites
and histories can intersect and overlap without apparent conflict or
contradiction.[23] And no matter that religion in Leo seems a matter
more of history than of faith, and a secondary one at that. If we
want to know more about Mohammedism, the one religion Leo
takes up at length, we must look, Leo tells us, at his published
'Commentaries' (III:886), not here.[24] No matter: a dangerous Africa
requires a Moor; it also makes imperative the Moor's conversion.

Thus, in the *History*, Pory's exoticization of Africa and of Leo's
travels not only seems out of place beside the claims to objectivity
and reliability that marks the main part of both Leo's and Pory's
accounts. Rather than nailing the Moor down to a fixed impression,
the exoticism also 'un-Moors' him, contributing to two contradictory judgements of the Moor, whose Moorishness both saves and
damns him. Africa's dangers, it is clear, define the Moor. What is
not – and cannot be – clear is, ironically, *how* they define him.

This, then, is the passage that lies at the core of Othello's
testimony – a passage which undermines the authority which it
attempts to claim. Its fantasies resonate as just that, fantasies whose
ideological bearings are, because contextually out of synch and contradictory, also undecipherable. Though the passage means to produce a definitive Moor, we can read in it neither Pory nor the Moor.

In importing this particular excerpt from Pory, Shakespeare imports as well its contradictions, putting in Othello's mouth echoes of a European representation which fails to define its subject, the Moor, in any stable way. That Shakespeare refuses to specify his Moor's religion may underscore further the conflicts embedded in Pory's text, which tries, in the matter of religion, to have it both ways, to excuse the Moslem and celebrate the Christian, by means of an exotic African score. In any case, in grounding the identity of his Moor on a moment in Pory that is so contextually and ideologically conflicted, Shakespeare ungrounds both Pory and the Moor. The exotic African scene that Pory has produced is not – and, because of Pory, cannot be – here simply the signpost of colonialist discourse and Othello's circumscription within that discourse, which the passage has been taken for. Rather, it marks the limits of European discourse, which Shakespeare turns over to Othello, to judge, limit and delimit the Moor.

In fact, although Othello produces 'the story of his life' as he stands before the Venetian court (and so, before us) ostensibly to be judged, Shakespeare suggests that moment of judgement as moot.[25] The advances of the Turks have already made clear where Othello's future lies, and it is not in some prison in Venice. Othello has been 'hotly' (1.2.44) called to court to receive his already established commission. And despite Brabantio's best efforts to draw attention to the domestic crisis, to accusations that the Duke will tellingly call 'thin habits and poor likelihoods / Of modern [that is, commonplace] seeming' (1.3.108–9), it is the movement of the Turks, and not the 'mangled matter' (1.3.173) of the Moor, that the court assesses with a contrasting degree of scrutiny. Though members of the court do prompt and probe, Othello himself directs the proceedings, breaking legal and marital precedent to dictate that his wife speak for him, and, in the interim, deciding to 'confess the vices of [his] blood' (1.3.123) himself. And the senators are at least as ready to hear that the marriage came about 'by request, and such fair question / As soul to soul affordeth' as they are to find that Othello 'by indirect and forced courses / Subdue[d] and poison[ed]' Desdemona's 'affections' (1.3.111–14), as I have argued elsewhere.[26]

Dramatically, too, the verdict is in before Othello even speaks. Although we do not yet know that the imperialist crisis will dissolve, we need Othello to play out the domestic tragedy that has begun to lurk along the edges of his military progress, need to see the intimate mix of black and white that Iago – with his vulgar vision of an 'old black ram' 'tupping' a 'white ewe' (1.1.88–9) – has seeded in our imaginary, and need to see how Iago (who, rather than the court, is clearly Othello's nemesis) will do Othello in.[27] However Othello might represent himself, whatever stories he might tell, the services he has done and must do for the state, as for the play, have already 'out-tongued' Brabantio's complaints. Dramatic structure and political expediency demand it.

Though set up as a trial, then, the context surrounding Othello's testimony is rather a scene of judgement *manqué*, a scene which ultimately refuses – and emphasizes its refusal – to put Othello on the spot.[28] If anyone is being judged here, it is the irate Brabantio and the circuitous Turks. Othello's testimony turns the tables too and, in its incorporation and contextualization of the Pory passage, makes clear that what is at stake here is not, in fact, the identity of the Moor but rather Europe's inscription of that identity. The central subject of Othello's narrative is obviously not his exotic history, which appears only in outline, but rather Desdemona's, and briefly Brabantio's, reactions to that history. As an acting 'I', Othello is barely present within his list of adventures. He appears instead as he describes himself describing his adventures – as the 'I' who, at Brabantio's prodding, 'ran through' the story of his life and 'spoke', on cue, of 'disastrous chances'; the 'I' who observed Desdemona 'devour[ing]' his discourse and 'found good means / To draw from her a prayer of earnest heart' (1.3.150–2); the 'I' who, by recounting 'some distressful stroke', 'did beguile her of her tears' (1.3.156–7), and so on. What frames and fills the testimony are the responses of his audience – with Brabantio providing the starting point ('Her father lov'd me' [1.3.128]) and Desdemona, the end ('She lov'd me for the dangers I had pass'd / And I lov'd her that she did pity them' [1.3.167–8]). We watch as they eat his stories up, as it were, buying into what the Pory intertext and the courtroom context undermine as a definitive subtext.

Yet while they eat, Othello's representation of their responses further undermines the veracity, and the importance of the veracity, behind his tales. For starters, he depicts Desdemona as a cannibal, 'devour[ing]' his discourse with 'a greedy ear' (1.3.149–50), an image critics have read as a symptom of Othello's own exoticism, his preoccupation with the marvellous or monstrous, manifest in his life story as here.[29] Yet unlike the all-too-familiar figures within that exotic story, the image of Desdemona eating through her ears is jarringly disfigured – as if the image cannot carry, and carry meaning, out of its fixed and more obviously fictional place into a present and unprescribed reality, as if that image is, finally, all image, an incomplete and untranslatable sign. Although the image does not translate, Othello's depiction of Desdemona leads us to believe that the story does, as a seductive commodity almost anyone could sell. Desdemona 'bade me', Othello narrates, 'if I had a friend that lov'd her, / I should but teach him how to tell my story, / And that would woo her' (1.3.163–5). As Othello tells it, Desdemona treats 'his' story as fungible, transmissable from suitor to suitor (and not necessarily to an African suitor), with only a little coaching from him. The remark figures, of course, as a come-on, inviting Othello, in particular, to profess his love. But the words Othello puts in Desdemona's mouth here also undermine the truth value of that story, which, circulated between suitors, would carry meaning only insofar as it would be detached from any historical reality, speaker or event. Its value in the imagined interaction would be rather in its familiarity as seductive exotica, not in its pretensions (if it had any) to a truth it could not possibly claim.

Thus, as Othello tells a story – or rather, tells of telling a story – that pivots on and reiterates the unreal, unreliable and unreadable edge of the Pory text, his narrative produces not a believably exoticized Moor, but Europeans embracing an unbelievably exoticized Moor.[30] And the crucial question is: who knows it? Who guides the suggestive interplay of texts and shapes a scene that puts the Venetians, in lieu of the Moor, pointedly on the spot, Shakespeare or Othello? And to what end? If Othello's place is not determined by the exotic history he once told, then where does he stand in relation to the *present* telling of that *past* scene of telling? In the representation of the Moor, where does circumscription end and circumspection begin?

Importantly, there are several competing possibilities. It may be that the ruling subjectivity is only Shakespeare's – that he, in incorporating Pory, distances Othello from the exotic text and shows as fiction what Othello and the Venetians accept as fact. Othello would thus be unwittingly trapped by an exoticizing European discourse which he and the Venetians, but neither Shakespeare nor we, believe. And the tragedy, which Shakespeare shows us, would be the familiar tragedy of colonialism, leaving the Moor open to the kind of makeover which Iago plays insidiously out on him. Or, along similar lines, it may be that Shakespeare assigns Othello a subjectivity which, though circumspective, is also circumscribed. It may be, that is, that while Othello does not buy into Europe's fantasies, he knows that Europe does and so feeds Europe its own fantasies, as critics have suggested, because he can see or imagine no other choice. His tragedy would be of colonialism's making too – and his limited subjectivity, as I've suggested, about the farthest critics who read Othello as a subject of colonialism are willing or able to go.

Yet the play allows us to go farther. For it may also be that Shakespeare produces an Othello who neither believes nor expects the ruling Venetians to believe his prefabricated stories – an Othello who, like Shakespeare, is aware of the ironies of his narrative and uses them to show his persuasive dominance over a disruptive senator and a subversive daughter, who, he assures the court, will never make 'a skillet of [his] helm' (1.3.272). It is, after all, only those two subjects, obviously alienated from the court, whom Othello offers as approving listeners. Otherwise, he does not invite his present audience to engage in his exotic stories, which appear as an abbreviated catalogue; he invites them only to scrutinize those who do. And significantly, the Duke responds with the open-ended declaration, 'I think this tale would win my daughter too' (1.3.171), indicating not only what most readings assume, that the Duke (like Desdemona) is drawn into these fantasies, but, what the language also suggests, that he sees these fantasies as the stuff daughters' (but not his) dreams are made on. 'I think this tale would win *my daughter* too', as it has won Desdemona, the unruly daughter on display. In this case, Othello would then stand outside the fictions he produces, registering his prowess not only as a persuasive suitor but also as a reader of Europe's gaze. If, as I've argued, his political position is secure and his trial is ultimately moot, then his testimony may be more critique than apology, more offence than defence. Instead of following Europe's fantasy, Othello could be exposing its limits and coming out as Moor in his own terms – as subject who can read Europe and read Europe reading, or misreading, him.

Though *any* of these readings is possible, what is crucially important here is that they *all* are. Othello may well be a precariously situated 'alien', who plays into Europe's clichés because he either knows no better or knows no other choice. Or he may be a secure and authoritative witness, who plays against those fictions, insisting on their circumscription while defying his. Or his footing may fall somewhere in between. Rather than giving him a certain, prefabricated definition, the exoticism within his script forces those who would produce him theatrically or critically to confront the Moor as

subject – a subject whose own perspective, rather than, or in addition to Europe's, may determine how we read those exotic features,
Africa and the Moor.

Tellingly, the same is true for the two other moments I have identified as part of Othello's self-defining discourse and will only gesture
towards here: his representation of Desdemona's handkerchief and
his final representation of his tragedy. Both call up an exoticism that
they then either reinscribe or defy and, through it, build an indelible
flexibility into the figure of the Moor. Desdemona's handkerchief
first becomes a loaded prop in its displacement, when Emilia secretly
steals it, noting that it was Desdemona's 'first remembrance from the
Moor', who 'conjur'd her she should ever keep it' (3.3.291, 294).[31]
Yet it is only later, when Othello calls Desdemona to account for it,
as for her chastity, and gets a troubled resistance in reply, that he
puts 'magic' (3.4.69) in its web, asserting that an 'Egyptian', 'a
charmer' who 'could almost read the thoughts of people' (3.4.56–8),
gave it to his mother, to secure her husband's love. Desdemona interrupts twice to ask 'Is't possible?' and 'is't true?' (3.4.68, 75), as if this
history is indeed news to her – and consequently, as if it is, on
Othello's part, more vehicle than truth. With this exotic precedent
behind him (in lieu of other ocular proof), Othello can and does
press on Desdemona's fidelity, cautioning her to 'take heed' (3.4.65)
lest she, in losing or giving the handkerchief away, bring 'such perdition' on herself, 'as nothing else could match' (3.4.67, 68). Because
he uses the exotic story to gain leverage at a point of obvious crisis,
and uses it to manipulate someone whom he has already represented
as susceptible to his exotica, we are bound to suspect its veracity,
bound to wonder whether the enchanted past Othello produces is,
to his mind, finally his.[32]

At the end of the play, we face a similar dilemma as Othello
provides Venice the terms for the retelling of his story, directing his
audience to speak:

> Of one that lov'd not wisely but too well;
> Of one not easily jealous, but being wrought,
> Perplexed in the extreme; of one whose hand,
> (Like the base [Indian]) threw a pearl away
> Richer than all his tribe; of one whose subdu'd eyes,
> Albeit unused to the melting mood,
> Drops tears as fast as the Arabian trees
> Their medicinable gum.
>
> (5.2.344–51)

At this point, the images Othello evokes to exoticize his story figure explicitly as just that, exotic images: he is 'like' the base Indian (or Judean) and his eyes drop tears 'as fast as' Arabian trees drop gum. These pictures are displaced almost as quickly as they appear, as Othello then reproduces (and destroys) himself in terms of an imagined conflict between Venetians and Turks, becoming the figure in Aleppo who 'took by th' throat' and 'smote' 'a malignant and a turban'd Turk', who, in turn, once 'beat a Venetian and traduc'd the state' (5.2.353–6).

This final set of images, in its concreteness, plays so clearly against the images which precede – and which wander, in contrast and in more detail, across an abstract and shifting metaphorical terrain – and, in its stereotyping, plays so squarely into Venetian politics, that it puts a strategic spin on the act and intent of representation here.[33] Lodovico, who presides as Venice's representative, makes sense of the tragedy and its villain Iago through epithets – '[damned] slave' and 'damned villain' (5.2.292, 316) – and his terms are well answered by Othello's 'malignant' 'Turk' and 'circumcised dog' (5.2.355). But, as before, it is the relation between Othello and his audience, between his stories and Europe's, that is ultimately unclear. Is Othello, with or without knowing it, giving the Venetians the stories and the Moors of their choice? Or is he, via the obvious shifts and discontinuities between his images, 'marr[ing]' 'all that is spoke' (5.2.357), refusing yet again the terms that would nail him down? John Bernard has argued that this final scene 'transcends the represented character, Othello, and embraces the representing theatrical apparatus itself, that is, the entire panoply of production, including the audience, that constitutes the play's ultimate interpretive authority'.[34] Yet as we watch Othello supply his audience a series of different stories, it is his interpretive authority, his embrace or rejection of an exotic history, that we must question first.

The range of options, evident at each of the signal moments when Othello emphasizes his identity as Moor, is not only crucial but, in fact, distinctive. For importantly, not all parts of the play – and, I would argue, any Renaissance play – are equally open. If Robert Weimann is right, the Renaissance stage was still partially defined by the medieval divisions of *locus* and *platea* acting spaces, characters and styles, with the *locus* harbouring the dramatic illusion, its characters and action creating a reality that absorbs us and them, and the *platea* constituted by stock figures, who, in contrast, break the frame of that illusion and undermine its truth.[35] Though, as

Weimann suggests, the lines between the *locus* and *platea* were becoming increasingly faint by Shakespeare's time, we still see in Shakespeare a substantial difference between the more predictable characters such as Iago, who emerges, like the related Vice, from a *platea* tradition and who is, at base, a stock type, and less predictable characters such as Hamlet who would, if they could, be real.[36] There is notable room for movement, for the surprising inscription of subjectivity, within the more conventional, *platea* parts, as I've argued elsewhere.[37] At the same time, however, these roles are significantly more fixed than *locus* parts, even in the case of characters such as Iago, whose motives and sexualities will always elude our grasp. Iago may never be what he is, but his unreadability is, to a significant degree, a readable part of the package of malignancy he, from his first step on stage, comes in with – an expected, if not conventional, sign that he is unquestionably, because motivelessly, evil.[38]

Stage traditions had already found a similarly prescribed place for the Moor. Shakespeare himself had produced the infamous Aaron, of *Titus Andronicus* (1593–94), who, like and even more than Iago, was dressed in the familiar trappings of stereotype. Yet even though dramatic precedent, some of Shakespeare's own making, dictated otherwise, Othello is decidedly not a stock, *platea* type. It seems no coincidence that, in the Restoration, when Thomas Porter refashioned *Othello* into a 'villain play' – entitled, in fact, *The Villain* (1662) – Othello's role faded into that of 'two barely distinguishable gentlemen', while the Iago figure, Maligni, prevailed.[39] Virginia Mason Vaughan reads this emphasis on the Iago part as a sign that, in the Restoration, '*Othello* was perceived as a villain play'.[40] Yet this emphasis might also (or rather) suggest that, whatever Restoration playwrights thought about the play, when they looked to *Othello* for material that would best fit their exaggerating play of types, they looked to the European Iago, *not* to the Moor – as if it was impossible, even as colonialism and New World slavery were beginning to emerge as a visible future, to typecast Shakespeare's Moor.

Colonialism and postcolonialism eventually would find ways to nail him down. Olivier's *Othello*, a film which is untroubled by having Laurence Olivier, a standard-bearer of the white British and Shakespearean elite, play the Moor in black-face, produces the Moor, with his Caribbean accent and Catholic cross, as a Europeanized subject, who bonds with Venice's ruling men by proving his power over women, using the shared ground of gender to compensate for differences of race. As a postcolonial protest against that kind of unreflective colonial circumscription, Salih's Mustapha Sa'eed would revive Othello as a 'lie', using his own 'fabricated stories about deserts of golden sands and jungles' to seduce European women, prompting them to envision him as 'a naked, primitive creature, a spear in one hand and arrows in the other' (38). And he would distinguish himself from Othello ('I am no Othello') for knowing what he assumes Othello does not know: that in thus 'stir[ring] the pool' of the white woman's emotions he could play upon the 'taut strings' of her desires, in his words, 'as I wish' (38). Yet the Othello that persists in Shakespeare's play, and underlies these renovations, is the Othello that depends upon and up-ends exoticizing representation such as Pory's, a Moor that could as easily be self-possessing as he could be dispossessed.

Critics tend to treat the malleability of a dramatic text as something the playwright would rather do without – as, for example, an unwelcome, if not also unanticipated, after-effect of theatrical or textual production, determined more by the changing cultural climate that demands a changed play, for political, economic or ideological reasons, than by the playwright.[41] The flexibility within a given version of a play appears often as a sign or source of the playwright's or culture's anxiety, ambivalence or indecision about some issue or ideology that is fixed, or threatens to be fixed, more solidly somewhere else.[42] Yet it seems very likely that a playwright such as Shakespeare, who was intimately involved in the theatrical production of his work, had to be aware that each of his plays would undergo continual revision from production to production, during and after his time. If he was to have any impact on the effect (not to mention marketability and lifespan) of his plays, he necessarily had to work with rather than against what was an indelible fact of dramatic life – to build into his plays an openness that allowed, if not invited, certain change as well as certain kinds of changes. He had to allow room for revision of those subjects, in particular, whose fate, though scrutinized, was not yet sealed. The resulting openness that emerges prominently within clearly select parts of his plays, then, would register not, or not just, anxiety or ambivalence about some set position it could not adequately support or supplant. Rather it would suggest the ongoing indeterminacy and multiplicity of attitudes that were not yet, but were likely to be, targeted, with the selected subjects, for codification, stabilization and even institutionalization.

Shakespeare probably could not have predicted, in 1604, the course that history, especially New World and African history, would take. Yet that he would build into the characterization of his Moor multiple possibilities for playing suggests that he was aware of the Moor as a potentially controversial figure – a figure, for example, like Hamlet, whose search for interiority, during a period when the self was not necessarily 'in', was bound to hit a few nerves.[43] What makes Shakespeare's representation of Othello's representation of himself such a remarkable discursive coup is that, rather than playing anxiously into or against a set field of ideologies, it capitalizes on the very openness of that context and challenges us to rethink the historical moment as one which itself was open-ended, even, if not especially, as imperialist and colonialist politics were beginning to take shape. For even as Shakespeare draws upon what seem relatively fixed European fantasies, he puts them on a par with the Moor as equally vulnerable to manipulation, leaving the door open for Othello to stand apart from as well as within their forms. In the end, the Moor that emerges from the self-defining histories he does and does not claim is a figure that Europe imagined not only looking at but also looking back – a figure, therefore, for whom the jury, though assembled, is still and necessarily out.

Emily C. Bartels' essay is published here for the first time.

NOTES

[Emily Bartels has written extensively on the meanings of race and nationality in early modern literature and culture, and her research in the field continues in this chapter, never before published. 'Othello on Trial' bridges the distance between historicist research and postcolonial criticism. As a man of the theatre, Bartels argues, Shakespeare would have known that his plays would mutate over time and in different venues, and so he would have built into them the openness that has allowed them to be so infinitely productive of new meanings and effects ever since. The old argument between A. C. Bradley and F. R. Leavis about Othello's character was ultimately sterile, as Bartels shows here. She argues that the 'multiple possibilities' of the Moor are inherent to the text. This is a way of rethinking not only *Othello* but also history. Both, according to Bartels, are 'open-ended' – or receptive of our continuing investigation. Ed.]

1. Tayeb Salih, *Season of Migration to the North*, trans. Denys Johnson-Davies (London: Heinemann, 1969), p. 95. This text was brought to my attention by Jyotsna Singh, 'Othello's Identity, Postcolonial Theory, and

Contemporary African Rewritings of *Othello*', in *Women, 'Race' and Writing in the Early Modern Period*, ed. Margo Hendricks and Patricia Parker (London: Routledge, 1994), pp. 287–99 [reprinted as chapter 7 in this collection]. I have presented versions of this essay at the Bread Loaf School of English, Middlebury College, Middlebury, VT (July 1997) and at the Rutgers Center for Historical Analysis, Rutgers University, New Brunswick, NJ (February 1998), and am grateful to all who responded there.

2. From the subtitle. All quotations from Shakespeare come from William Shakespeare, *The Riverside Shakespeare*, ed. G. Blakemore Evans *et al.* (Boston: Houghton Mifflin, 1974).

3. See, for example, Ania Loomba, 'Sexuality and Racial Difference', in *Critical Essays on Shakespeare's 'Othello'*, ed. Anthony Gerard Barthelemy (New York: G. K. Hall, 1994), pp. 162–86, especially p. 173; and Virginia Mason Vaughan, *'Othello': A Contextual History* (Cambridge: Cambridge University Press, 1994), especially pp. 65–9. For a contrasting view, see Martin Orkin, 'Othello and the "Plain Face" of Racism', *Shakespeare Quarterly*, 38 (1987), 166–88.

4. On the impact of the miscegenation, see: Karen Newman, ' "And Wash the Ethiop White": Femininity and the Monstrous in *Othello*', in *Shakespeare Reproduced: The Text in History & Ideology*, ed. Jean E. Howard and Marion F. O'Connor (New York: Routledge, 1987), pp. 143–62; Loomba; and Michael Neill, 'Unproper Beds: Race, Adultery, and the Hideous in *Othello*', *Shakespeare Quarterly*, 40 (1989), 383–412. On the related issue of misogyny, see Valerie Wayne, 'Historical Differences: Misogyny and *Othello*', in *The Matter of Difference: Materialist Feminist Criticism of Shakespeare*, ed. Valerie Wayne (Ithaca: Cornell University Press, 1991), pp. 153–79.

5. I talk about Hakluyt's distinction between Negroes and Moors in 'Imperialist Beginnings: Richard Hakluyt and the Construction of Africa', *Criticism*, 34 (1992), 517–38.

6. Michael D. Bristol, *Big-Time Shakespeare* (London: Routledge, 1996), p. 185; Loomba, p. 171. See also Stephen Greenblatt, *Renaissance Self-Fashioning: From More to Shakespeare* (Chicago: University of Chicago Press, 1980), pp. 222–54. Other examples include Dympna Callaghan, ' "Othello was a White Man": Properties of Race on Shakespeare's Stage', in *Alternative Shakespeares 2*, ed. Terence Hawkes (London: Routledge, 1996), pp. 192–215, who argues that 'the physical presence of a black man is always already an exhibition of monstrosity' on the Renaissance stage (p. 209); and Barthelemy, 'Ethiops Washed White: Moors of the Nonvillainous Type', in *Critical Essays*, pp. 91–103, who sees in Othello 'fear of being a stereotypical stage Moor' (p. 95).

7. Loomba, 'Shakespeare and Cultural Difference', in *Alternative Shakespeares 2*, p. 180, and 'Sexuality and Racial Difference', p. 177. See also Singh.

OTHELLO ON TRIAL *167*

OTHELLO ON TRIAL *167*

8. Alessandro Serpieri, 'Reading the Signs: Towards a Semiotics of Shakespearean Drama', trans. Keir Elam, in *Alternative Shakespeares*, ed. John Drakakis (London: Routledge, 1985), p. 140.

9. I discuss the play's treatment of imperialism in '*Othello* and Africa: Postcolonialism Reconsidered', *William and Mary Quarterly*, 54 (1997), 45–64.

10. Other subtexts which rehearse catalogues of such marvels include *Mandeville's Travels* (1499), Ralegh's *The Discovery of Guiana* (1595), Richard Hakluyt's *Principal Navigations* (1600), and classical cosmographies such as Pliny's *Naturall History*, translated by Philemon Holland. For a good note on these texts, see *A New Variorum Edition of 'Othello'*, ed. Horace Howard Furness (New York: Dover, 1963), pp. 56–7, note to 1.3.167. For further background on representations of Africa circulating in the Renaissance, see Alden T. Vaughan and Virginia Mason Vaughan, 'Before *Othello*: Elizabethan Representations of Sub-Saharan Africans', *William and Mary Quarterly*, 54 (1997), 19–44, who stress the negative edge; and Martin Van Wyk Smith, 'Othello and the Narrative of Africa', *Shakespeare in Southern Africa*, 4 (1990–91), 11–30. I am grateful to David Brown for prompting me to think of the implications of Montaigne here, and to Stephanie Moss for alerting me to the Smith essay.

11. Singh, pp. 288, 299; and Newman, p. 150.

12. On the place of the exotic in cross-cultural descriptions, see Stephen Greenblatt, *Marvelous Possessions: The Wonder of the New World* (Chicago: University of Chicago Press, 1991); Mary B. Campbell, *The Witness and the Other World: Exotic European Travel Writing 400–1600* (Ithaca: Cornell University Press, 1988); and Newman, p. 148.

13. See Lois Whitney, 'Did Shakespeare Know *Leo Africanus*?', *Publication of the Modern Language Association*, 37 (1922), 470–83; Eldred D. Jones, *The Elizabethan Image of Africa* (Charlottesville: University of Virginia Press, 1971); and Rosalind Johnson, 'The African Presence in Shakespearean Drama: Parallels between Othello and the Historical Leo Africanus', *Journal of African Civilization*, 7 (1985), 276–87. I have discussed the *Othello*/Africanus relation in 'Making More of the Moor: Aaron, Othello, and Renaissance Refashionings of Race', *Shakespeare Quarterly*, 41 (1990), 433–54, and hope to complicate parts of its argument about Pory here.

14. Al-Hassan Ibn-Mohammed Al-Wezâz Al-Fâsi, *The History and Description of Africa*, 3 vols., trans. John Pory, ed. Robert Brown (New York: Burt Franklin, 1846). As here, all references to this text will appear in my text. The italics that appear in this quote and others are as in Pory.

15. One important exception is Kim F. Hall, *Things of Darkness: Economies of Race and Gender in Early Modern England* (Ithaca: Cornell University Press, 1995), pp. 28–40, who sees Pory's relation to Leo's text as 'fascinatingly complex' (p. 30), though she ultimately stresses Pory's 'anxiety' about Leo's 'cultural difference' (p. 31).

16. William S. Powell, *John Pory, 1572–1636: The Life and Letters of a Man of Many Parts* (Chapel Hill: University of North Carolina Press, 1977), p. 16. Pory's cultivation of the text's reliability may also be seen as promotion of his own; see Andrew Mousley, 'Self, State, and Seventeenth Century News', *The Seventeenth Century*, 6 (1991), 149–68, especially pp. 156–7. For Leo's references to the chroniclers, see I:133, I:201n.11, I:208n.26 and III:956.

17. See, for example, Barthelemy, 'Ethiops Washed White', p. 96; and Elliot Tokson, *The Popular Image of the Black Man in English Drama, 1550–1688* (Boston: G. K. Hall, 1982), p. 17. See also Patricia Parker, 'Fantasies of "Race" and "Gender": Africa, *Othello* and bringing to light', in *Women, 'Race', and Writing*, pp. 84–100, especially pp. 84–90, who sees in Pory a 'language of dilating, opening, or unfolding' (p. 92).

18. For instance, see II:226, II:231, II:232, II:239, II:292, II:428, III:869, III:949, III:956, III:971 – and the list could go on.

19. See II:235, II:276 and II:685.

20. For the example cited below, see I:170–4. Other instances include: I:158, I:170, II:231, II:239, II:461, II:665, III:884 and III:888.

21. Powell, p. 51. See Powell on Pory and Hakluyt (pp. 9–12) and on the Ortelius collection (pp. 19–24).

22. Mousley, p. 152.

23. See also II:422, II:428 and II:504.

24. See also II:288 and II:453.

25. Compare Parker, '*Othello* and *Hamlet*: Dilation, Spying, and the "Secret Place" of Woman', in *Shakespeare Reread: The Texts in New Contexts*, ed. Russ McDonald (Ithaca: Cornell University Press, 1994), pp. 105–46, especially p. 109.

26. 'Making More of the Moor', p. 449.

27. On the ways the play prompts our desires to see the married couple and marriage bed, see Neill.

28. Interestingly, when critics identify a scene of judgement, it is often Othello's trial of Desdemona that they focus on. See, for example, Katherine Eisaman Maus, *Inwardness and Theater in the English Renaissance* (Chicago: University of Chicago Press, 1995), pp. 104–27.

29. For alternative readings of the exoticization of Desdemona and how it plays into the representation of Othello, see Newman and Parker, 'Fantasies of "Race" and "Gender"'.

30. Compare Greenblatt, *Renaissance Self-Fashioning*, who sees 'this tale' of 'the telling of tales' as a sign of Othello's 'submission to narrativity' (p. 237) and 'loss of his own origins' (p. 245); and Maus, who sees in Othello's retelling of the scene of telling one of many signs of his 'energetic guilelessness', his 'denial or avoidance of potential discrepancies between surface and interior' (p. 121). See also Newman's critique of Greenblatt, pp. 130–1, and John Gillies, *Shakespeare and the Geography of Difference* (Cambridge: Cambridge University Press, 1994), especially pp. 28–34, who sees in the speech a classically prescribed exoticism that marks Othello's difference.

31. We may have seen the token before if, as Emilia describes, Desdemona always 'reserve[d] it evermore about her / To kiss and talk to' (3.3.297–8). The seminal essay on the handkerchief is Lynda Boose's, 'Othello's Handkerchief: "The Recognizance and Pledge of Love"', in Barthelemy, pp. 55–67.

32. Compare Boose, who argues that the history Othello assigns the handkerchief is 'removed from the objective action of the drama' and 'directs us back into the sphere of myth, custom, and symbolism, the precise level at which we are to identify the handkerchief' (p. 59).

33. Compare Wayne, who sees Othello here 'killing that self who is the other, the Turk or the Moor, as an act of Venetian patriotism' (p. 168).

34. John Bernard, 'Theatricality and Textuality: The Example of *Othello*', *New Literary History*, 26:4 (1995), 942. On the theatrical representation of this scene, see James R. Siemon, '"Nay, that's not next": *Othello*, V.ii. in Performance, 1760–1900', *Shakespeare Quarterly*, 37 (1986), 38–51.

35. Robert Weimann, *Shakespeare and the Popular Tradition in the Theater: Studies in the Social Dimension of Dramatic Form and Function*, ed. Robert Schwartz (Baltimore: Johns Hopkins University Press, 1978), especially pp. 73–85.

36. Compare Weimann, who sees Hamlet as a transitional figure, in which the two traditions collapse.

37. 'Breaking the Illusion of Being: Shakespeare and the Performance of Self', *Theatre Journal*, 24 (1994), 171–86.

38. Compare Mark Breitenberg, *Anxious Masculinity in Early Modern England* (Cambridge: Cambridge University Press, 1996), pp. 175–201, who reads Iago as a character 'not without motive but rather as articulating and activating the cultural anxieties that produce jealousy

as a condition of romantic love, indeed, of male subjectivity itself' (p. 176).

39. Virginia Vaughan, *Othello*, pp. 101, 103. The label 'villain play' comes from Robert D. Hume, *The Development of Drama in the Late Seventeenth Century* (Oxford: Clarendon Press, 1976), cited in Vaughan.

40. Vaughan, *Othello*, p. 111.

41. Compare Paul Yachnin's treatment of multiple theatrical and critical interpretations of Desdemona, in *Stage-wrights: Shakespeare, Jonson, Middleton, and the Making of Theatrical Value* (Philadelphia: University of Pennsylvania Press, 1997), especially pp. 25–35. For an excellent example of the contextualization of competing texts, see also Leah S. Marcus, 'Textual Indeterminacy and Ideological Difference: The Case of *Doctor Faustus*', *Renaissance Drama*, 20 (1989), 1–29. See also Steven Urkowitz, *Shakespeare's Revisions of 'King Lear'* (Princeton: Princeton University Press, 1980), and Marion Trousdale, 'A Trip Through the Divided Kingdoms', *Shakespeare Quarterly*, 37 (1986), 218–23.

42. On Othello as a register of anxiety, see, for example, Breitenberg, who reads Othello 'as the everyman of male sexual anxiety' (p. 176), and also Greenblatt, *Renaissance Self-Fashioning*, and Newman.

43. For a provocative reading of *Hamlet* and the issue of self-discovery, see Neill, *Issues of Death: Mortality and Identity in English Renaissance Tragedy* (Oxford: Oxford University Press, 1997).

7

Othello's Identity, Postcolonial Theory and Contemporary African Rewritings of *Othello*

JYOTSNA SINGH

...it would be something monstrous to conceive this beautiful Venetian girl falling in love with a veritable Negro.

(S. T. Coleridge)

[there is] something extremely revolting in the courtship and wedded caresses of Othello and Desdemona.

(Charles Lamb)[1]

I accept!

And my special geography too; the world map made for my own use, not tinted with the arbitrary colors of scholars, but with the geometry of my spilled blood, I accept both the determination of my biology, not a prisoner to a facial angle, to a type of hair, to a well-flattened nose, to a clearly Melanin coloring, and negritude... but measured by the compass of suffering and the Negro every day more base, more cowardly, more sterile, less profound, more spilled out of himself, more separated from himself, more wily with himself, less immediate to himself, I accept, I accept it all.... And there are those who will never get over not being made in the likeness of God but of the devil, those who believe that being a nigger is like being a second-class clerk ... those who say to Europe: 'You see I *can* bow and scrape, like you I pay my respects, in short, I am no different from you; pay no attention to my black skin: the sun did it.'

(Aimé Césaire)[2]

At the end of Shakespeare's *Othello*, after the Moor murders Desdemona and recognizes his tragic error, he is concerned about how he will be remembered in Venice – and by implication, in history: 'When you shall these unlucky deeds relate, / Speak of me as I am. Nothing extenuate, / Nor set down aught in malice'.[3] A few moments later, Othello's firm claim to an identity is undermined, when he identifies with the 'malignant and turbanned Turk', while '[dying] upon a kiss' as Shakespeare's tragic hero. Does the play's conclusion offer a clear, 'moral' resolution to the tragedy, as critics have often suggested?[4] I would suggest that it simply lets the murderous deed 'be hid', blocking off any further consideration of the social and psychic divisions which Othello experiences through the play, and which remain with him till the end, when he straddles contradictory roles – as 'both infidel and defender of the faith'.[5] Thus we cannot really 'Speak of [Othello as he is]', for his 'otherness' as a black man cannot be contained within the dominant, Western fantasy of a singular, unified identity.

From the opening scenes of the play, we quickly note how Othello experiences his identity in contradictory terms set by the Venetians. His belief in his own integrity ('My parts, my title, and my perfect soul / Shall manifest me rightly' [1.2.30–1]) is predicated on the fact of his service to Venice: 'My services which I have done the Signiory / Shall out-tongue his [Brabantio's] complaints' (1.2.18–19). However, while the Venetians honour him for his military skills, they do not question the racist European ideology whereby Othello is variously marked as an 'old black ram', 'a barbary horse', and 'a thing...to fear, and not to delight'. So when the Duke of Venice defends Othello to Brabantio, he simply perpetuates the negative connotations of the word 'black': 'Your son-in-law is far more fair than black' (1.3.285). And it is also questionable whether Desdemona knows Othello any better when she declares that she sees his 'visage in his mind' and binds herself to him for 'his honors and his valiant parts' (1.3.249–50). Desdemona's love for Othello comes to life in the stories he tells about his past. And who is Othello in these stories of slavery and adventure? He is simply a 'character' in an imaginary landscape which viewers, then and now, recognize as a semifictional creation of colonialist travel narratives – from antiquity through the nineteenth century. These are accounts of 'being taken by the insolent foe / And sold to slavery...[and of] anters vast and deserts idle, / Rough quarries, rocks, and hills whose heads touch / heaven, ...And of Cannibals that each other eat, / The Anthropophagi, and men whose heads / Grew beneath their shoulders' (1.3.136–44). Thus, as some critics have suggested, Othello can gain access to his own origins only 'through the ascriptions of European colonial discourses'.[6] And these discourses do not so much reveal Othello's origins as they ideologically produce his 'identity' as a black man within a configuration of familiar signifiers: slaves, 'Cannibals' and 'Anthropophagi'. When Desdemona responds to these stories with 'tears' and 'pity' for 'the dangers [he] had passed' (1.3.166), she also, at least initially, loves Othello as a fictional character of these exotic narratives.

Generations of Western critics largely ignored these ideological underpinnings of Othello's identity and focused instead on the Moor's character in terms of psychological realism. However, in doing so, as the literary history of the play testifies, they had difficulty in reconciling Othello's role as a tragic hero with his blackness. Commentaries ranging from Coleridge's assertion that Othello was not intended to be black to A. C. Bradley's acknowledgement of the 'aversion of our blood' to the sight of a black Othello ironically, and perhaps unwittingly, echo some of the Venetian voices in Shakespeare's play.[7] Like Brabantio and Iago, critics such as Charles Lamb, for instance, activate stereotypes of the Moor's 'bestiality' *prior* to the murderous deed.[8] They rarely question Brabantio's view of Othello as a 'civilized' Christian citizen in so far as he is the pliant servant of the Venetian State, though as Desdemona's husband he cannot escape the racist stereotypes pervasive in the culture. Overall, the Western literary tradition, until recently, has inevitably judged Othello as heroic only in terms of qualities that are considered Western, Venetian, Christian and 'civilized'.

Today, in the postmodern, Anglo-American academy, most of us discount this earlier critical tradition as being implicitly racist and outmoded at best. Yet, because ideological divisions between the 'civilized' West and 'backward and uncivilized' non-Europeans continue to shape the popular imagination of the West, the old stereotypes sometimes reappear in contemporary discourses about the play. For instance, when undergraduates read the Introduction to the Signet Classic edition of *Othello*, they are introduced to the figure of the Moor as a stereotypical 'character' within a 'symbolic map' which naturalizes a division between the Western 'civilized' world and the 'barbarian' non-Christians:

> Here then are the two major reference points on the map of the world
> of *Othello*: out at the far edge are the Turks, barbarism, disorder, and

> amoral destructive powers; closer and more familiar is Venice, the
> City, order, law, reason.... [in Cyprus] passions are more explosive
> and closer to the surface than in Venice, and here, instead of the
> ancient order... of the City, there is only one man to control vio-
> lence and defend civilization – the Moor Othello, himself of savage
> origins and a converted Christian.[9]

While such a discourse is certainly not in the forefront of contemporary critical practices, and in this instance takes the form of an
obligatory 'innocuous' Introduction, it nonetheless reinforces essentialist categories of difference between races that already exist in the
minds of some in our society. It does so by reinscribing the map of a
'symbolic geography' which continues to perpetuate racial divisions
within today's postcolonial world. Before further examining the
implications of these 'symbolic' divisions, let us first turn to the
political approaches to Shakespeare's *Othello* which, with the hind-
sight of history, have attempted revisionist readings that reveal the
ideological underpinning of racist and sexist discourses of the play –
and of its subsequent reproductions in the West.[10] For instance,
Karen Newman, in an influential essay, shows us the relation
between the play's racist discourses and the early phases of Western
colonialism, examining the ways in which the play 'stands in a contestatory relation to the hegemonic ideologies of race and class in
early modern England'.[11] She reads *Othello* in terms of an identification between black male sexuality and [white] femininity/female
desire, both of which are perceived as a 'monstrous' threat to the
'white male hegemony' in the play – a threat that is expressed in the
horror of miscegenation. Thus, Newman states:

> I want to argue... that femininity is not opposed to blackness and
> monstrosity, as white is to black, but identified with the monstrous, an
> identification that makes miscegenation doubly fearful. The play is
> structured around a cultural aporia, miscegenation.[12]

While the critic usefully points to certain parallels in the Renaissance
attitudes towards racial and sexual difference, her conceptual scheme
elides the condition of black masculinity with that of white femininity. Historically, we know that the taboo of miscegenation was not
so much based on the fear of the femininity of white women as it was
on the potential phallic threat of black men, who, incidentally, bore
the brunt of the punishment for violating this taboo.[13] Newman's
formulation suggests a seamless conflation of the different forms of

prejudice when she conclusively defines her perspective:

> [it] seeks to displace conventional interpretations by exposing the extraordinary fascination with and fear of racial and sexual difference which characterizes Elizabethan and Jacobean culture. Desdemona and Othello, woman and black man, are represented by discourses about femininity and blackness which managed and produced difference in early modern England.[14]

This neat elision – of categories like 'woman' and 'black man', 'femininity' and 'blackness' – obscures the *specific* effects of stereotyping in the play, whereby Othello self-destructively internalizes the prevailing racism, while Desdemona does not enact or internalize the stereotypes of women's sexual 'monstrosity'. In fact, to the end, she remains an idealized, virtuous woman – keeping alive the image of a besieged, white femininity so crucial to the production of the black man as a 'savage'.

Overall, it seems, Newman's argument suggests a shared victimization of blacks and women, thus conflating the particular histories of white women's sexual oppression with the enslavement of black men. The scene of a 'barbaric' black man evoked by the play's conclusion not only haunted the Western imagination in the Renaissance, but remains an integral part of postcolonial history; and the sexism suffered by European women does not necessarily or inevitably configure in the same history. Thus, while Newman's subtle, deconstructive reading of *Othello* in the context of ideological struggle offers useful insights into the relation between race and gender codes of the time, it also reveals a tendency in contemporary, Western feminist engagements with race which, in trying to chart the complexities of the relation between race and gender oppressions, implicitly *collapse* the categories of difference by assuming a common history of marginalization. Non-European or Third World readers, as we will see, do not reveal a similar investment in discursively eliding the different forms of victimization – of white women and blacks, for instance – because they have been participants in a long history of violent racial divisions that produced complex, and often confusing, sexual politics. African responses to Shakespeare's *Othello* during twentieth-century decolonization have radically resisted the image of Othello as a 'barbarian', even while the generic conventions of tragedy, as well as the 'civilizing' impulses of Western critics, have simply vindicated Othello as a tragic hero and 'converted Christian' who temporarily succumbs to his 'savage origins'.[15] Thus, not surprisingly, a number of African readings and revisions of the play have attempted to alter the European ideological and cultural codes that have discursively and materially produced the black man as a violent 'other' while marking the white woman as his innocent, and often idealized, victim. From their perspective, the end of Shakespeare's play *cannot foresee* the violence and conflict of colonial history, and even in his dying moments, Othello perpetuates the dichotomy between 'civilized' Venetians and 'barbaric' non-Europeans: for instance, he chastises himself as a 'base Judean' who 'threw a pearl away', and in stabbing himself ('I took the circumcised dog by the throat') he implicitly identifies with the 'malignant and turbanned Turk'. However, finally, he dies as a tragic hero within the 'moral' resolution of the play, whereby the violence is displaced upon the demonized, 'malignant' Turk, while Lodovico quickly hides the sin of murder that is also the sin of miscegenation on the marriage bed: 'The object poisons sight; / Let it be hid' (5.2.360–1).[16]

Europeans can turn their eyes away from this spectacle of violence – and from the 'poisons' of racism in the play – through a disidentification with the black man, but for African viewers and readers, the deed cannot 'be hid', as its image has proliferated through the centuries, making it a site for the production of troubled and contradictory colonial/postcolonial identities. Not surprisingly, then, the 'new' literatures of Africa and the West Indies often have as their theme the divided subjectivity of the black man, aptly defined by Frantz Fanon as the 'Black Skin, White Masks' syndrome.[17] Thus, while Alvin Kernan displaces the tensions of Othello's split identity – as both 'the infidel and the defender of the faith' – onto a benign landscape of a 'morality play, offering an allegorical journey between heaven and hell', African revisions historicize Othello's wrenching psychic conflicts within the violence of colonial/postcolonial history.[18] And when they read the play in the context of this revisionist history, they do not view the black man as a homogeneous, coherent subject, the universal 'victim', but rather attempt to map the shifting boundaries of colonial identity – seemingly overdetermined by political forces and yet never statically held in place. One important effect of this historicization has been to *disarticulate* the connections between the victimization of black men and white women in ways that reveal the complexities of gender struggle within the patriarchy of European imperialism. There is, of course, a familiar tradition in Western scientific and social discourse of using analogies between females and people of 'inferior' races and groups.[19] But these discursive analogies do not always conform to the material conditions within which different groups and races exist and which create different histories.

When Shakespeare's *Othello* – like other Western, canonical works – is read as a part of the 'civilizing mission' of colonial history, then it tells a story of the empire's African subjects which is generally missing in critical accounts of the play. It is ironic that a work like *Othello* should have been part of a project by which English literary works were to aid in the manufacture of a native elite class, who would then be a 'conduit of Western thought and ideas'. Cultural values, as the colonists perceived them, moved downwards from a position of power.[20] A number of postcolonial studies persuasively show how the British colonial administrators found an ally in English literature to support them in maintaining control over the natives under the guise of a liberal education. This was achieved by representing Western literary knowledge as universal, transhistorical and rational and by disguising its hegemonic impulses as a humanizing activity that created a class of persons non-European 'in blood and color, but English in tastes, in opinion, in morals and intellect'.[21]

By all accounts, the success of the empire depended on the production of the 'mimic man' who was 'whitewashed' by Western culture, and yet excluded from its full entitlements.[22] Postcolonial theorists like Frantz Fanon, and more recently Homi Bhabha, have identified 'mimicry' as a crucial aspect of relations between the Europeans and non-Europeans in a colonial/postcolonial situation. For the black man, Fanon argues, pressures to imitate whites produce a pathological self-alienation: 'He becomes whiter as he renounces his blackness, his jungle'.[23] Bhabha theorizes the effects of mimicry to point to the ambivalences of colonial authority as it constructs the 'other', whereby the colonial subject both resembles and differs from the master, 'not quite/not white'.[24] Those Africans or Indians who mediated between the imperial authorities and the native subjects were in certain ways to become 'English', often Christianized, and yet, according to Bhabha, the creation of these mock Englishmen was also troubling because 'mimicry is at once a resemblance and a menace'.[25] Mimicry thus becomes a condition of the native's divided subjectivity and self-alienation as well as a means of resistance. It is on the nexus of this split between identity and difference that Africans have struggled to negotiate their identities through colonial/postcolonial history. The complex ironies of this dilemma are perhaps most vividly evoked by Aimé Césaire when his 'Negro' defiantly 'accepts' being 'separated from himself' and yet parodies his own mimicry of Europeans: 'You see I can bow and scrape, like you I pay my respects, in short, I am no different from you: pay no attention to my black skin, the sun did it'.[26]

In this context, when Africans see themselves represented in the figure of Shakespeare's Othello – and in numerous Western interpretations of his character – they quite understandably resist the dichotomy of 'civilization' and 'barbarism' in terms of which Othello is judged. Recognizing that even in sympathetic readings, such essentialist categories demonize the black races and occlude the material conditions of their struggle, African writers have sought to historicize the production of Othello's divided subjectivity as a 'mimic man'. In Murray Carlin's revision of *Othello, Not now, sweet Desdemona*, the playwright reminds us that Shakespeare's play as it exists today cannot escape the burden of history: 'This play is not a critical essay on Shakespeare. ... my play ... is about the race conflict in the twentieth century'.[27] This race conflict is articulated by a black actor playing Othello who rejects the image of Shakespeare's hero, 'civilized' and Christianized by the Europeans. In the plot of the play, two actors, who are also lovers offstage, are rehearsing for a pro- duction of Shakespeare's *Othello* in London. The male lead, known to us as 'Othello', is a black from Trinidad and the woman, known as 'Desdemona', is a white, South African heiress. The central ques- tion raised by both the playwright and his protagonist is 'Why is Othello a black man?' This ironically refers to the frequent denial of Othello's real race in Western performance history when white actors played the role and usually not as 'a Negro [but] done up – in a romantic, hawk-nosed sort of way, very reassuring to white audi- ences'.[28] Questioning the cultural validity of this practice, Carlin's black actor wants to disrupt its signification when he suggests to 'Desdemona': 'Suppose I play Othello in white makeup? ... white actors have always played Othello in blackface. Why shouldn't a black actor play him in whiteface?' (p. 15). Mimicry, in this formulation, clearly scrambles and complicates colonial notions of difference where subjects were considered mere imitations of the rulers.

In many instances, Carlin's actor from Trinidad recognizes his own colonized persona as he does Othello's: 'I was born in the English language. ... I was born in the language that William Shakespeare is talking' (p. 31). Because of this awareness he resists an easy identity with Shakespeare's protagonist, who, in his eyes, is also represented as a European creation, 'a black liberal' (p. 44). The female lead, 'Desdemona', however, denies the impact of colonial history and reads the play as a 'universal' story of love and jealousy: 'Othello is a jealous man. ... She is a faithful, and loving innocent. And he's jealous. And there's your play' (p. 28). Her lover, in contrast, seems self-righteously preoccupied with the Africans' historical struggle for identity. As a result he attempts to open the play to colonial history, and ironically does so by ascribing a transcendent vision to the bard:

> When the play was written the Age of Imperialism had already begun. ... And Shakespeare ... understood and foresaw all the problems of that Age. It is the first play about color that was ever written. ... Here stands Othello, the negro, the black man   the only black man among hundreds of white people.
>
> (pp. 32–3)

Not only does Carlin's 'Othello' articulate the alienation experienced by blacks through history, but he also attempts to revise the discursive configuration in which the black man is invariably cast as a sexual predator on innocent, white women. Challenging Shakespeare's image of a pure and devoted heroine, Carlin's 'Othello' is obsessively preoccupied with Desdemona's power over the Moor. Repressing any empathy for her as a woman, he forces his co-star to confront Desdemona's dominant position within colonialist ideology:

> Desdemona is the first of the White Liberals. Yes she is a real white liberal. She wants power, through love – power, yes. They tell themselves they are on the side of the black man – they are fighting for him against the oppressors – but what they really want is to tell him what to do. That's your Desdemona. Othello is her personal black man. Hers because he is black – he's a slave. He must do what she says – and she won't leave him alone until he does.
>
> (pp. 37–8)

Carlin portrays his West Indian actor as a self-pitying neurotic, full of contradictions. He refuses to mimic the 'White Liberals', and wants to transmute Shakespeare's Othello into 'a passionate negro. All full of Bitterness and Suffering' (p. 44). Yet, with some irony, the audience can also recognize his claims to the 'authentic' 'negro' identity of Othello simply as another pose of self-aggrandizement before

his co-star. According to Fanon's theory of race and psychology in
Black Skin, White Masks, the actor's attraction and hostility for
the white woman is typical of the psychic divisions experienced by
black men during colonial rule in places such as Fanon's native
Martinique. According to Fanon, a 'Negro's' desire for a white
woman is 'a wish to be white. A Lust for revenge'.[29] Thus, his sexism thrives on the fantasy of the European female's power over black
men and, as Fanon suggests, he 'enjoy[s] the satisfaction of being the
master of a European woman...as a certain tang of proud revenge
enters into it'.[30] Clearly, then, gender struggle within European
imperialism reveals a more complicated and often contradictory
relation between discourses of race and gender than the standard
feminist position allows in its frequent insistence upon the shared
experiences of women and marginalized ethnic groups.[31]

Such complexities in the interplay of racial and sexual politics are
more vividly and wrenchingly brought to life in another non-
Western response to Shakespeare's *Othello*, the Sudanese author
Tayib Salih's novel, *Season of Migration to the North* (1969). This
work retells the story of a North African Othello, named Mustapha
Sa'eed, tracing his journey from his poor and obscure origins in a village outside Khartoum to Cairo and then to London, where he wins
acclaim as a scholar and economist, and back again to the Sudan
where he lives as a humble farmer and a family man on the banks of
the Nile. While in London, Mustapha spends seven years in prison
for murdering his English wife, Jean Morris. Like Shakespeare's
Othello and Carlin's West Indian actor, Salih's enigmatic hero is
also caught up within the pressures of mimicry and self-alienation
in a colonial/postcolonial society. Repeatedly, through the narrative,
Mustapha Sa'eed self-consciously mimics Shakespeare's Moor
though often through ambivalence and denial. For instance, before
he meets Jean Morris, he seduces a number of European women
by self-consciously enacting the sentimentalized stereotypes of
Orientalism, often with starkly ironic, and sometimes parodic,
results:

> As we drank tea, she [Isabella Seymour] asked me about my home.
> I related to her fabricated stories about deserts and golden sands
> and jungles where non-existent animals called to one another. I told
> her the streets of my country teemed with crocodiles and lions and
> that during siesta time, crocodiles crawled through it. Half-credulous,
> half-disbelieving, she listened to me, laughing and closing her eyes.
> Sometimes she would hear me out in silence, a Christian sympathy in

her eyes. There came a moment when I felt I had been transformed into a naked, primitive creature, a spear in one hand and arrows in the other, hunting elephants and lions in the jungles. Curiosity had changed to gaiety, and gaiety to sympathy.... when I stir the pool in its depths the sympathy will be transformed into a desire upon whose taut strings I shall play as I wish.[32]

According to Barbara Harlow,

the fantasies in which these women indulge, which Mustapha caters to consciously and provocatively, are so hackneyed and over-used as to be not only crude but trite... commonplaces of a romantic convention infatuated [with]... images conjured by the *Thousand and One Nights*.[33]

Such images of sensuality and violence are not unlike those with which Othello wins Desdemona, over the objections of her father, in Shakespeare's play. 'My mother', Sheila Greenwood tells Mustapha, 'would go mad and my father would kill me if they knew I was in love with a black man', and then declares, 'how marvellous your black color is... the color of magic and mystery and obscenity' (p. 139). And Ann Hammond sees in his eyes 'the shimmer of mirages in hot deserts, ... in [his voice] she hears the screams of ferocious beasts in the jungles' (p. 145). The analogy with Shakespeare's protagonist is reinforced when Isabella Seymour asks him, 'What race are you?' and Mustapha Sa'eed replies, 'I am like Othello – Arab-African'. In order to live the Western fantasy of Othello with a literal vengeance, Mustapha Sa'eed creates in his room in London a 'den of lethal lies':

[with] the sandalwood and incense; the ostrich feathers and ivory and ebony figurines, the paintings and drawings of forests of palm trees along the shores of the Nile, boats with sails like doves' wings, suns setting over the mountains of the Red Sea, camel caravans wending their way along sand dunes....

The stereotypical setting of the room, seemingly a self-parody, is in effect a site of contamination, as the protagonist tells us: 'My bedroom was a well-spring of sorrow, the germ of a fatal disease. The infection had stricken these women a thousand years ago, but I had stirred up the latent depths... and had killed' (p. 34). It is not incidental that images of disease and violence permeate these exotic fabrications that Mustapha Sa'eed enacts and encourages. In these

Tayib Salih historicizes the cultural fantasies of the early travel narratives as they got transformed into the sentimental Orientalist myth by the nineteenth century. To some, this exoticism may seem benign, but at the time, with its heady mixture of intoxication and condemnation, it became a justification for continuing colonial domination, an excuse to 'civilize' and rule over the Orientals.[34] And the European women in *Season of Migration to the North* are also, like Sa'eed himself, both the instigators and victims of this myth, replicating the conflicts of East and West. Thus, in contrast to Shakespeare, and like Fanon, Salih shows that sexual relations within a colonial struggle rarely produce idealized Desdemonas. If Mustapha Sa'eed, as a colonizer of European women, denigrates their identities as desiring subjects, they in turn desire him only in the context of racist fantasies. Thus, they cast an ironic light on Desdemona's 'pity' and 'tears' for Othello. In the case of Jean Morris, his wife, Salih further complicates the issue of gender struggle. Her fantasies of desire turn pathological as she takes a sadomasochistic pleasure in playing both predator and prey, finally and inexplicably begging her husband to kill her. Repeatedly, Salih manipulates and inverts the relations between colonizer and colonized, as a particular form of 'revenge' that also shows, as Fanon has shown in *Black Skin, White Masks*, how political and racial power struggles produce psychic and sexual dislocations in gender relations.

Finally and inexorably, Tayib Salih makes Mustapha Sa'eed relive Othello's violent deed. When he kills his English wife, just as when he seduces the Englishwomen, he is aware of re-enacting Othello's life. Like Othello, he comes to Europe carried on the tide of colonial history and takes on an alien persona, but retrospectively he defines his cultural transformation as a European disease and repudiates not only his own resemblance to Othello, but also the Moor's very identity:

> They [the Europeans] imported to us the germ of the greatest...
> violence ... the germ of a deadly disease that struck them more than a
> thousand years ago. Yes my dears, I came as an invader into your very
> homes: a drop of poison which you have injected into the veins of
> history. 'I am no Othello. Othello was a lie'.

> (p. 95)

Such contradictions in the novel clearly make visible the complex production of a divided subjectivity in conditions in which it becomes impossible to 'speak' of Othello as he is. Unlike Shakespeare's

Othello, Mustapha Sa'eed is conscious of the way in which he is being defined by the West and he resists and manipulates the subject positions assigned to him within colonialist ideology. With some irony, Salih shows his protagonist willingly embracing the identity of a predator given to him by the British who initially 'civilized' him. One of his professors at Oxford, who chooses to defend him at the trial, had earlier declared: 'You Mr Sa'eed, are the best example of the fact that our civilizing mission in Africa is of no avail. After all the efforts ... to educate you, it's as if you'd come out of the jungle for the first time' (p. 94). To such assumptions, of which Sa'eed is keenly aware, his response is simply, 'I am the intruder. ... Yes my dear sirs, I came as an invader into your very homes' (pp. 94–5). While questioning Othello's identity as a 'civilized' servant of the Europeans, Mustapha Sa'eed nonetheless draws an analogy between his sexual colonization of European women and the British takeover of the Sudan, especially when he identifies with Lord Kitchener:

> When Mahmud Wad Ahmed was brought in shackles before Kitchener [in the Sudan], the intruder said to him, 'Why have you come to my country to lay waste and plunder?' It was the intruder who said this to the person whose land it was, and the owner of the land bowed his head and said nothing. So let it be with me.
>
> (p. 94)

Mustapha Sa'eed wants to rewrite the script of the colonial takeover of the Sudan. The period of the late nineteenth century into which he is born had already witnessed the consolidation of imperial power in North Africa. Thus, by playing the part of Lord Kitchener and others as an invader to England and a predator of English women, Mustapha Sa'eed feels he is reversing, in a way, 'the rattle of swords in Carthage and the clatter of the hooves of Allenby's horses desecrating the ground of Jerusalem' (pp. 94–5).

As a 'mimic man', and a violent, pathological reincarnation of Shakespeare's Othello, Mustapha Sa'eed is truly dangerous, both to himself and to his masters. If Othello was a man who 'loved not wisely, but too well', and who temporarily allowed his baser, 'savage' passions to overwhelm him, Salih's imitation of Shakespeare's hero incarnates a mind that never allows his feelings to overcome him – the 'civilized' man of reason, his mind is 'like a sharp knife, cutting with cold effectiveness'.[35] Chameleon-like, he emulates and mimics his rulers, constantly displacing the binary relations of the colonizer and colonized, yet unable entirely to cast off his European identity even when he returns to the village on the Nile. Here, after Mustapha's disappearance, the narrator finds in a locked room a replica of an English drawing room, lined with books found in many traditional European libraries. Like his garish room in London, this setting also seems artificial – 'a lie' that must remain hidden.

As a novel, a generic form imported by the Arabs from the West, *Season of Migration to the North* participates in what, by Arabic literary classification, is called a *mu aradeh*, literally 'opposition', 'contradiction', but meaning a formula whereby one person will write a poem, and another will retaliate along the same lines, but reversing the meaning'.[36] The 'symbolic geography' that Tayib Salih maps in this work points to complex interconnections between categories of difference that in Shakespeare's play, and in the old critical tradition, are represented as a simple division between the 'malignant' Turk and the Christian Moor as the tragedy heads towards its conventional, moral, 'resolution'. Salih reminds us that Africans, Turks, Moors, among others, recognize Shakespeare's Othello as a 'character' in a familiar, Orientalist landscape, both erotic and violent, a composite fantasy of the Europeans' 'colonial harem'.[37] As readers and viewers, they are drawn into both an identification with and disavowal of the Moor: living as 'mimic men', they recognize that Othello's claims to *any* identity – either as a 'savage' or as a Christian and a tragic hero – are tenuous and derivative. Clearly then, both *Season of Migration to the North* and *Not now, sweet Desdemona* remap the world of Shakespeare's *Othello*. Attempting to wrest it away from colonialist ideologies, they show how Shakespeare's play and its revisions are all inextricably tied to histories of racial conflict in the 'new world' of the Renaissance, which is the 'third world' of our postcolonial era.

Furthermore, it would be fair to suggest that these non-European, revisionist readings approximate what cultural theorists have called a counterdisciplinary practice whereby texts are read as multivocal sites of conflict and analysed at the level of the *specific* historical struggles by which they are shaped.[38] Written in the 1960s, and in the wake of the African independence movements, these works clearly embody a call for cultural decolonization. However, their engagement with their own history is also complex, and often troubling, as they focus on the psychic self-divisions experienced by colonial subjects. Not surprisingly, then, the 'characters' of Othello and Desdemona as incarnated by Carlin and Salih are caught up in a world of contradictory and complicated racial and sexual politics.

And in this world, discourses of resistance to racism and sexism often work in *opposition* rather than in *collaboration* with one another: for instance, it is clear that these African readings of 'race' in *Othello* and in colonial history deny white femininity its sanctified cultural space (there can be no virtuous and pure Desdemona), while disrupting the pervasive notion among feminists and other political critics in the West that victims of race and gender oppression are bound by a common struggle. Implicitly, at least, in their discursive configuration, Desdemona, like Miranda, colludes in creating the 'otherness' of the black man.

To conclude, both *Not now, sweet Desdemona* and *Season of Migration to the North* question whether Shakespeare's *Othello* can be read and appreciated (as conservatives would insist) without the interventions of its non-European revisions. Of course, in terms of conventional reading practices, *Othello* remains an autonomous text, which is guaranteed its canonical status in the West. However, I would argue that it is crucial to expose the ideologies that secure the pleasure and 'understanding' of most European audiences – an understanding that *separates* the play from our colonial legacy of continuing racial conflicts. Thus, to understand *Othello*'s place in the postcolonial moment is to open the play to the competing ideologies of multiple interpretations, some of which will enable Othello's descendants to claim their own histories and Desdemona's descendants to understand their complicity in the production of the 'exotic' Moor.

From *Women, 'Race', and Writing in the Early Modern Period*, ed. Margo Hendricks and Patricia Parker (London, 1994), pp. 287–99.

NOTES

[Singh's essay operates on two planes, as a reading of *Othello* and also as a reading of *Othello* criticism. It observes parallels, for example, between Desdemona, the 'first of the white liberals', and liberal criticism, such as feminist work that seems to 'collapse the categories of difference [gender and race] by assuming a common history of marginalization'. This is, Singh shows, a false equivalence. She also writes about the ways Shakespeare has been used as a 'civilizing' agent in non-Western cultures. One of the most strenuous ambitions of recent criticism, and especially that produced by cultural materialists, has been to counter old assumptions about Shakespeare's universality. To claim that Shakespeare is the poet of all humanity is, among other things, to attempt to naturalize European values and beliefs among non-European peoples. In the wake of decolonization, Singh therefore argues, there is a continued need for 'cultural decolonization'. One way to open the play to the 'competing ideologies of multiple interpretations' is to read it in tandem with works like those by Murray Carlin and Tayib Salih. This essay was originally printed in an important collection, *Women, 'Race', and Writing in the Early Modern Period*, edited by Margo Hendricks and Patricia Parker. Ed.]

My thanks to Don Wayne for his critique and comments.

1. Quotes from Lamb and Coleridge are cited by Sylvan Barnet, '*Othello* on Stage and Screen', reprinted in *Othello*, ed. Alvin Kernan (New York: Signet Classic, 1986), p. 273.

2. Aimé Césaire, *Selected Poetry*, trans. Clayton Eshleman and Annette Smith (Berkeley: University of California Press, 1983), pp. 77–9.

3. William Shakespeare, *Othello*, ed. Alvin Kernan (New York: Signet Classic, 1989), 5.2.338–9. All subsequent references will be from this edition of the text.

4. See Alvin Kernan, 'Introduction' to *Othello*, Signet Classic pp. xxiii–xxxv, for one such moral reading.

5. Ibid., p. xxxiii.

6. Karen Newman, ' "And wash the Ethiop white": Femininity and the Monstrous in *Othello*', in *Shakespeare Reproduced*, ed. Jean E. Howard and Marion O'Connor (London: Methuen, 1987), p. 150.

7. For a discussion of the play's critical history, see Michael Neill, 'Unproper Beds: Race, Adultery, and the Hideous in *Othello*', *Shakespeare Quarterly*, 41, 4 (Winter 1989), 391–2. Also see Newman, ' "And wash the Ethiop white" ', pp. 143–5.

8. Cited by Neill, 'Unproper Beds', p. 392.

9. Kernan, 'Introduction', pp. xxvi–xxvii.

10. Essays by Newman, ' "And wash the Ethiop white" ', and Neill, 'Unproper Beds', cited earlier, are representative of the recent interest in the reproduction of *Othello* within colonialist and racist ideologies. Also see Martin Orkin, 'Othello and the "Plain Face" of Racism', *Shakespeare Quarterly*, 38 (1987), 166–88, and Eldred Jones, *Othello's Countrymen: The African in English Renaissance Drama* (London: Oxford University Press, 1965). For a feminist analysis of Othello's self-divisions, see Dympna Callaghan's *Woman and Gender in Renaissance Drama* (Atlantic Highlands: Humanities Press, 1989).

11. Newman, p. 157.

12. Ibid., p. 145.

13. See Angela Davis, *Women, Race, and Class* (New York: Vintage Books, 1983), pp. 172–201, for her discussion of the myth of the black rapist and how it led to mass lynchings of black men in America after the Civil War. This myth has had many earlier incarnations throughout colonial history, whereby black men were cast as sexual predators. I am also grateful to Dympna Callaghan for her astute analysis of this subject in our frequent discussions.

14. Newman, ' "And wash the Ethiop white" ', p. 157.

15. Kernan, 'Introduction', p. xxvii.

16. For a perceptive discussion of the play's final scene, see Neill, 'Unproper Beds', pp. 411–12. I am also indebted to Michael Neill for his comments on my reading of *Othello*.

17. In *Black Skin, White Masks*, trans. Charles Markmann (New York: Grove Press, 1969), Frantz Fanon develops a detailed theory of the struggle for black identity within European colonialism – a struggle that is self-defeating because it is underpinned by a 'wish to be white' (p. 14). I use the term 'black man' throughout the chapter, not generically to refer to people, but specifically, to identify black men of all ethnic groups in African history.

18. See Kernan's formulation of *Othello* as a 'morality play, offering an allegorical journey' ('Introduction', pp. xxxiv–xxxv).

19. Nancy Leys Stepan's essay, 'Race and Gender: The Role of Analogy in Science', in *Anatomy of Racism*, ed. David Theo Goldberg (Minneapolis: University of Minnesota Press, 1990), pp. 38–57, elucidates on the discursive strategies of nineteenth-century scientists in which 'gender was found to be remarkably analogous to race, such that the scientist could use racial difference to explain gender difference and vice versa' (p. 39). Even though today we recognize the dangerous elisions between racism and sexism in such 'scientific' formulations, many political critics still seem to collapse the categories of race and gender, though often for progressive social goals.

20. A number of studies have noted that English literature played a role in ensuring the hegemony of the British empire. A representative work is Gauri Vishwanathan's essay, 'The Beginnings of English Literary Study in India', *Oxford Literary Review*, 9 (1987), 2–26. Also see my essay, 'Different Shakespeare: The Bard in Colonial/Postcolonial India', *Theatre Journal*, 41, 4 (December 1989), 445–58.

21. Quote from Thomas Babington Macaulay's 1835 *Minute on Colonial Education*, cited by Ania Loomba, *Gender, Race, Renaissance Drama* (Manchester: Manchester University Press, 1989), p. 31.

22. See Jean Paul Sartre's 'Preface' to Frantz Fanon's *The Wretched of the Earth* (New York: Grove Press, 1963), pp. 8–9, in which he discusses

Fanon's resistance to 'becoming European' and to the 'nauseating mimicry' of the colonized races. Fanon's resistance and critique of the ways in which the empire produced subservient, though Europeanized, subjects is a theme in many postcolonial works. V. S. Naipaul's famous title, *The Mimic Men*, captures the postcolonial dilemma that others like Homi Bhabha have theorized more fully.

23. Fanon, *Black Skin, White Masks*, p. 18.

24. Homi Bhabha, 'Of Mimicry and Man: The Ambivalence of Colonial Discourse', *October*, 28 (1984), 132.

25. Robert Young's analysis of Bhabha's theory in *White Mythologies: Writing History and the West* (London: Routledge, 1990), pp. 146–8, specifically draws on the essay 'Of Mimicry and Man: The Ambivalence of Colonial Discourse' to point to the complexities of mimicry.

26. Césaire, *Selected Poetry*, p. 79.

27. Murray Carlin, *Not now, sweet Desdemona* (Nairobi and Lusaka: Oxford University Press, 1969), pp. 2–5. All quotes will be taken from this edition of the text.

28. Ibid., p. 2.

29. Fanon, *Black Skin, White Masks*, p. 14.

30. Ibid., p. 69.

31. Western feminists have recently offered useful insights into the ways in which race, gender and class oppressions interact. In many instances, however, they tend to collapse these categories as a convenient discursive strategy that often makes their critique somewhat apolitical. For instance, Elizabeth Foxe-Genovese, in *Feminism Without Illusions: A Critique of Individualism* (Chapel Hill: University of North Carolina Press, 1991), cites W. E. B. Du Bois's theory of the feeling of 'twoness' among African-Americans and applies it to the experience of women. She preempts a critique of such a move by stating:

> It is no part of my intention to trivialize the particular meaning of Du Bois's words by equating female and African-American experience. But however different the problems and histories of women and African-Americans, the living of twoness applies to both.
>
> (p. 139)

This emphasis on shared experience, while well-intentioned, is ultimately a move to elide very *distinct* histories, even while the critic acknowledges the differences among them.

32. Tayib Salih, *Season of Migration to the North*, trans. Denys Johnson-Davies (Washington, DC: Three Continents Press, 1969), p. 38. All quotes will be taken from this edition of the text.

33. Barbara Harlow, 'Othello's Season of Migration', *Edebiyat: Journal of Comparative and Middle Eastern Literature*, 4 (1979), 166. This essay reads Salih's novel in the context of Arab encounters with colonialism and reinforces parts of my argument. I am grateful to Ruquayya Khan for recently bringing this piece to my attention.

34. By the nineteenth century, one 'idea' of the Orient (symbolically encompassing African and Arab cultures) that was passed off as 'knowledge' produced a sexual fantasy, reflected in works like *Madame Bovary* and Richard Burton's Introduction to his translation of *Thousand and One Nights*, and packed with 'Oriental clichés: harems, princesses, princes, slaves, veils, dancing girls'. See Edward Said, *Orientalism* (New York: Vintage Books, 1979), p. 190. Also see Harlow's account of such clichés in Burton and elsewhere, p. 166. The stereotypical images of non-Europeans from antiquity through Hakluyt's narratives of the early modern encounters with the 'New World' natives to Richard Burton's sentimentalized prurience are all largely a conglomeration of facts, exaggeration and pure fantasy. Therefore, similar images of 'cannibals', 'monsters' and 'harems' or of naked 'beasts' appear in haphazard combinations of 'facts' in texts ranging from Columbus's *Journals* to Conrad's *Heart of Darkness*.

35. I am indebted to Harlow's discussion of this quote from the novel, in 'Othello's Season of Migration', p. 166.

36. Ibid., p. 162.

37. See Malek Alloula, *Colonial Harem* (Minneapolis: University of Minnesota Press, 1987).

38. I am indebted to Patrick Brantlinger's analysis of cultural studies as a counterdisciplinary practice, especially as it has been articulated by Raymond Williams. See P. Brantlinger's *Crusoe's Footprints: Cultural Studies in Britain and America* (London: Routledge, 1990), p. 42.

8

Race-ing *Othello*: Re-Engendering White-Out

BARBARA HODGDON

On Friday, 17 June 1994, Shakespeare became a voice-over for a moment of American cultural history. Reporting that a suicidal O. J. Simpson lay in the back of his Ford Bronco holding a gun to his head, CBS television anchor Dan Rather glossed the flickering image of the vehicle, parked before Simpson's Brentwood home, by saying that he was reminded of *Othello*, in which a black man, suspecting his white wife of adultery, kills her and then himself. As though shopping for a good story, Rather had mined the literary archive to imagine an ending which, by courting the obsessive fictions that attach to Othello's colour, could mask the culture's racism in Shakespearean suicide and its attendant admission of guilt. What was later dubbed 'The Night of the White Bronco' did not of course replicate *Othello*'s ending, but in the days immediately following Simpson's arrest, charged with the murder of Nicole Brown Simpson and her friend Ronald Goldman, further evidence (in this instance, as in the play, a *media*-ted term) connecting these events to the critical, theatrical and cultural legacy of Shakespeare's play proliferated.

There was, for instance, the uncanny resemblance between Othello's final speech ('speak / Of one that loved not wisely but too well') and Simpson's 'suicide note' ('If we had problems it's because I loved her too much').[1] And, as though echoing the famous 'dirty still' from Laurence Olivier's 1964 *Othello*, in which Olivier's black make-up has smudged Maggie Smith's white cheek, *Time*'s 27 June cover framed a blacked-up police mug shot of Simpson with the headline banner, 'An American Tragedy'. Even the (patriarchal) state agreed. For after all, Simpson had done it some service, and they knew it. On 23 June, Richard Halverson, Chaplain of the US Senate, evoking II Samuel 1:25 ('How are the mighty fallen'), spoke of how 'our Nation has been traumatized by the fall of a great hero', to ask consolation to 'the unnumbered, who have been disillusioned by the fall of their idol', and to pray 'for a special dispensation of grace for this American hero, his loved ones and all who are hurting irreparably by this event'.[2] In this narrative, Simpson moves from 'great hero' to 'American hero' isolated in tragic splendour; never named, Nicole Brown Simpson and Ronald Goldman are simply dismissed as 'victims'.

Wrapping Simpson's heroic identity in classical ghosts that position him as the noble protagonist in a tale of love and betrayal relies on a time-honoured humanist reading that harnesses Shakespeare's text to a stable order of meaning which excludes the unruly issues of gender, class and race. Or seems to. Yet by omission and avoidance, such strategies silently subscribe to a racist discourse which *Time*'s cover image, as well as a range of Internet jokes, makes overt.[3] A particularly brutal one asked, 'Have you heard about O. J.'s new defense strategy?' and answered, 'He's going to say that he was just following his coach's game plan: cut to the left, cut to the right, and run like hell'.[4] Although absent from the joke, race matters here: the myth of the black man as an icon of (regulated) performative violence in American (sports) culture, coupled with a prevailing cultural misogyny, makes the joke a 'joke' – at least for a potential Iago. Marking the intersection of Simpson's identities as star athlete and defendant, the joke frames an emergent narrative of O. J. as criminal in terms of an established narrative of O. J. as sports hero – contradictory constructions that not only threaten to turn him, like Othello, into a split subject ('Please think of the real O. J. and not this lost person') but also seek to undo Simpson's efforts to white out his race ('I have worked all my life to get people to look at me like a man first, not a black man').[5]

To make his (de)construction as Othello complete, Simpson's history of wife-battering mobilized other cultural myths, yoking the (white supremacist) fear of miscegenation invoked by his marriage to an archetypal blonde beauty with a stereotype of animalistic black male sexuality – violent, monstrous, even deadly to the (forbidden) white woman. As jury selection proceeded, the 3 January *National Enquirer* printed a 'computer-enhanced' photograph of Nicole, purportedly taken by her sister and later seized by authorities, showing injuries she had sustained in a 1989 beating: a blackened eye, a split lip and the imprint of a hand on her neck. Framed in the American symbolic imaginary between *Time*'s darkened mug shot and the *Enquirer*'s equally doctored photograph, the case went to trial anchored by an iconography through which ideologies of race, gender, power, sexuality, pleasure and pain became a visible, even tangible body of evidence.

POSTCOLONIAL TERRITORIES: A RE-MEDIATION

This moment in American mass culture frames my viewing of two made-for-television *Othello*s, Janet Suzman's film of her 1987 production at Johannesburg's Market Theatre and Trevor Nunn's film of his 1989 production at Stratford's The Other Place.[6] Aside from Liz White's noncommercially released *Othello*, starring Yaphet Kotto,[7] the two were (until the December 1995 release of Oliver Parker's *Othello*, with Laurence Fishburne) the only filmed representations of the play featuring black actors in the title role – South African John Kani, winner of a 1975 Tony Award for his performance in Athol Fugard's *Sizwe Banzi Is Dead*, and Jamaican-born American Willard White, an operatic bass-baritone whose performance at Glyndebourne as Porgy in Nunn's staging of Gershwin's *Porgy and Bess* brought him wide acclaim. Both involve the return of cultural 'parents' to their origins: Suzman, an RSC associate and co-founder of Market Theatre, to her native South Africa despite an international cultural boycott in protest of apartheid ('Putting on *Othello* with John Kani', she remarked, 'is infinitely more important than stamping my foot and saying, "I won't set foot in the country" '); Nunn, the RSC's former artistic director, to follow a series of glitzy, big-money hits (*Cats, Starlight Express, Les Miserables, Aspects of Love*) with a small-scale *Othello* in Stratford's most intimate venue. Both are postcolonial representations in which mise-en-scène evokes particular colonialist histories, narratives and ideologies. Conceiving *Othello* as High Renaissance tragedy, Suzman dresses it in Jacobean silhouettes – a move designed to 'focus spectators' minds on the dreadful story' and to avoid 'imposed anachronisms that might hinder their self-recognition'. Asked why she had not updated the setting, she replied, 'Where do you suggest, post-revolutionary Pretoria?'[8] Deliberately calling attention to the absence of such a utopian social (or theatrical) space, Suzman appropriates *Othello* as a mirror in which South Africans might confront the racism of their prevailing social order. Nunn's strategy is decidedly less overt. Veiling his project in Shakespearean 'authenticity' and claiming to reproduce 'original' staging conditions similar to those of recorded performances at Court,[9] he chooses a milieu reminiscent of the US Civil War or of a nineteenth-century colonial outpost that might be anywhere in Britain's Empire – territories that spawned racist-orientalist discourses, among them slavery narratives, which not only mark the turn of the century but also resonate in early modern culture. In Nunn's postcolonial theatre, Empire becomes a displaced sign of the Elizabethan–Jacobean period, a site where contemporary Britons can both discern and misrecognize themselves.

Today, I experience a somewhat similar collapse of history, for Elizabeth I's correspondence with the Privy Council seeking to deport eighty-nine black people and the subsequent warrant issued on 18 July 1596 contrasting blacks ('those kinde of people') with her white subjects ('Christian people')[10] resembles immigration bans and deportation schemes currently under consideration in the United States – moves that recall the turn-of-the-century cult of Anglo-Saxon heritage[11] and reinvoke the idea of 'purifying' America through proposed legislation aimed at eroding recent initiatives, both within and outside the academy, affirming multiculturalism and racial diversity. At a moment when past traditions of hatred are being appropriated to support such new expediencies, to renegotiate *Othello*'s territory is to situate oneself at the intersection of overlapping, conflicting discourses, to remediate already mediated representations, including the Simpson trial, which haunts my looking. I am interested in how these two *Othello*s circulate metanarratives of race and gender and cultural tropes of assimilation and domestic violence. How, I want to ask, do such discursive frameworks monitor looking relations? And how do the discourses surrounding these representations work to secure spectators' pleasure and to keep *Othello*, and Othello, in place?

BLACKING UP

'Look, a Negro!'
(Frantz Fanon, 1952)

Othello represents a site through which the problem of the black body in the white imaginary becomes visible, gets worked through. Consider, first, a theatrical passing narrative. In his autobiography, Laurence Olivier speaks of transforming himself into Othello, 'creating the image which now looked back at me from the mirror':

> Black all over my body, Max Factor 2880, then a lighter brown, then Negro No. 2, a stronger brown. Brown on black to give a rich mahogany. Then the great trick: that glorious half-yard of chiffon with which I polished myself all over until I shone....The lips blue-berry, the tight curled wig, the white of the eyes, whiter than ever and the black, black sheen that covered my flesh and bones, glistening in the dressing-room lights. ...I am, I...I am Othello...but Olivier is in charge. The actor is in control. The actor breathes into the nos-trils of the character and the character comes to life. For this moment in my time, Othello is my character – he's mine. He belongs to no one else; he belongs to me.[12]

Fetishizing his blackened body, Olivier erases distinctions between self and other to take ownership of Othello, claiming the character ('he belongs to me') as though he were colonial property. Although he admits that 'throwing away the white man was difficult but fas-cinating', he imagines that he can 'feel black down to [his] soul' and 'look out from a black man's world',[13] as though mimicry might efface notions of difference and dissemble the complexity of power relations between black and white bodies into the satisfying whole-ness of an ultimate cultural impersonation.

Olivier's Othello confirms an absolute fidelity to white stereotypes of blackness and to the fantasies, cultural as well as theatrical, that such stereotypes engender. Layered onto the body, 'blackness' (like femininity) may be constructed – and viewed – as a performance, the theatrical equivalent of what Charles Lamb termed 'the beautiful compromise we make in reading'.[14] The 'real' black body, and the histories it carries, can be elided, displaced into and contained by theatricality, which embraces a long tradition of whites blacking up, primarily for comic effect, in minstrelsy.[15] Such impersonation prob-lematizes looking relations precisely because it deflects analysis by aligning racist ideology with theatrical pleasure.[16] Most importantly, a made-up Othello ensures that both blackness and whiteness remain separate, unsullied. Putting race matters succinctly, blacking up is whiting out.

Olivier's position of stardom in the Shakespearean theatrical (and cinematic) pantheon not only makes his Othello a structuring absence for both films (though in radically different ways) but operates as a kind of spectatorial counter-memory that any actor of the role, white or black, encounters. Suzman's film recalls his image at Othello's first appearance, where (as Olivier had done in 1964) Kani poses against a wall, brushing a red rose across his lips. By quoting Olivier's fetish-African as Kani's ghosted other, the film marks the difference between the painted-on identity of Othello's (colonial) theatrical history and the 'real thing', calling attention to the situatedness of an actor who, like Frantz Fanon's 'Negro', experiences first-hand what it means to be black in a pervasively negrophobic society where blackness, in the colonizer's perspective, is simultaneously a point of identity and a problem.[17] Like Othello in Venice, Kani is an outsider in his own land, an alien without citizenship – an irony underlined daily as he travelled from Soweto 'through ... road blocks, *terra incognita* to the rest of the cast'.[18] As Homi Bhabha writes of Fanon's split subject, 'Black skin, white masks is not ... a neat division; it is a doubling, dissembling image of being in at least two places at once which makes it impossible for the devalued ... to accept the colonizer's invitation to identity'.[19] Or even, in Kani's case, to play Othello. As he himself put it, 'There goes the native causing more trouble, and this time he has Shakespeare to do it for him.'[20]

Kani's Othello does not resemble the commanding figure imagined by critical discourse (his generalship, writes Suzman, is 'modeled on Alexander, Napoleon, Montgomery, rather than a tank')[21] and exemplified in theatrical culture by Paul Robeson and James Earl Jones. Keyed to follow his slim, light-skinned body, the camera captures (in long and mid-shots) its full range of movement within the frame, producing the illusion that he controls the space and is free within it. Costumed in a flowing white shirt which accentuates his colour, black military trousers, polished black over-the-knee boots, and a magnificent red floor-length cloak, he is an exquisitely elegant Titian-esque figure; a golden circlet, from which hangs a small case, surrounds his neck – a sign of national or tribal identity, of a mysterious otherness (what slavery was he sold into, and how redeemed from it?). But his gestures, as much as his colour and attire, distinguish him from the rest: in the Senate scene, for example, broad arm movements open his whole body to the gaze, marking his confidence, his exoticism and his vulnerability, especially in contrast to Richard Haddon Haines's stolidly built, exhibitionistic Iago, beside whom Kani's presence pales, registering a subdued, even 'feminine' passivity. Yet the dynamic between the two never suggests a homoerotic (or even homosocial) bond; instead, Suzman's film rather precisely reveals how such an interpretive strategy masks the implications of race and so evades what Ben Okri calls 'the terrors that are at the heart of the play'.[22] Produced a year after the repeal of the Immorality Act, which criminalized sexual encounters between blacks and whites[23] and subjected the black male gaze to state control, the film condenses these looking relations into Iago's surveillance. Haines's Iago sets out to destroy Othello and Desdemona 'with all the relish of a Eugene Terreblanche': a bluff loudmouth whose vulgar crotch- and nose-grabbing bespeaks his fear of and disgust with sexuality, he cannot touch Othello without afterwards wiping the taint of blackness from his hand. Even five years after Nelson Mandela walked free, his performance highlights the body politics of the apartheid state and invites spectators to resist his blatantly racist inscription of Othello.[24]

For black South African viewers, that invitation was enhanced by Kani's star presence, through which Othello's descendants might lay claim to their own histories.[25] And it is through Desdemona (Joanna Weinberg) that Othello's body becomes the object of the gaze for the pleasure – or displeasure – of the dominant (white) spectator. Although Iago may take *linguistic* control over that body, because the film insists that it is *Desdemona*'s trajectory of desire rather than Iago's that initiates the narrative (observed by Iago, she first appears as a shadowy figure leaving her father's house), it is primarily her look that keys a white woman spectator into Kani's exoticism and the sexual bond between them. The gaze of this blonde, dignified Botticelli beauty who is as much wooer as wooed not only fetishizes Othello but works to resituate Iago's racist looking relations. Yet if her forthright desire shatters the myth that black men need to force their attention on white women, it also suggests how white women collude in constructing the black man's exotic sexuality. Suzman's theatre production had confronted spectators with memories of a past history still threatening enough to make some white South Africans walk out at the first embrace between Desdemona and Othello, a gentle kiss in the Senate scene after Desdemona has been rejected by her father. In the film, the sexual attraction between the two does not remain just beyond representation until the close, where it becomes aligned with death, but is boldly – and repeatedly – staged. One effect is to reveal how sexual intimacy between black and white bodies drives Iago's fantasies and how private looking relations intrusively invade upon, and problematize, his racist representations.

That is most sharply articulated as Desdemona and Othello meet at Cyprus. When Othello is announced, Desdemona takes Cassio's sword and, standing at the bottom of the stairs as he descends to her, raises it high in salute, prompting his 'O, my fair warrior'. His line keys music, and the sequence glides into slow motion, alternating between Desdemona's point of view of Othello and his of her, an editing pattern that suggests their shared passion. Both music and slow motion not only function to romanticize their meeting – expressed in a full, sensual embrace – but to separate their seemingly ideal relationship from its perception by others, which is further marked off by a cut to Iago's 'O you are well tun'd now, / But I'll set down the pegs that make this music, / As honest as I am'. Because this sudden stylistic shift draws attention to their harmony, it is all the more startling when, midway through the temptation sequence (and again in the so-called whorehouse scene) Othello's 'barbaric' sexuality explodes.[26] Pulling Desdemona to him and thrusting his body against hers, he takes her breath away with a rough kiss and pulls down her dress to kiss her breasts, leaving her stunned at a seeming rupture in his identity which destabilizes her own. Although this moment may play into some viewers' desire to see an Othello dominated by passion who fulfills their expectations of 'wild' primitive blackness, it is important to remember that, in South Africa, black and white discourses differ markedly on precisely how such qualities are valued.[27] Yet if Suzman's film evokes such stereotypes and myths, it appropriates them not as denigrating narratives of cultural othering but, by trivializing and problematizing their racist content, turns them into positive modes of self-definition.

Significantly, it is not only through Desdemona that a white spectator has access to Othello's subjectivity, for the film positions Cassio both as his 'other' in loving Desdemona and as Desdemona's 'twin' in his devotion to and worship of Othello. Highlighting the similarities between these two blond 'curled darlings', Suzman stages a moment which, by embodying the possible liaison between them, constructs a screen for Iago's fantasies. After Othello's triumph, Cassio presents Desdemona with a bouquet of daffodils, and she kisses his cheek, but when Othello joins her, he quickly moves away. As the camera isolates Othello and Desdemona, it pans down their joined figures to Desdemona's hand: rapt with Othello, she drops the bouquet, and as Othello leads her off, he directs a low laugh and a salute to the watching Cassio, relegated to wishing himself in Othello's place as he stands guard over their love-making. Crossing to the discarded flowers, he picks them up as though to relish Desdemona's lingering touch; but once Iago emerges from the shadows, offering him an occasion to recuperate his rejected manhood, he drops the bouquet and stumbles off. Having baited his snare, Iago picks up a daffodil, smacks it against the wall, and the flower head falls off.[28] As this treatment of the daffodil suggests, Cassio's lovesickness gets displaced into Iago's destructive jealousy; for Cassio's part, his frank admiration for and loyalty to his commander is intensified when, after a gloating Iago rips off his badge of office, he echoes Othello's own gesture ('My life upon her faith') – a fist brought to the chest in a 'Roman' salute. By securely marking these two moments, Suzman's film positions the cashiered Cassio to anticipate the rejected Desdemona, pulling the two into a shared space of loyalty and desire, misread by Othello as double betrayal.

Just as Cassio's salute offers to efface the conflict between races, cultures and histories which *Othello* dramatizes, and which constitutes South Africans' lived experience, the film's final scene, where the intersection of race and sex are most fiercely contested, reinstates that conflict only to call it into question. Put simplistically, this scene articulates a demand for 'the negro' that Suzman's representation of the negro disrupts. Following the street quarrel (where Bianca as well as Roderigo is killed), a white scrim descends, and a brief blackout yields to brilliant white light as the camera pans across the bedsheets draping Desdemona's sleeping form, materializing her body as the alabaster monument of Othello's description. Backlit, Othello's magnified figure appears silhouetted on the scrim, making him into the featureless black devil of a colonial fantasy the film imposes only to deconstruct, framing it as a literal projection. Yet once he enters the chamber – nude to the waist, barefoot, and wearing black harem-like trousers – costume codes a return to 'native' manners, and his movements parody the primitive animalism so desired by the white imaginary. Turning murder into ritual sacrifice, Kani's Othello *performs* the 'other': at once a substitute for the stereotype and its shadow, he simultaneously evokes and deflects the narratives of black males' violence against women that accede to the colonizer's wildest dreams. After the murder – an embrace which Desdemona even seems to welcome – he kneels, yoga-style, on the bed, swaying back and forth in a histrionic lament that pulls him into the space of femininity Catherine Clement marks as characteristic of opera's heroes, who die like heroines: like them, he seems 'excluded, marked by some initial strangeness,...doomed to [his own] undoing'.[29] Immobilized by Emilia's revelations about the handkerchief, he is unable to stop Iago from killing her and, as the music which marked his reunion with Desdemona at Cyprus plays under her reaffirmations of her mistress' chastity and devotion, he watches transfixed as she inches towards the bed to take Desdemona's hand, then reaches out to close her eyes. Once Iago is brought back, however, he returns to the 'he that was Othello'. Crab-walking towards Iago, he raises his curved weapon up to Iago's crotch and castrates him, not only reversing power relations between black and white bodies but literally enacting an even deeper political and social fear of white disempowerment. Almost as an anticlimax, he moves back to the bed, where he slits his jugular with a tiny knife taken from the golden case round his neck.

Like most filmed *Othellos*, Suzman's turns Desdemona's body into a muse; unlike most, the shot that records Othello's death pans across the bed to show Emilia's body and then up to Cassio, whose Roman salute to his dead commander connects him once again to the silenced Desdemona. Putting his head in his hands to mask his own gaze keys a dissolve to the film's final shot, of Desdemona and Othello on the bed, entwined together in a last embrace. Although elsewhere the film insists that *Iago*, not the dead Othello and Desdemona, is the 'object' that 'poisons sight' and must be hid, this shot also calls attention to how, especially for South African viewers, the deed cannot be hid, for as Jyotsna Singh writes, 'its image has proliferated through the centuries, making it a site for the production of troubled and contradictory colonial/postcolonial identities'.[30] By freeze-framing this image, Suzman both aestheticizes it and makes its political resonances inescapable, and that is underscored when, as the film's credits roll up, all colour fades away, forever fixing *Othello*'s ending in the binary it knows best: black and white. Deeply ambiguous, this still asks viewers to meditate on, even to radically revise, their racist memories.

If Suzman's film deliberately confronts South African spectators, white as well as black, with their own histories, Nunn's seems acutely conscious of catering to a white (British) imaginary, especially in selecting an ambiguously colonial locale where any racist burrs can be attributed to a past historical moment. Although Nunn maintains that casting a black actor was essential 'for political reasons', he conveniently elides what these might be for late 1980s Britain to wrap his decision in Shakespearean aesthetics – 'integrity to the play' – and 'sheer theatrical practicality': 'a white Othello in black make-up comes off on Desdemona'.[31] But if Nunn throws off Olivier's blacking-up, choosing Jamaican-American Willard White evokes another ghost – that of American Paul Robeson, the *only* black actor to play Othello (in 1959) in Stratford. As a (post)colonial subject and a newcomer to Stratford's theatrical culture, White goes Othello one better by occupying two alien categories. Although White's American-ness is acknowledged, even 'celebrated', by the Civil War echoes that give him something like an old Kentucky home in Cyprus, his position as an opera star marks him as an outsider both to Shakespeare and to Stratford. As it turned out, that alien identity allowed reviewers to smooth over, even erase, questions of race, turning it into a language game, a playful accident of naming. Stanley Wells, for instance, noted what he called a double irony: that 'the black Othello was played by a negro called White, while Bianca – whose name means white – was played by a black actress'.[32]

In spite of Nunn's claim that race matters in *Othello*, such an awareness need not automatically correspond with politicization. Certainly both his production and the later film offer few ruptures where a spectator, whether black or white, can resist Iago's racist inscriptions.[33] In part, this is a function of casting, which overturns Suzman's physical typing to pit White's statuesque, coal-black Othello – looking every inch the military hero – against Ian McKellen's slight, tightly reined-in Iago, an inscrutable, smiling psychopath with a Führer moustache, dead eyes and officious manners who is consumed by sexual and professional jealousies. When Othello first appears, he bursts open the doors and enters striding, his commanding figure filling the entire frame. Yet from this point forward, the film contains his body ever more closely, producing the illusion that Iago may be in cahoots with both the cameraman and the editing process – an illusion that carries over into costuming. A Franco-Prussian black uniform and polished knee-high boots encase the black body, turning White's avuncular figure from a potential Uncle Tom into a very English Othello whose exotic origins as well as his sexuality are buttoned up and whose assimilation seems (comfortably) complete. Yet even though his still, compelling presence gives him the *look* of a complete Othello, his broadly sketched performance makes him prey to McKellen's precise, transfixing Iago. Indeed, their relationship reproduces the stereotypical opposition between instinctive, emotional 'natural' power attributable to the 'native' other and the intelligent, rational judgment of the (civilized) colonizer – and is most clearly worked out in terms of the selective representation of performative bodies.

As Iago, McKellen delivers a riveting performance, recorded primarily through close-ups that capture his developing paranoia or through framing that stresses his omnipresent voyeurism – as when, entering Desdemona's bedroom for the first time, he maps it with a furtive glance, fixing its geography as though to give his fantasies a local habitation. Brother, father, valet, mother hen, his military discipline takes form as obsessive tidiness: straightening papers, adjusting Roderigo's collar, mixing the brew that will make Cassio drunk (and cleaning up after him), saving cigarette stubs in a little silver box, he seems indispensable to the garrison's domestic order. The technical precision of his performance tropes his mastery over the narrative, and because he also controls the material objects that mark the film's densely particularized attention to social detail (Nunn's neo-Brechtian trademark), it is he who anatomizes and manipulates its optical economy, as through the eyepiece of a microscope. One effect of this accumulative detail is that, by explaining Iago's actions, it not only exposes his 'motiveless malignity' as a critical fiction but also points to how Coleridge's famous phrase serves to wrap both Iago's racism and that of a critic in a convenient abstraction.[34] Tellingly, McKellen's Iago touches everyone *except* Othello – shoulder pats and hair-ruffling for his fellow-soldiers, contemptuous kisses for Emilia, a comforting embrace for Desdemona; through handling the handkerchief – the feminine sign binding Desdemona to Othello's maternal origins – his misogyny taints all the women, including Bianca. Moreover, this absolute control figures his technique in framing Othello, who becomes simply another pawn to manoeuvre on his screen of desires. Not only does he use whatever evidence he finds at hand, he manufactures it. The most striking instance occurs when, after tucking Cassio into bed following the drinking bout, Iago perches at the edge of Cassio's cot, straightening his kit as he soliloquizes on villainy. Turning in drunken slumber, Cassio throws a leg over Iago's lap: startled, Iago shies away from Cassio's touch; later, he uses the moment to construct 'ocular proof' of Desdemona's infidelity.

Proceeding from a heightened realism full of minute quirks and Brechtian gests, Iago's intellectual control over looking relations also drives the film's sex/gender economy. That he is able to do so depends in part on how the film represents the relationship between

White's dignified, massive Othello and Imogen Stubbs's fragile, naive Desdemona (who anticipates going to Cyprus as her first trip abroad), a Scarlett O'Hara-like figure who assumes that everything will be all right tomorrow.[35] While the bond between Weinberg's Desdemona and Kani's Othello is clearly erotic, that between Stubbs and White seems like a curiously old-fashioned attraction between an older man and a much younger woman, a marital arrangement that passes Desdemona from one father figure to another. As though playing house, Stubbs's Desdemona chides and cajoles White like a child; she sits on his lap, twisting him around her finger, and he treats her as a prized possession – like the chocolates that are Cassio's tribute to her, a delicious confection.

The moment that marks their relationship occurs, as in Suzman's film, in the quayside scene, where, as before, it distinguishes public from private spheres. In Nunn's film, however, passion remains offstage. As Othello enters, Desdemona starts towards him, but he stops her by extending the flat of his hand to keep her away; lifting her onto a pile of luggage, he circles around her, fetishizing her body, even (literally) positioning her as the cultural capital which has made him an honorary white Venetian; as he finishes speaking his blazon, she throws herself into his arms.[36] Except for this embrace, any expression of physical desire comes from Desdemona; the public view of their relationship exhibits a highly British restraint, deriving both from Nunn's textual fidelity and from casting, but also (perhaps) indicative of anxieties about representing an erotic bond between a black man and a white woman. Whatever the case, because any trace of Othello's sexuality is absent from representation until the close, it remains entrenched in Iago's – and a spectator's – imaginary, where it can be staged, in terms of all the myths associated with the black male's sexual potency, by a spokesman for the white patriarchy who would protect all white women from black men.

That staging becomes most pertinent at the close, where a high-angle shot captures Iago's point of view of Othello's body covering Desdemona's in a last orgasmic embrace, revealing, at last, the image that has haunted his desires. But it is not that image with which the film ends. Instead, the final shot frames Iago, his arms folded across his body as though to maintain his distance from both site and sight. And as the camera dollies in to isolate his face in close-up, it registers, first, his disinterested glance at the dead and then, as he raises his eyes to stare straight at the camera, a dead-eyed gaze that seems to acknowledge, even proclaim, his complicity in the colonial project. All has been done strictly according to the book: spectators meet Iago's eyes only to discover that he is us. Presiding over his private vision of Empire, Iago's look bringing to mind a terrifying nostalgia for the good old days when Kipling's 'Proper Sort', and the racist ideologies which firmly ensconced them at the top of a hierarchy, might flourish. Those who might wish to claim that Nunn's *Othello* – a production with a black actor at its centre – is not 'about' race may be right, but not in the way they might think. It is about who controls the narrative of racism. Speaking for many who saw Nunn's *Othello* as Iago's – and McKellen's – play, one critic mentions (without citing White's name) 'in a subsidiary role, a particularly attractive performance from a black opera singer'.[37] But if the film's take on how race matters is most acutely realized through performative bodies, racist ideologies become even more visible in the discourses surrounding it, where, Iago-like, they monitor, interpret and (at times) punish Othello's performance.

'SAY IT, OTHELLO'

You're your country's lost property
with no office to claim you back.
You're polluting our sounds. You're so rude.
'Get back to your language', they say.
                    (Adil Jussawalla, 1976)

Commenting on these lines from *Missing Person*, Homi Bhabha writes of the difficulty of comprehending 'the anxiety provoked by the hybridizing of language, activated in the anguish associated with vacillating *boundaries* – physic, cultural, territorial – of which these verses speak'.[38] Such anxiety, of course, does not belong exclusively to the colonized other, especially when Shakespeare's language is in question. Stanley Wells, for example, writes that 'White's speech rhythms were sometimes at odds with the iambic patterns of Shakespeare's verse, resulting in a less than thorough exploration of verbal meaning'; nonetheless, he concedes, 'emotional truth overcame technical limitations' to produce a noteworthy performance.[39] Although faulting an actor's speaking performance gets consistently evoked in critical discourse to register how far he (or she) falls short of an imaginary Shakespearean ideal, that phenomenon has a long history for Othellos, especially when, as with Paul Robeson and James Earl Jones, the most renowned twentieth-century Othellos, they happen to be black. In marking White's inferiority as a Shakespeare speaker while simultaneously praising the emotional truth of his performance, Wells (consciously? unconsciously?) not only expresses a desire to erase any spoken sign of the 'other' in the actor's speech but subscribes to an essentialism that aligns emotionality with blackness. If, as John Barton argues, 'Shakespeare *is* his text',[40] then disturbing iambic pentameters violates authorial authenticity, threatens to turn Shakespeare 'black'.

What is at stake in this fear of linguistic miscegenation? More, it would seem, than a white auditor's trouble with blackness 'polluting' a language. Words, after all, are Othello's primary instrument of expression, but *whose* expression, exactly, do they represent? Written by a white playwright for a white actor, his language is marked, in the play's linguistic context, by its *difference*: characterized by the large phrase, by repeated metaphysical abstractions (light/dark, heaven/hell), it spans a height and depth of reference embraced by no other speaker in the play.[41] A role identified by and treasured for its glorious sound – what G. Wilson Knight long ago called 'the Othello music'[42] – its canonical performances are often described by critics in musical terms. One hears Olivier singing the lines, building to agonized crescendo on 'Othello's occupation's *gone*', or Anthony Hopkins sliding into Welsh accents in the explosive rages: speaking Othello's words generates a 'different' language, one which tempts a white British performer to slide from Received Standard Pronunciation into a 'native' – or othered – tongue. What is going on here? If speaking Othello's language can mark the *white* performing body with linguistic otherness, what does it *do* to the black performer? If its rhetorical display mimics an excess which stands in for what Bhabha calls the fading identity of the colonized subject through his inscription in the colonizer's language,[43] then the question for a black actor becomes how to 'posit a full and sufficient self in a language in which blackness is a sign of absence'[44] – a problem intensified when that language represents a sign of Anglo-European dominance and has high cultural status. Always already perceived as a translation from a 'master text', black Othellos' 'rude speech' positions them as imperfect slaves who perform disservice to Shakespeare's canonical word.

By casting Kani, whose mother tongue is Xhosa, as Othello, Suzman deliberately challenges the national linguistic stronghold which claims that appropriating Shakespeare's language to the lived experience of the other censors its potential range.[45] Reflecting on the production as it moved into film, Suzman writes: 'Not even Paul Robeson, I imagined, could have said "Rude am I in my speech", and be entirely believed. In the event, it gave John an innocence, a sense of struggle, that a more Promethean actor, at home in the tongue, couldn't possibly achieve. Better still, it gave him a mystery, an unknowable past, that would attract Desdemona and worry the hell out of most whites'.[46] Yet however politically astute Suzman may be about energizing Kani's black body, and its 'native' identity, so as to trouble white spectators, she herself speaks a curiously conflicted language that, if not entirely accepting the text's (racist) dictates, pulls in terms – 'innocence', 'mystery', 'an unknowable past' – common to British colonialist discourse about Africa and especially prominent in Conrad's *Heart of Darkness*. That Suzman is caught up in such discursive formations becomes pertinent in the context of critical frameworks current in South Africa at the time. Martin Orkin writes of how South African academics who do discuss *Othello* rarely touch on its concern with race but instead, by seeking refuge in idealist abstractions about tragedy, 'human nature', and interiority, continue, by omission and avoidance, to underwrite the hegemony of the prevailing social order.[47]

Similar strategies surface in two academic reviews of Suzman's production, both written by white women South Africans. Commenting on Suzman's 'care and respect for the language' and on her 'orchestration' of its 'poetic music', Elisabeth Lickindorf especially admires Brabantio, Desdemona and Lodovico for 'appropriate' verse-speaking that made their roles intelligible (read, identifiably 'white'?) but faults Haines's Iago for 'disturb[ing] the auditory composition of the play' and reducing the 'diabolical manipulations of the tragedy' to a 'shouting match' in which his was the more powerful voice. Although she praises Kani for avoiding the histrionics of Olivier's 'highflown and unconvincing hyperbole', Lickindorf finds his Othello most moving in the final act, where he was able to convey 'the entire quality of sound that belonged to each verbal cluster and to each facet of anguish'.[48] Also remarking on Kani's final scenes, Hilary Semple speaks a more racially coded language: 'dressed in a dark sarong and bootless in his bechamber, [Kani's] movements had grace and were eloquent. ... At appropriate moments he squatted easily back on his heels in the fashion of Africa, ... keen[ing] his anguish and grief in tones and cadences our ears could recognize as familiar. In such moments he was an exciting and powerful figure, his dilemma and experiences immediate to his audience.'[49] Most 'Othello' when dressed in native garb, his body fashioned by African gestures and his speech inflected by a 'black' sound familiar to white South African ears, Kani becomes constructed as the reviewer's exotic other, most sharply recognizable once he conforms to closural expectations by killing a white woman and then victimizing himself. In labelling Suzman's production 'a metaphor for South Africa', Semple's comments call attention to how perceptions of that staging remain imbricated in the colonial legacy, for as she takes up her part in that metaphor, she speaks to the need to keep a black Othello in his place in order to secure her own pleasure and understanding of 'Shakespearean tragedy'.

A somewhat similar desire to mark off blackness surfaces in the British critical response to White's Othello. Here, however, racist ideologies masquerade under the guise of an aestheticized 'correctness' which measures White's verbal performance against an imaginary audition driven by a mix of Knightean and Leavisite reading formations and past theatrical practice. Unlike Kani, White was born into the language Shakespeare speaks, but, by assuming that his 'native' language is opera, the review discourse marks the high risks that attach to the outsider attempting to enter the confines of Stratford's Shakespearean precincts. Michael Ratcliffe, for instance, remarks that 'the narrative breathing techniques demanded by Shakespeare and Wagner are quite unalike: White's voice resonates where it should colour and remains earthbound where it should rise'; Nicholas de Jongh concurs: 'He is an opera singer and it shows…: [he] misses out on vulnerability; high notes of desperation and wildness pass him by; he never says farewell to greatness at all'.[50] Like de Jongh, Michael Coveney misses Knight's 'Othello music': White, he notes, 'has lungs but not the slightest indication toward rhetoric…[his] velvety rich voice lies many fathoms deep, but neither sings nor intones'.[51] Those who, like Charles Osborne, thought White's Othello 'a remarkably impressive achievement for a singer with little experience of speaking dialogue, and none of Shakespeare', almost invariably evoked Paul Robeson, a move that permitted identifying White's inability to 'immerse [himself] very deeply in the character' as characteristic of the (black) operatic outsider.[52]

Strikingly, most reviewers avoid mentioning White's colour: instead, 'opera singer' and 'Robeson' became coded terms for the lacks of a performance that 'does not take audiences on the kind of dramatic journey undertaken by McKellen's Iago' and that 'needs to tap a deeper layer of emotions to match the rest of the company'.[53] Because such comments also fix White's blackness, it is useful to recall how the desire for a 'savage' Othello traced through (white) critics' discourse about Robeson's Othello. Although he faulted Robeson's mastery of Shakespeare's verse, James Agate praised Robeson's performance for those moments in which, at play's end, his Othello 'ceased to be human and became a gibbering primeval man'. Once the production reached New York, Robeson, his verse-speaking improved, was playing Othello as a man of dignity whose racial honour is betrayed: now, however, Rosamund Gilder noted that his 'savagery [was] not believable, the core of violence is lacking'.[54]

In attempting to fashion a colour-blind critical subjectivity, reviewers construct a curiously double discourse which makes the notion of 'race', as it circulates in the white imaginary, painfully visible. Watching Othello, it would seem, activates the desire for a stereotypical, mythical blackness out of which the critic may (re)construct his own whiteness. In this regard, Michael Billington's comments were the most telling. With Leavis firmly entrenched in his back pocket, Billington waited in vain for Othello's time-honoured 'heroic self-dramatization' to break out; the production, he concludes, 'ultimately misses the sound we long for in a tragedy: the agonized cry of a cornered human soul'. Titling his review 'A tiger tamed', Billington not only embraces Leavis's (seemingly) colour-blind reading rules but also faults White for not being Salvini, for not demonstrating the famous actor's 'tiger-like bestiality'.[55] He does not say that White is not black enough; rather, his comment suggests that he cannot match the constructed blackness of the white imaginary. In a curious variant of the assimilation narrative, Billington elevates White by comparing him to the great Salvini, but that move arrests White in a historical moment which the critic, who owns the theatrical history, can transcend. Overall, the act of diss-ing White's performance works to 'out' a white, predominantly male, racist ideology which reasserts a Shakespearean hegemony that, by aligning blackness with its mythic preconceptions, reminds the critic of his own dominant class status.[56] But if watching a black actor perform Othello awakens anxieties that enable critics to secure their own historical, or Shakespearean, real,[57] what may be most troubling is that, in returning to Stratford for a 'farewell' *Othello* which stages the death of a black man and closes the doors on the theatre where he lies, Nunn himself becomes a kind of hero for the white majority. So enclosed, White's Othello can remain shrouded in a theatrical – or televisual – representational domain in which racist ideologies can appear simply as functions of material theatrical culture, never breaching the boundaries separating Shakespearean theatrical politics from those of the social real.

OUTING ABUSE

So far, my account has privileged race almost to the exclusion of gender. Certainly Kani's and White's performances direct particular attention to how race and racializations circulate in these *Othellos* and are re-mediated by the discursive formations surrounding them. But I also have wished to avoid collapsing race and gender into the same marginal space, a move which blurs the distinctions between black masculinity and white femininity, separating the histories of black men's enslavement from those of women's sexual oppression.[58] Uncannily, that strategy has parallels to what occurred in both the Simpson trial and its media coverage, where Nicole Brown Simpson virtually disappeared from accounts of her own murder, replaced by the iconic and symbolic power of a national and local history whose touchstones were the lynched nigger and the 1991 Rodney King beating and the subsequent Simi Valley jury that acquitted his white police assailants of any wrongdoing.[59] Blatantly oversimplified, that cultural history almost mandated a choice between combating racism and combating sexism; moreover, that narrative already had an antecedent in the Anita Hill–Clarence Thomas Senate hearings.[60] As the trial began, however, domestic violence, not race, was its crucial plot-line. Los Angeles Deputy District Attorney Christopher Darden's opening statement, for instance, represented the defendant as a possessive man caught in a recurring cycle of behaviours – seventeen years of violent physical and psychic abuse leading to apology and to further control over Nicole Brown Simpson, ensuring her economic as well as physical dependence on him.[61] It would be tempting to call this 'the Othello prosecution': certainly all signs indicated that Nicole's murder would be represented as the final, inevitable act of a jealous wife-batterer, an abusive – and abused – control freak (the 28 June 1994 *Village Voice* reported Simpson as saying, 'If I can't have [Nicole], no one else can'; his 'suicide note' claimed that at times he had 'felt like a battered husband or boy friend but I loved her'). At least until L.A. police detective Mark Fuhrman, accused of planting the bloody glove at Simpson's Rockingham estate and of being a 'genocidal racist', surfaced as the event's 'real' Iago, prosecutors seemed to be framing Simpson *as* Iago; more precisely, it was as if hero and villain had been collapsed into a Janus-faced identity which revealed, under the smiling public figure of the Hertz commercials who had so successfully converted himself into white America's idea of an acceptably colourless black man, a private face that more closely resembled their most deeply racialized fantasies.

In Shakespeare's text, 'abuse' is a conflicted term that slips easily from voice to body, from meaning 'wrong with words' (Iago's 'I'll abuse him to the Moor') to 'misuse' (Brabantio's 'she is abus'd, stol'n from me and corrupted') and 'deception' (Emilia's 'the Moor's abus'd by some outrageous knave'). Tellingly, Brabantio calls Othello 'an abuser of the world'; and Desdemona, remembering her Willow Song's 'you'll couch with more men', asks Emilia whether she thinks 'in conscience' that 'there be women do abuse their husbands / In such gross kind'. Characteristically, Desdemona internalizes the cultural prerogatives which justify misogyny, displacing its 'cause' onto women and positioning herself ('Nobody, I myself') in the space of shame allotted to her by men. In both the play and its critical reproductions, abuse is traditionally understood primarily in terms of Iago's 'practise' on Othello, his elaboration of a perverse scenario in which racism and misogyny become energized as theatrical pleasure – especially, though arguably, the pleasure of male spectators. But that scenario, which constructs Desdemona as whore, prompting Othello to strike her in public, to misuse her in the so-called whorehouse scene and, finally, to kill her, displaces and represses another narrative of spousal battery, that between Iago and Emilia.

By staging that repressed narrative, Nunn's film reveals how Iago's abuse of Emilia becomes displaced onto and appropriated by Othello, who turns it on Desdemona. Signs of Iago's possessiveness appear first in the Cyprus quayside scene when, as Cassio greets Zoe Wanamaker's Emilia with a kiss on both cheeks, McKellen's Iago quickly moves to re-establish her body as his territory, marking (with a false heartiness and a proffered shot of brandy) his wife as (necessary) domestic property. Later, as he watches Othello and Desdemona kiss, Iago wrenches Emilia's head towards his, staking out his claim with a hard, passionate kiss which belies his thought that the 'Moor has done [his] office' – a gesture to which Emilia responds with startled incomprehension. Although Iago is the film's most obvious voyeur, Emilia is equally omnipresent: in a performance constructed out of loss, misused desire, frustration and constant fear of Iago's displeasure, she watches Othello's adoration of Desdemona and Desdemona's playful confidence in her love with defeated silence. The grounds for that become most apparent when, after retrieving the handkerchief, she muses that she has no such token to 'kiss, and talk to', a lack that prompts her to offer it to an Iago who pulls her onto his lap, kisses her, puts a hand up her dress and, through a near-magical sleight of hand, takes both the handkerchief and her pipe, which he puts in his mouth and lights, puffing smoke in her face and laughing as he thrusts her away.[62]

Emilia's own history of verbal, psychological and physical abuse surfaces once she sees Desdemona subjected to similar treatment in the whorehouse scene and recognizes, in Othello, the symptoms of the jealous batterer. But even in the Willow Song scene, where Desdemona guiltily takes Cassio's box of chocolates from her dressing table and the two share a sweet, Emilia can speak only in general terms of 'husbands' faults' and women's desires, not of her own experience. As that scene ends, Emilia hesitates before leaving, as if she would say more. The text, which gives her no 'good night' in response to Desdemona's, marks her role by silence and Desdemona's with a prayer; the play's ending, of course, overturns this verbal economy to punish Desdemona for her silence, Emilia for her speech. Domestic violence offers yet another site for exploring the relations between women's speech and silence in *Othello*, one that aligns with recent studies citing women's unwillingness to file charges against spouses who have abused them or to seek their arrest.[63] An even more particular link ties Emilia and Desdemona to Nicole Brown Simpson, whose voice apparently went unheard when, after Simpson had beaten her in 1989, she called police to her home. Tellingly, her statements to relatives and friends about her fears that Simpson would kill her were kept out of representation at the trial. Like *Othello*'s women, her voice was silenced, cut-off – that is, until the end of Chief Prosecutor Marcia Clark's closing statement, when, as though mimicking Shakespeare, Nicole's voice, on the famous 911 tape, filled Judge Ito's courtroom as well as millions of domestic spaces worldwide. Still, neither Nicole's voice nor Clark's strategy influenced proceedings in which Fuhrman's Iago-like inventions, including his alleged use of 'the n-word' that re-marked O. J. as a black man (and Johnnie Cochran's insistence that no one forget it), had, as in Shakespeare's play, stopped all ears.

Not unexpectedly, the patterns of abusive behaviour towards women that surface in Nunn's *Othello* also went unnoticed by reviewers, who contained and re-mediated such narratives of domestic abuse as 'male effects' – either taking them as a given, constructed by 'Shakespeare', or as resulting from McKellen's meticulous performance (as in Michael Coveney's 'Iago's marriage has gone cold and dead').[64] One might conclude that abuse represents a symptom apparently so dangerous to the psychic health of the (usually) male critic that it must be consistently repressed. Too fascinating, however, to repress successfully, for what surfaces in its place is a desire for feminine victimization. As Elisabeth Bronfen writes, 'Representations as symptoms articulate unconscious knowledge and desires in a displaced, recorded, and translated manner'.[65] All too willingly, or willfully, the review discourse constructs Emilia as well as Desdemona in terms of their appearances and feminine traits – figured as 'some shining Burne-Jones heroine', Desdemona becomes a 'young bride with Rapunzel hair'; Emilia is marked as 'strong' yet 'slow-burning, sickly-sad'[66] – or as potential victims – '[Emilia's] face speak[s] if not volumes then at least a complete Victorian novel'; by contrast, Stubbs's Desdemona is 'a study of innocence out of its depth' who displays an 'empty-headedness [which] makes the last scenes especially moving' as she becomes 'a painful, pitiful victim in the clutches of incomprehensible evil'.[67]

This desire for the victim symptomatic of *Othello*'s reviewers aligns with the discourse surrounding the Simpson trial, where the question of how it was that a *black* man's spousal abuse prompted a faddish fascination with domestic violence which was displaced into a near-hysterical tabloid discourse that made Nicole Brown Simpson's body, and her sexual conduct, less a site for evaluating her ex-husband's criminal responsibility than for shoring up his masculine mystique. At the same time the Brown family announced plans for a foundation for abused women in Nicole's name and accepted a cheque for $50,000 from No Excuses jeans, photographs of Nicole embracing Ronald Goldman or nude in a hot tub with three (white) male 'lovers' circulated Iago-like proofs of her promiscuity in a series of panic body images; stories of her affair with Simpson's friend Marcus Allen, of her pleas to a minister to 'save her from a lesbian hell', and of her drug addiction hinted at 'unnatural' behaviours designed to demonize her with the signs of her own undoing. As in *Othello*, blackness became a category that could magically disappear and reappear, marking all the women connected with the case; with the trial in session, the tabloids extended their surveillance. The 14 February *National Enquirer* featured a double-page spread on Marcia Clark's 'topless fling' fifteen years ago with her 'hustler hubby'; the *Star* headlined Nicole's sister, Denise, and her 'jealous' attraction to O. J. Simpson; both fantasized a romantic relationship between Clark and fellow prosecutor Darden. Even more troubling was a 28 February *Star* exposé entitled 'Marcia and Johnnie: Johnnie Cochran puts the smile back on Marcia Clark's face', which printed a series of photos showing Cochran touching Clark (from behind). Clark, the piece claims, was 'all business' until, sensing Cochran's touch, she recalled the 'correct' relations between a man and a woman: 'the thought turns her girlish for a microsecond – and she lowers her eyes', while 'ladies' man O. J.' looks on in 'total glee'. Turning the relation between the two trial lawyers into a version of Nicole and O. J., this spread not only 'normalizes' the positions of 'man' and 'woman' but also evokes a familiar scenario – 'she's asking for it' – which works to strip Clark of her professional status and to displace responsibility for any 'crime' from the male defendant to the female prosecutor.

By coincidence, the day the verdict was announced was also the day that President Clinton declared October Domestic Violence Awareness month. But long before Cochran was rereading the beating that prompted Nicole's 911 phone call as 'an unfortunate incident between two people who were married' and reminding jurors that Simpson is a 'human being' who, like all of us, is not perfect, black and white women had sharply divided responses to the trial. As race became genderized, even black women who thought O. J. was or might be guilty embraced his acquittal: although the verdict spurred a renewed focus on domestic violence at shelters for abused women all around the country, black women in one Chicago shelter stood to cheer his triumph, and Camille Paglia told *Playboy* that Nicole's frantic call for help proved she was a tease who enjoyed playing sadomasochistic games.[68] And, some nine months following his acquittal, O. J. hosted a black-tie dinner, with security provided by the Nation of Islam, to oppose domestic violence.[69] 'If we cannot see things clearly', writes Freud, 'we will at least see clearly what the obscurities are'.[70] If what is at stake in reading the Simpson case is nothing less than a culture reading itself through a set of heavily coded, highly mediated discourses, the *Othello* connection provides a literary logic not only for containing blackness within the white imaginary but also, by dreaming the death of 'woman', for re-enclosing women's voices and bodies within a male imaginary that sanctions its own destructive desires. At a moment when the law, and the ideal of justice behind it, has become a televisual theatrical commodity, that dream is more than a transhistorical literary trope. If Lodovico's 'Let it be hid' seems symptomatic of a refusal to address domestic violence shared by early modern and late twentieth-century cultures, there is a radical difference between the image of Nicole's battered, bloody body – too sensational to be viewed by eyes other than those in the courtroom (until, on the day the verdict was announced, the *Globe* published 'exclusive' photos under the headline 'Don't Free O.J. to Kill Again') – and the serene, alabaster-like Desdemona, safely confined within the boundaries of a discrete, authoritatively Shakespearean tragedy. Or at least one would like to think so.

From *Shakespeare the Movie: Popularizing the Plays on Film, TV, and Video*, ed. Lynda E. Boose and Richard Burt (London, 1997), pp. 23–44.

NOTES

['Race-ing *Othello*' is an example of how performance history can be cultural history. Barbara Hodgdon discusses two theatrical productions of *Othello* that had colonial settings but that nonetheless betrayed the contourings of a persistent white imaginary. In both, actors of colour played the lead role; in both, they were criticized on the seemingly impartial ground of their inadequate skill in speaking verse. Thus these *Othello*s worked to reify old racial divisions as well as to reinforce continuing stereotypes. Hodgdon is particularly concerned with the perceived relationship between race and violence, and this leads to a concluding section on spousal abuse. Hodgdon makes enlightening connections between the two productions of *Othello* and the O. J. Simpson trial in California. As was true of that trial, so, too, for *Othello*: whether in the way it is presented to us or in the way we read it, it is a symptom of important cultural conditions. This essay appeared in *Shakespeare the Movie: Popularizing the Plays on Film, TV, and Video*, edited by Lynda E. Boose and Richard Burt. For a longer version, see Barbara Hodgdon's book, *The Shakespeare Trade: Performances and Appropriations* (Philadelphia: University of Pennsylvania Press, 1998). Ed.]

1. Read by his friend Robert Kardashian at a 17 June news conference, Simpson's letter circulated widely in print and television news, in the tabloids and on the Internet.

2. *Congressional Record*, vol. 140, no. 81 (1994).

3. Reacting to outraged response, *Time*'s next issue printed a full-page apology for what the editors called a 'photo illustration', claiming that all they had done was 'improve on reality'. The magazine has refused permission to reprint the cover image.

4. My thanks to Jonathan Shectman for calling my attention to this 'joke'. See Chris Lamb, 'The Popularity of O.J. Simpson Jokes: The More We Know, the More We Laugh', *Journal of Popular Culture*, 28.1 (Summer 1994), 223–31.

5. Simpson letter; see also Ellis Cose, 'Caught Between Two Worlds: Why Simpson couldn't overcome the barriers of race', *Newsweek* (11 July 1994), 28.

6. Although I refer to both *Othello*s as 'films', a more accurate label is 'video text', for both use video technology and both were screened on Britain's Channel 4 – Suzman's in January 1989, Nunn's in late Spring 1990. Although I base my descriptions and analyses on these video texts, I rely on reviews of the stage productions. This is a discrepancy I ask readers to accept, and for two reasons. For one, both video texts represent records of theatrical performances; for another, the only commentary on the videos falls into the category of 'puff' pieces. See, for example, (on Suzman) Peter Lennon, 'Catching His Soul', *The Listener* (5 January 1989), 38–9; and (on Nunn) Robert Gore-Langton, 'A Round, Unvarnish'd Tale', *The Listener* (1 February 1990), 36–7 and Peter Conrad, 'When Less Means Moor', *Observer Magazine* (24 April 1990), 24–5.

7. On White's film, see Peter S. Donaldson, ' "Haply for I am Black": Liz White's *Othello*', in *Shakespearean Films/Shakespearean Directors* (Boston: Unwin Hyman, 1990), pp. 127–44.

8. All citations are from Janet Suzman, 'Othello Goes to Market', *Punch* (26 August 1988), 49.

9. Alex Renton, 'Honest Conversation', interview with Trevor Nunn, *Independent* (17 August 1989).

10. Elizabeth's warrant is quoted in Ruth Cowhig, 'Blacks in English Renaissance Drama and the Role of Shakespeare's *Othello*', in *The Black Presence in English Literature*, ed. David Dabydeen (Manchester: Manchester University Press, 1985), pp. 1–25 (I quote from p. 6).

11. See, for instance, Owen Wister, 'The Evolution of the Cow-Puncher', *Harper's Monthly*, 91 (September 1895), 602–17; Herbert N. Casson, 'The Americans in America', *Munsey's Magazine*, 36 (January 1907),

432–6; and Brander Matthews, 'The American of the Future', *Century Illustrated*, 74 (July 1907), 474–80. My thanks to Richard Abel for calling these texts to my attention and for commenting on drafts of this essay.

12. Laurence Olivier, *On Acting* (New York: Simon and Schuster, 1986), pp. 158–9.

13. Ibid., p. 153.

14. See Charles Lamb, 'On the Tragedies of Shakespeare' (1811). Reprinted in *Charles Lamb on Shakespeare*, ed. Joan Coldwell (New York: Harper and Row, 1978), p. 38. On femininity as performance, see Judith Butler, *Gender Trouble: Feminism and the Subversion of Identity* (London: Routledge, 1990), especially pp. 128–41.

15. And in eighteenth- and nineteenth-century burlesques of *Othello*. See Stanley Wells, ed., *Nineteenth-Century Shakespeare Burlesques* (London: Diploma Press, 1977–78), 5 vols. See also Ray B. Browne, 'Shakespeare in American Vaudeville and Negro Minstrelsy', *American Quarterly*, 12 (1960), 374–91; and Joyce Green Macdonald, 'Acting Black: *Othello*, *Othello* Burlesques, and the Performance of Blackness', *Theatre Journal*, 46 (1994), 231–49.

16. See bell hooks, 'The Oppositional Gaze: Black Female Spectators', in *Black American Cinema*, ed. Manthia Diawara (New York: Routledge, 1993), pp. 288–302 (I quote from p. 293).

17. One of Kani's brothers was sentenced to prison in 1962 for furthering the aims of the outlawed National Congress; another, Xolile, was killed (at the age of 26) during the 1985 riots. See John D. Battersby, 'The Drama of Staging *Othello* in Johannesburg', *New York Times* (26 October 1987), C16.

18. Suzman, 'Othello Goes to Market', p. 49.

19. Homi K. Bhabha, Introduction to Franz Fanon, *Black Skin, White Masks*, trans. Charles Lam Markmann (London and Sydney: Pluto Press, 1986), p. xvi.

20. Kani quoted in Battersby, 'The Drama'.

21. Suzman, 'Othello Goes to Market', p. 49.

22. Ben Okri, 'Meditations on Othello', *West Africa* (March 1987), 562–3 (I quote from p. 562).

23. For a dramatization of this issue, see Athol Fugard, *Statements After An Arrest Under the Immorality Act* (New York: Theatre Communications Group, Inc., 1986).

24. Janet Suzman, Private communication, 31 January 1995. Terreblanche is the leader of the Afrikaner Resistance Movement (ARM), engaged in

terrorism against blacks. Ninety per cent of the audience for Suzman's production had never seen the play before; for the first time, Market's black audience 'jumped from the usual 10% or 15% for a European classic, to double and treble that number'. See Suzman, '*Othello* – A Belated Reply', *Shakespeare in Southern Africa: Journal of the Shakespeare Society of Southern Africa*, 2 (1988), 90–6.

25. Speculating on why black audiences came to see *Othello*, Suzman writes: 'they enjoyed it because they had seen nothing like it before in their lives. ... They enjoyed it because the black guy gets to be in charge of his own death at the end, and because the white guy gets found out'. Private communication.

26. The only other cinematic 'trick' occurs in the temptation scene, where Kani's look off left frame keys two inset shots, one of Desdemona and Cassio kissing, another of the two parting. Both are moments he (and viewers) have seen before; repeating them stresses how, once Iago's fantasy has taken hold of Othello, he rereads what he has previously witnessed.

27. Such distinctions were evident among theatrical spectators. 'White couples hissing at blacks to shhhh! Blacks shouting "look out behind you!" as Iago stabs Emilia. ... Blacks laughing in the quiet bits because tragedy is an unknown form in Africa. They are not as well-schooled as whites in the manners of the theatre. Thank God. "You could have heard a pin drop" is the greatest accolade you can pay to a moment of high drama in European theatre. In Africa silence is threatening, as if the lights had fused. ... The nub of it is, that a black audience is a vociferous thing, and likes to express itself (cf. black church services and sung responses), and a white audience is schooled in polite silence.' Suzman, Private communication.

28. In protest of apartheid, Stratford's 1987 Birthday Celebrations Committee decided not to invite representatives from South Africa, a move that met with considerable resistance from the District Council, the Stratford Council and the Birthplace Trust. Philip Brockbank mourns the dissent which transformed 'a once inconsequential and delightful festival [the Grammar School's annual daffodil festival] into a local as well as a national political forum'. See Philip Brockbank, 'Shakespeare's Stratford and South Africa', *Shakespeare Quarterly*, 38 (Winter 1987), 481. Suzman's choice of daffodils, however, was accidental: on any night, the properties manager would snatch up whatever flowers were available from the precinct's stalls. Suzman, Private communication.

29. See Catherine Clement, *Opera, or The Undoing of Women*, trans. Betsy Wing (Minneapolis: University of Minnesota, 1988), p. 118.

30. Jyotsna Singh, 'Othello's Identity, Postcolonial Theory, and Contemporary Rewritings of *Othello*', in *Women, 'Race', and Writing in the*

Early Modern Period, ed. Margo Hendricks and Patricia Parker (London: Routledge, 1994), pp. 287–99 [reprinted as chapter 7 in this collection] (I quote from p. 291).

31. Nunn quoted in Alex Renton, 'Honest Conversation', interview with Trevor Nunn, *Independent* (17 August 1989).

32. Stanley Wells, 'Shakespeare Production in England in 1989', *Shakespeare Survey*, 43 (1990), 183–203 (I quote from p. 194).

33. See Manthia Diawara, 'Black Spectatorship: Problems of Identification and Resistance', in *Black American Cinema*, ed. Diawara, pp. 211–12.

34. See Paul Taylor, who writes: the 'close-up, detailed approach ... paradoxically diminishes Iago because it encourages the belief that he can be realistically "explained" like a figure in a novel'. *Independent* (2 October 1989).

35. Stubbs comments on her role in Gwyn Morgan, 'Three Women in *Othello*', *Plays and Players* (October 1989), 16–18.

36. This stylization is repeated in the whorehouse scene, where once again a circling camera embodies Othello's point of view as he surveys Desdemona's body, now a scorned object.

37. Rhoda Koenig, *Punch* (13 October 1989).

38. Homi K. Bhabha, 'Interrogating Identity: The Postcolonial Prerogative', *Anatomy of Racism*, ed. David Theo Goldberg (Minneapolis: University of Minnesota Press, 1990), pp. 183–209 (I quote from p. 202).

39. Wells, 'Shakespeare Production', p. 194.

40. John Barton, *Playing Shakespeare* (London: Methuen, 1984), p. 168.

41. See James L. Calderwood, 'Speech and Self in *Othello*', *Shakespeare Quarterly*, 38 (Autumn 1987), 293–303.

42. See G. Wilson Knight, 'The *Othello* Music', in *The Wheel of Fire* (London: Methuen 1949), pp. 97–119.

43. Bhabha, 'Interrogating', p. 202.

44. See Henry Louis Gates, 'Writing, "Race" and the Difference It Makes', Editor's Introduction to *Critical Inquiry*, 12 (Autumn 1985), 1–20 (I quote from p. 12).

45. While this does pertain to a postcolonial Othello, it may not apply to performers working from a translation, who are perceived as able to leap over or transcend language barriers. See John Russell Brown, 'Foreign Shakespeare and English-speaking audiences', *Foreign Shakespeare: Contemporary Performance*, ed. Dennis Kennedy (Cambridge: Cambridge University Press, 1993), pp. 21–35.

46. Suzman, 'Othello Goes to Market', p. 49.

47. See Martin Orkin, 'Othello and the "Plain Face" of Racism', *Shakespeare Quarterly*, 38 (Summer 1987), 166–88; and *Shakespeare Against Apartheid* (Craighall: A. D. Donker, 1987).

48. Elisabeth Lickindorf, 'The Verse Music of Suzman's *Othello*', *Shakespeare in Southern Africa: Journal of the Shakespeare Society of Southern Africa*, 1 (1987), 69–70.

49. Hilary Semple, '*Othello*: An Historic Milestone', *Shakespeare in Southern Africa: Journal of the Shakespeare Society of Southern Africa*, 1 (1987), 69.

50. Michael Ratcliffe, 'Disgust of the Blue-eyed Monster', *Observer* (27 August 1989); Nicholas de Jongh, 'When Less Means Moor', *Guardian* (7 October 1989). These and other reviews are collected in scrapbooks at the Shakespeare Centre Library.

51. Michael Coveney, 'A Monumental Othello', *Financial Times* (26 August 1989).

52. Charles Osborne, 'The Pity of It', *Daily Telegraph* (26 August 1989).

53. Ratcliffe, 'Disgust of the Blue-eyed Monster'; David Nathan, *Jewish Chronicle* (6 October 1989).

54. Agate and Gilder are cited in Richard Dyer, *Heavenly Bodies: Film Stars and Society* (London: Macmillan Education Ltd, 1987), p. 77.

55. Michael Billington, 'A Tiger Tamed', *Guardian* (26 August 1989). See also F. R. Leavis, 'Diabolic Intellect and the Noble Hero: or The Sentimentalist's Othello', in *The Common Pursuit* (London: Chatto and Windus, 1952), pp. 136–59; and, on Salvini, John Gillies, 'Stanislavski, *Othello* and the Motives of Eloquence', paper read at the Sixth World Shakespeare Congress, Los Angeles, April 1996.

56. I am indebted to Mark Fransiscus for the idea of outing racist ideology.

57. For a pertinent discussion of the historical real, see Janet Staiger, 'Securing the Fictional Narrative as a Tale of the Historical Real', *South Atlantic Quarterly*, 88 (1989), 393–414.

58. In 'Othello's Identity' (pp. 290–2), Singh critiques Karen Newman's ' "And was the Ethiop white" ', in *Fashioning Femininity and English Renaissance Drama* (Chicago: University of Chicago Press, 1991), pp. 71–94. See also Ania Loomba, 'Sexuality and racial difference', *Gender, Race, Renaissance Drama* (Manchester: Manchester University Press, 1989), p. 63n4.

59. See, for instance, Robert Gooding-Williams (ed.), *Reading Rodney King, Reading Urban Uprising* (New York and London: Routledge, 1993). The jury for the Rodney King trial consisted of ten whites, one Asian and one Hispanic.

60. See Toni Morrison (ed.), *Race-ing Justice, En-gendering Power: Essays on Anita Hill, Clarence Thomas, and the Construction of Social Reality* (New York: Pantheon Books, 1992); and Robert Chrisman and Robert L. Allen (eds.), *Court of Appeal: The Black Community Speaks Out on the Racial and Sexual Politics of Thomas vs. Hill* (New York: Ballantine Books, 1992).

61. See Sheila Weller, *Raging Heart: the Intimate Story of the Tragic Marriage of O.J. and Nicole Brown Simpson* (New York: Pocket Books, 1995). For other perspectives, see Faye D. Resnick, with Mike Walker, *Nicole Brown Simpson: The Private Diary of a Life Interrupted* (Beverly Hills, CA: Dove Books, 1994); O.J. Simpson, *I Want to Tell You: My Response to Your Letters, Your Messages, Your Questions* (Boston: Little, Brown, 1995); and David Bender, *The O.J. Simpson Confession, A Work of Fiction* (New York: Berkeley Books, 1997).

62. Although Suzman's film also stages moments of domestic violence (Iago slaps Emilia on several occasions), it emphasizes race more than gender.

63. See, for instance, Anne Jones, *Next Time She'll Be Dead: Battering and How to Stop It* (Boston: Beacon Press, 1994).

64. Covency, 'A Monumental Othello'.

65. Elisabeth Bronfen, *Over Her Dead Body: Death, Femininity and The Aesthetic* (New York: Routledge, 1992), p. xi.

66. In order, the quotes are from Jack Tinker, 'Catching the Soul of the Eternal Outsider', *Daily Mail* (26 August 1989); Coveney, 'A Monumental Othello'; Osborne, 'The Pity of It'; Coveney.

67. In order, the quotations are from de Jongh, 'When Less Means Moor'; Osborne, 'The Pity of It'; and Helene Barratt, 'Military Study of Evil', *Coventry Evening Telegraph* (25 August 1989).

68. *New York Times* (13 October 1995), A1, A12; Paglia's comment reported by Katha Pollitt in *The Nation* (23 October 1995), 457. See also E. R. Shipp, 'OJ and the Black Media', *Columbia Journalism Review*, 33 (November/December 1994), 39–41.

69. David E. Thigpen, 'Black Tie, but Presumably No Gloves', *Time* (8 July 1996), 73.

70. Sigmund Freud, *Inhibitions, Symptoms and Anxiety*, Standard Edition XXI (London: Hogarth Press, 1926), p. 125.

9

Black and White, and Dread All Over: The Shakespeare Theatre's 'Photonegative' *Othello* and the Body of Desdemona

DENISE ALBANESE

This essay is sparked by a singular and idiosyncratic staging of *Othello* that resonates beyond its particular theatrical boundaries.[1] Offered by the Washington Shakespeare Theatre in the fall of 1997, the production was characterized by those involved in it as 'photonegative'. Unusually for recent productions, the title role was taken by a white actor; almost every other speaking part, however, featured an actor of African descent, so that the racial dynamics of the script were visually reversed.[2] Although the lead actor, Patrick Stewart, did not modify his appearance to portray Othello, the script's colour-coding of the central character as markedly black remained unmodified. For reasons I'll go on to suggest, I consider this production to have been problematic – indeed, unsuccessful, to use the aestheticized and evaluative language of the reviewer. Nevertheless, my aim is less to evaluate it than to consider how director Jude Kelly's realization of 'photonegativity', while perhaps a foreseeable consequence of the theatre's efforts at colour-blind casting, offers a contradictory view of raced masculinity to be read against conflicts about integration and affirmative action in the

United States at the end of the twentieth century on the one hand, and against the body of a woman on the other.[3]

It has been recognized for some time that *Othello*'s performance history, in which the lead was generally assumed by a white actor wearing blackface make-up, affords ample evidence for racist theatrical practices. Othello has often been played according to dominant and quixotic stereotypes of black deportment (most recently, perhaps, by Laurence Olivier), and the play became, in effect, the elite cultural counterpart of black minstrel shows pervasive in the nineteenth and early twentieth centuries in the United States – with which, ironically, many Shakespearean productions might then have shared the bill.[4] In light of the historical affront its production history represents, the title role has in recent decades become the all-but-inalienable province of black actors; indeed, sometimes other parts – notably, Iago – have been given over to actors of African descent, as well.[5] In attempting to see the play still differently from these corrective productions, the Washington photonegative staging offered a representation of blackness – and, by extension, whiteness, since race properly cannot but be constructed relationally – that was both incoherent and resonant. It proved impossible for many members of the audience to recode raced bodies via the polarities of the photographic image from which the production apparently drew its inspiration; the failure of the conceit, as well as the fact of its having been undertaken, reveal a great deal about the state of race consciousness in the United States at the end of the millennium.

Given the potential box-office appeal of Patrick Stewart, it is likely that the Washington Shakespeare Theatre *Othello* represents first and foremost the opportunistic casting of a famous white actor with a production built around him that minimized offensive racial impersonation. Nevertheless, the production's racial reversals seem to imply the prior existence of an extra-theatrical context where race – not simply Othello's race, but all racial identity – can be seen as a performance, a series of discursive positions potentially available to all regardless of birth, rather as gender theorists have already claimed about femininity and masculinity.[6] Yet just as in practice it has gone far harder with women who dare to impersonate maleness than for men who impersonate femininity, what undoes this particular attempt to render race performative is the intransigent asymmetry of overtly raced positions, rather than the particularity of Stewart's 'failure' to convince the audience he is a Moor.[7] This asymmetry must be linked not only to minstrel-show practices, but also to dominant casting practices for classical dramatic texts, both in the theatre and in Hollywood, that aspire to an enlightened blindness about colour. Thus the stage and screen are asked, in effect, to model a utopian space where race doesn't 'matter' any more – especially when it comes to Shakespeare, who has long been positioned as the universal property of all humanity. Productions like this one, however, reveal the extent to which the purported insignificance of race is largely a one-sided affair. And perhaps that word 'affair' bears more than its usual freight of meaning: as my analysis will reveal, it is often around the problem of cross-racial desire that the return of the racial repressed cannot but force itself on a viewing public otherwise conditioned to look past the overt signs of race in productions of Shakespeare.

I

If viewers were (able) to take the Washington Shakespeare Theatre production at its word, what could they have been meant to see in a 'photonegative' staging of *Othello*? The question concerns whether the production accomplished what the term 'photonegative' implies, and whether that term offered the audience a coherent rubric for the experience of spectatorship. Is the demand, as I have argued, that race be seen simply as a form of performance, with an optically sensitive correction reregistering the staged bodies the production arrays to view, which would still leave 'blackness' as the term in crisis while visually substituting for 'thick lips' Stewart's thin-pursed mouth?[8] Even if so, such a correction would in itself be far from simple, since it depends for its efficacy upon the authority of the text – specifically the *Shakespearean* text – in dominating, overriding, the script provided by Stewart's body, just as it generally does when actors of African descent take part in 'colour-blind' productions. Kelly needed the audience to recolour the actors as embodied subjects, to accept Shakespeare's words as arbiter of their perception: it, and she, demanded that they read 'black' for 'white' with Stewart, as well as 'white' for 'black' for the rest of the cast. To understand the complex negotiation between ideology on the one hand, and perception on the other, involved in this demand, consider what would have happened had Kelly changed some of the more charged descriptions of Othello's appearance to suit Stewart's whiteness (and modifications to the language are sometimes made with other

Shakespearean scripts). In that case, Kelly would have been deprived of the graphic qualities of a 'photonegative' production – but she also would not have offered a challenge to the audience members to rationalize the discrepancy between what they saw and what they heard, a discrepancy which, as I've argued, pressures the boundaries that separate performance from inalienable somatic identity. Some actors can play 'against' their race; others, it seems, cannot.

Kelly's decision to fret the relationship between signs and referents, between words of self-representation and the embodied subject articulating them, manifested at least in part the differential investment between director and audience in the authority of Shakespeare's words. However contingent the occasion, they have long been presumed to put on offer a universalizable tragic experience addressed to a universalized audience: hence the wide acceptance accorded to mixed-race performances. But what happened was far different from a realization of a universalist Shakespeare: Kelly's respectful fidelity to the script was not echoed by the subject position of her audience – at least that segment of the audience which laughed when Stewart pronounced on his blackness.[9] Apparently the visual disparity between Stewart and his proclaimed self-representation broke the fiction of the performance in a way that having black actors in Shakespeare customarily does not, enabling the audience to assert a 'commonsense', empirically based response to an apparently absurdist moment. This reaction certainly arose because Stewart's prior reputation might have made it particularly difficult to absorb him into the dramatic fiction, a point to which I'll later return. Nevertheless, it might not have occurred if, as I aver, the audience was united (with Kelly?) in a worshipful dispensation towards Shakespeare. But without the audience's complete surrender to the imaginative and ideological control of *Othello*, the scene became incoherent, risible – and telling.

Much could be said about the evidence of dissent from the reflexive worship of Shakespeare such tendencies to mock betoken.[10] Indeed, even to ask how the production was intended to be viewed is to take its discursive cues to the audience as likely to interpellate them authoritatively, and so to ignore the extent to which Shakespeare, in the theatre as in the classroom and the public sphere, represents the contested terrain that elite culture has become at the beginning of the twenty-first century. However tempting it might be to pursue this line of argument, it risks misrecognizing that in the asymmetry of response I've described, the Washington *Othello* might be read as an ideological symptom of something 'larger' than a formation around Shakespeare – a symptom, that is, of an underlying shift in the conjuncture around race, specifically concerning affirmative action, at the present moment. Indeed, it is only by virtue of addressing the production as symptomatic that its incoherence about race can be put into an explanatory structure. That structure is bipartite: it involves both understanding how the Shakespearean theatrical practice privileges hegemonic forms of racial identity, and acknowledging that that racial hegemony may be inadvertently denaturalized when the staging of cross-raced heterosexual conduct forces the issue of what performative race represses.

The failure in interchangeability of white for black that rendered the Washington *Othello* flawed reveals the asymmetry underlying the supposedly 'colour-blind' casting practices that currently obtain whenever elite theatrical texts are reproduced in the United States.[11] In general, convention seems to demand that when non-white actors are cast in Shakespearean roles, their colour fades in significance; they are meant to be taken in some sense as indistinguishable from white actors. Indeed, this indistinguishability is not only the result of a classical dramatic training system through which most Shakespearean actors pass; it may also be its point. The disciplinary regime of dramatic training, which manifests itself through a demand for uniformity of voice and bodily decorum, ensures a uniformity of effect among cast members – the better to reproduce what Susan Bennett has called a 'monolithic Shakespearean voice', which is only the most privileged marker of an equally monolithic identity as a 'Shakespearean actor'.[12] While I do not wish to essentialize what are, after all, only conventional markers of racial identity, temporally and geographically contingent, the vocal form of the Shakespearean actor usually naturalized in mainstream theatre in the United States, as Bennett's phrase indicates, is informed already by the theatrical values of the dominant – which is, to put it with an undeniable lack of argumentative suppleness, 'white', developed in relation to a European, indeed British, acting and elocutionary tradition, Method acting notwithstanding. Even as theatrical practitioners have come to recognize the salutary nature of diversity on stage, there remains a grounding conviction that the universalizing power claimed for Shakespeare's words must be secured by the sacrifice of vocal particularity. Thus the vocal coach Kristin Linklater has claimed that 'the actor who allows Shakespeare's text to influence and shape him as any good actor must, will be fulfilling the rich variety of sounds that great poetry demands, and will naturally remove the limiting stamp of regionality'.[13] As the performance theorist W. B. Worthen has written, 'The complicity of actor training in ideological formation is nowhere more visible than at this point: "Shakespeare" becomes a naturalizing metaphor on the body itself, representing the universal, transcendent, and natural in ways that both legitimate and render unquestionable the dominant discourse of the stage'.[14]

For obvious reasons, such training has not always characterized African-American actors who perform Shakespeare. In fact, it was not all that long ago that many were criticized for their perceived verbal and vocal inadequacy to the theatrical task: in 1963 the conservative theatre critic John Simon wrote of 'the sad fact … that, through no fault of their own, Negro [sic] actors often lack even the rudiments of Standard American speech'.[15] Simon's dated disparagement of alternative vocal models reveals his investment in policing (among other things) the sound of Shakespeare, in keeping the Shakespearean voice monolithic and hegemonic, but it is an investment that goes beyond him and still obtains, albeit in a less fractiously condescending and exclusionary form.[16] For those who have taken the necessity of a 'universal' and classic elocutionary tradition as a natural consequence of understanding Shakespearean verse, any difference in articulation is understood pejoratively, as a fall from verbal grace and rectitude.[17] But the training more widely extended to African-American actors (some of it fostered by the Shakespeare Theatre) has delegitimated the basis of such criticism, even as it confirms the ideological character of the Shakespearean aesthetic. Indeed, as African-American actors have come under the dispensation of the 'naturalized' Shakespeare to which Worthen refers, mixed-race performances have come to seem unremarkable – indeed, natural. This may explain why the analytical problem posed by the *Othello* I'm discussing does not map out onto Ron Canada's Iago, Franchelle Stewart Dorn's Emilia, Teagle F. Bougere's Cassio, or Patrice Johnson's Desdemona, at least not as black actors playing 'white' parts.[18] Certainly Washington audiences have been conditioned to seeing these African-American actors, and others, play a variety of Shakespearean roles, even if not within so foregrounded a governing fiction of whiteness. But that foregrounding, as I'll later suggest, raises problems of its own.

If actors of African descent are at this moment readily taken for 'white', the situation cannot be symmetrically reversed when white actors are asked to impersonate black characters. Through its reverse casting, the Washington *Othello* denies the material consequences of racial identity, skirts the risk of making race a latter-day minstrel show in its performativity, lacking only the final embarrassment of a blackface fraught with discredited practices. Indeed, so loaded with the possibility for offence is this impersonation that it is not at all clear what it ought to mean for Stewart to indicate that he is 'black' – especially within the regime of training I have described and especially for a British actor versed in classical technique. At the same time, the significance of Shakespeare to ideological formations around literature as an imaginative resource for human identity connects Stewart's casting to the larger social fabric that informs, and is informed by, the influential position occupied by *Othello*'s representation of blackness. If the meaning of race is constructed relationally, as I earlier suggested, against what hegemonic practices, what perceived essences was Stewart's Othello to be launched – apart, that is, from the authority of the Shakespearean text and an impugned history of production? When the stage is generally integrated and when actors of African descent are conventionally taken for 'white', Stewart's colour cannot mean in opposition and as pure figuration. But then what can it mean, given such a production?

The asymmetry of casting practices I have described, in which black can be taken for white but, it seems, not the reverse, reveals a theatrical problem erected on a much larger social fault. 'Whiteness', as many critics have suggested, still remains in the United States as the invisible, because culturally dominant, state. To take it as under siege while signifying its opposite may demand an act of double vision audiences may not have been prompted to undertake, within the terms the production itself puts on offer – or able to undertake under any circumstances at this particular historical conjuncture. Indeed, as I shall later suggest, the staging of Othello's anger against Desdemona before he murders her introduces a hauntingly (in)apposite juxtaposition of white male body against black female that makes it especially difficult to view Stewart as the racially beleaguered subject of the play.[19]

Critical responses to the immediate challenge of the lines notwithstanding, however, recent legislative and juridical actions indicate that a sizeable portion of the American population feels that whiteness, its own whiteness, is indeed beleaguered, under siege; this is surely one way to read anti-affirmative action measures in California and Texas. Or perhaps more clearly and less tendentiously, reverse-discrimination cases that have been brought in light of Allan Bakke's landmark 1978 Supreme Court victory concerning the University of California Medical School's racially preferential admissions policies, which marked perhaps the first salvo in the battle against the institutional legacy of the civil rights movement. Given the political terrain of the late twentieth century into which Kelly's 'photonegative' *Othello* has been inserted (and beyond its own ambiguous/incoherent staging of race), the issue it raises becomes not simply whether white can be read for black, and so the role available again (dare I say rescued?) for a white actor – this time without the unacceptable stigma of blackface. Rather, the production demands we consider whether its spectacular reversal of the play's racial valences becomes potentially symptomatic of the current American conjuncture around black–white relations, particularly concerning affirmative action since *Regents of the University of California v. Bakke*.

Although it is surely obvious that racism is alive and well in many corners of the United States, I want to use repudiations of affirmative action policies as my particular focus for two reasons. First, because arguments about the unjust structures of compensation that are its legacy have become an increasingly legitimated aspect of public discourse, and as such are strenuously separated from the more overt forms of white supremacy with which they nevertheless have much in common. The second follows from the first, in that the integration of the Shakespearean stage is itself a legacy of the civil rights era; indeed, Kelly's production can be considered a symptom if not a direct result of the playing out, and subsequent dismantling, of that legacy. If, in the conservative dispensation that permeates public discourse on race, governmental measures designed to compensate for wholesale discrimination in the past have resulted in a hypercorrective set of practices made rigid by force of law, the perceived offence of affirmative action policies lies in having set off a new system of inequity symmetrical with, and complementary to, the old ones, with whiteness now occupying the place of formerly disempowered blackness.[20] Thus what calcified liberal agendas around civil rights have institutionalized is a fetishization of quotas, a knee-jerk privileging of minorities which has, so it is argued, come to displace the receding democratic dream of a nation blind to colour and alive only to merit.[21]

Such arguments are, I am sure, highly familiar to most readers, precisely because they have been seen as legitimate and 'disinterested' objections to affirmative action (yet for all their exquisite attention

to the rights of Asian-Americans, such objections always seem mobilized by the pathos of the white subject who feels discriminated
against). Given the absence of a widely attended-to counterargu-
ment, the claim that affirmative action has 'gone too far' constitutes
the received wisdom of the day. Even in a world that sees affirmative action as symmetrical discrimination, however, it may yet
be 'going too far' to consider *Othello* safe again for white actors.
Nevertheless, Kelly's production gives us access to a view implicit in
such anti-affirmative action movements, albeit not acknowledged, or
even necessarily intended, as such. In casting a white man to play a
subject increasingly embattled and disempowered by virtue of his
race, Kelly summons forth a world where black men have the preferences, the apparently secure hold on 'occupations', a world where
inertial structures that cannot but favour the status quo, the normative vision, seem to have been obliterated. Left in their wake is
Stewart's Othello: not so much the character of the script as the icon
of a movement, he offers the spectacle of an aggrieved and displaced
white subject, railing against the motivated alienation of a power
that he blindly believes is his by merit rather than as an extension of
the colour of his skin.

That so suggestive and troubling a reading was only intermittently
resonant with the experience yielded by the production is undeniable; after all, the script itself militates against too sure a view of
Othello's blind privilege. Still, there was an arresting scene, one that
does not directly involve Othello, that brought the reverse subtext
I have outlined to the threshold of overtness. Shortly after landing on
Cyprus, the Venetians – played, as I have indicated, by African-
American actors – begin to mingle with, surround, and ultimately
menace the Cypriots, who happen to be played by the few white
actors other than Stewart in the production. The sense of menace
was underscored by the rhythmic stomping of feet which began as
the action escalated, and by the rough handling of a female Cyprian
soldier. If any scene affected me as spectacle – and I do want to
emphasize my position as a white audience member in recording my
reaction – it was this one. But at what ideological cost? Why might
this scene 'work' when, as I have already indicated, those that
demand positioning Stewart as disempowered do not? What aspect
of the white Imaginary is being engaged in seeing black – their
Venetian-ness is forgotten for all intents and purposes – soldiers act
out of control?

How the Washington production engaged the white Imaginary that is the legacy of race relations in the United States speaks to the 'dread' of my title: the rough handling of a white woman, accompanied by the primitivism of stomping feet, reiterates the staging of a racist nationhood that cannot be meant as interrogative, given the aims of the production. But its echo of an old racial drama, and its engagement with the ideological conditions of its far more suave recrudescence, have the ambiguous virtue of an inadvertent analytic. The phantasmatic spectacle of black men manhandling a white woman Kelly provides is disturbing in itself, given the shopworn fantasies of black male predation it reiterates. But when white Othello's abuse and murder of the black Desdemona is set against the scene in Cyprus, these climactic actions cannot but stand as the historical correction of white mythologies about dark male bodies, sex and violence with which the production has, whether inadvertently or not, trafficked.

My previous analysis of the homogenizing vocal and bodily decorum of the actor leaves aside the extent to which 'blind' casting, at this moment in Shakespearean productions, often reveals a subtext that is not blind at all. Before proceeding to consider how the final moments of the play blow apart the fiction of white beleaguerment, I want to show that this production, which I have already deemed idiosyncratic, actually constitutes part of a terrain: reading it against a selective account of recent colour-blind theatrical and cinematic instantiations of Shakespeare makes clear the potentially unintended resonances provided by bodies interacting, put on view, and pressured by the history surrounding the moment of viewing. After all, it is only when race is deployed as though it bore no weight, were yet another neutral variable, like eye or hair colour, that it can be flipped, reversed, as well as cast against, indifferently. And that race can be so deployed because systematic discrimination is a thing of the past, and whiteness not the structural basis of privilege, is contiguous with the basis upon which recent challenges to affirmative action have launched themselves.

II

Since the innovative casting work performed by Joseph Papp in New York in the 1960s, it has become an uncontroversial position that actors of other than white skin should and ought to be able to act in productions of Shakespeare.[22] Still, what may be less easy to assume – or more properly, what may be easier to assume than to consider critically and responsibly – is that casting parts without respect to the colour of the actors always remains unproblematic as it has become a widely accepted practice. Indeed, even to raise questions about race and casting is to risk being associated with the unpalatable views of such reactionary critics as John Simon, historically antagonistic to Papp's long-standing advocacy of colour-blind casting. I have already quoted Simon's disparagement of the speech patterns of African-American actors, but it is worth examining his remarks at greater length, the better to make clear how colour-blind casting at the moment of its emergence was understood to reflect political intentions by one of its most virulent opponents:

> Out of a laudable integrationist zeal, Mr. Papp has seen fit to populate his Shakespeare with a high percentage of Negro [*sic*] performers. But the sad fact is that, through no fault of their own, Negro actors often lack even the rudiments of Standard American speech. ... It is not only aurally that Negro actors present a problem; they do not look right in parts that historically demand white performers. ...
>
> The critical evaluations of Papp's enterprise have been consistently and thoroughly misleading, whether because of the assumption that something free of charge and for the people must be evaluated along democratic, not dramatic, lines, or simply because of the reviewers' abysmal lack of sophistication, it would be difficult to say.[23]

In deriding the 'integrationist' valence of Papp's casting decisions, Simon attempts to separate the stage from the state, and thus to insist on the theatre as pure aesthetic practice, to be evaluated on 'dramatic' rather than 'democratic' criteria. However, the rhetorical framework he establishes for his analysis betrays how theatre necessarily serves as a *representative*, as well as representational, cultural practice: looking 'right' for the part is inextricably tied to being *seen* on the stage, to participating fully in a dramatic polity that is also a professional workplace from which actors of non-European descent were long debarred, except in the all-black productions that preceded less restrictive mainstream casting.[24] Understood in this way, the stage offers an approximation, however partial and rarefied, of the space of national civic life. Hence Papp's casting decisions in the 1960s could not but be of a piece with the social agendas in which it is enmeshed.

Unlike Simon, I take the political nature of casting as a given within a progressive cultural politics. But I also want to question whether colour-blind casting, understood as symbolic practice, achieves what might have been vaunted for it since the breakthrough practices of Papp. Hence, I want to consider what happens when Shakespearean plays are cast unreflexively, without a sense of the resonances the extra-theatrical or -diegetic material world, the world of significantly raced bodies, social inequities, and histories of physical and sexual domination and expropriated labour, provides for the space of representation. Productions, of course, are not conceptualized apart from a specific historical moment, so that in speaking about such resonances I am necessarily also inquiring into the way a given production offers itself as an aesthetic artefact mounted within a particular ideological dispensation. Very different questions could be asked regarding Papp's initial practices on New York City stages in the heady aftermath of the civil rights movement, and the way such casting operates in the 1990s, when it has partly become a reflex (if not self-reflexive) practice, and as affirmative action itself has come under criticism – from the standpoint of progressives as well as of conservatives. In the space of this essay, I cannot do justice to the practice of colour-blind casting at the moment of emergence; however, given the sketch of context I've provided earlier in the essay, the reason for my interest in productions roughly contemporaneous with the Washington *Othello* is clear.

In general, stage productions of Shakespearean plays, especially productions not constrained by realist settings and mechanisms of verisimilitude, are less vexed with such extra-theatrical and -diegetic resonances. But that theatrical space is not exempt is evinced by a 1997 production of *The Tempest* by the Shakespeare Theatre that preceded the *Othello* under discussion, and that offered a white Prospero played against a black Caliban. Although such casting, seemingly anything but 'blind', might have opened the play up to a critical encounter with its own significant imbrication in the discourse and material practice of slavery and colonialism – and just as significant, given the venue, with the history of slavery in the United States – the fact is that in this production such possibilities went unexplored. The Prospero of Ted van Griethuysen was played as querulous but mostly benign, and the Caliban, Chad L. Coleman, was a physically commanding and attractive man who nevertheless seemed never to speak with politically informed defiance: indeed, the actor was apparently directed never to stand wholly upright. Moreover, with the exception of Ariel, all the island's spirits who appeared in the masque and elsewhere were played, wordlessly, of course, by black actors, who in the event looked to be nothing more than impassive slaves. But given the inscrutable interactions between Prospero and Caliban, to what end were such resonances, such performances of 'blackness', invoked? As Barbara Hodgdon has written in another context, production claims that race matters (as the casting choices seem to suggest) 'need not automatically correspond with politicization'.[25] In this case, the casting of white master and black slaves alludes to a history of racial domination familiar to American audiences. But it only alludes to them, preferring, it appears, not to use the stage to insist on a dialectical relationship between aesthetic artefact and a legacy of material exploitation.

The disturbing set of casting decisions undertaken in Washington could not have been intended as regressive at this late historical moment. In fact, the issue, contrary to Hodgdon's words, is whether race was overtly acknowledged to matter at all here: an actor associated with the Theatre, although not part of this production, seemed convinced that the director had intended only to give more up-and-coming black actors theatrical work. Thus he was taken aback by the harsh criticism his casting choices received from one DC reviewer – who appeared to have been alone among his colleagues in noting the unreflexively (and, one would have thought, inescapably) racist overtones of the production.[26] However, my own observations, and those of several other attendees, suggest that while the largely white audiences for the Shakespeare Theatre were not notably disquieted, the more racially mixed school groups brought to the production manifested discomfort at Caliban's being played as cowering and, indeed, base, especially by an actor whose physical presence suggested the latent possibility of an alternative conception of the character. In the event, the production's resonances generated questions about the politics of casting that had nowhere to go within the production itself. Questions, that is, for selected segments of the audience, who were perhaps never intended as the primary addressees for the production.

Regardless of the director's own possible blindness to the histories his production was invoking and then denying, the fact remains that this *Tempest* (if his colleague's account is correct) provides a clear illustration of the conflicts between a space of imaginative representation, in which colour does not 'matter' enough to inflect the interpretation, and the space of reception, in which it still cannot but signify, even if recognition of that signification is unevenly distributed among the audience. This uneven distribution suggests that the representation of race is inevitably politicized, to modify Hodgdon's overcompressed statement: the question then becomes whose politics are represented as the neutral state, and whose are marginalized, unacknowledged. Thus the issue raised by the Washington *Tempest* becomes whether the politics it invokes by its racially charged (but colour-blind?) casting resist and complicate the history of the text and the moment of production and viewing, or whether they simply refer to history – one safely remote from the dominant audience segment, whose desires (and the Washington Shakespeare Theatre's) to disconnect aesthetic experience from historical oppression are represented and ratified in the name of a universalist Shakespeare.

If I turn to more widely available recent Shakespeare films for my texts, some further examples will make clear the potential ideological dissonances of colour-blind casting in a representational space defined by the conventions of cinematic verisimilitude.[27] Kenneth Branagh's 1996 *Hamlet* sets the play in a fully realized nineteenth-century court; although certain aspects of the mise-en-scène are principally symbolic, the primary location is the resonant, and quite real and substantial, Blenheim Palace. Apparently to signify the Scandinavian ancestry that Hamlet is supposed to have, Branagh bleached his ordinarily red hair quite blond (an admittedly distracting move, which reinforces Branagh's star presence as much as it offers to subsume a distinctive personal attribute under the demands of the role).[28] Moreover, Branagh, who also directed, supplies a bedroom scene between Hamlet and Ophelia, all the better, one presumes, to ground concern about 'hot love' in a diegetic reality. What happens, then, given all the efforts to locate this *Hamlet* in a space of textual verisimilitude, when the seamless representation of the nineteenth-century mores and styles is entered by actors of African and Asian descent? A camera pans across the court assembled to hear Claudius's post-nuptial speech; occasionally it records brown and black faces among the courtiers as it records mostly white ones. What nineteenth-century nation could have had so integrated a citizenry, especially at the level of the courtly elite?

For Branagh, the answer lies less with seeing representations as bound to strict historical accuracy than in the film's status as a vehicle for a re-presented past, one which by the dispensation of Shakespeare becomes socially permeable, integrative, and hence utopian.[29] Indeed, an interview he gave shortly after the release of *Hamlet* indicates that the nineteenth-century setting was meant to signify a plausible site of racial and ethnic inclusiveness:

> part of the reason why our setting [is] more impressionistic than
> specific to a year in the nineteenth century is because I wanted not to
> worry about casting black actors, or Asian actors, or actors with dif-
> ferent accents. We have Russians in there, we have a Pole, we have a
> Frenchman. I also wanted each of the parts that I had felt over the
> years were most prone to a clichéd approach, the kind of thing that
> you fall into – I had seen many heavy-handed versions of the gravedig-
> ger scenes, and I wanted actors in the case of say, Billy and Robin,
> who would be funny but could also be real in the way I felt was
> necessary. ...
> There would be a price to pay for some people. I'm sure it won't
> work for everyone, but for me it was a great treat to see all those
> different approaches come together. I believe the man belongs to
> everyone, you know, across the world, and across cultures, across
> sexes, and so implicitly I wanted to suggest that with the accent-blind,
> nationality-blind, color-blind casting.[30]

It is, of course, a very different thing to have a Pole or a Frenchman
appear in a cinematic representation of a nineteenth-century
European court than it is to have an African or an Asian – or, for
that matter, an American. Indeed, it seems as if Branagh has allowed
the repudiation of slavery that occurred both in Britain and the
United States in the nineteenth century to dictate his sense of the representational possibilities inherent in *Hamlet*: for him as for many
theatrical practitioners, Shakespeare facilitates access to a utopian
vision of the past, where the 'openness' of the Shakespearean text to
all comers is translated into a corresponding absence of history's
material constraints on equal access to state power or even to literacy. Even in light of Branagh's words, however, it may seem that any
objection about colour-blind casting is based on too literal a reading
of the setting, a naive refusal to accept that movies traffic in illusion.
Or else a converse refusal to understand the politics of casting,
insofar as stars constitute a kind of capital on their own, without
which few cinematic endeavours, especially 'prestige' projects like
Shakespeare that too often lose money for their investors, can hope
for funding and distribution.[31]

But my point in the first case concerns production values, and the
naturalizing deployment of the camera by Branagh the director,
rather than a critique of the restorative function of historicity *per se*.
Regardless of the precise date in the 1800s in which his film is set –
and regardless of the naive utopianism that constitutes his sense of

the Shakespearean past – Branagh seems to have striven to render his setting unproblematic in terms of the conventions of Hollywood realism, and then undone the illusion of verisimilitude by means of casting bodies historically unavailable for the positions they are asked to take. Had Branagh not so relied on the techniques and apparatuses of cinematic verisimilitude, my questions could well substantially vanish, since the issue of their appropriateness is tied specifically to his conflicting desires for the play: both to ground it in a reality-effect concerning the past to which his words about the nineteenth century pay a kind of tribute; and to claim the text, despite its history and the larger histories he invokes, in a phantasmatic space of integration, to add people of colour into a history that in general excluded them, and certainly from positions of power and influence in the nineteenth-century European court. A check of the cast reveals the tokenism that pervades many such liberal formations around 'nationality-blind, colour-blind' Shakespeare. The actors of non-European descent, however much might be claimed for their belonging to the bardolatrous polity, appear only in the background, or in comparatively minor roles: only four speaking parts, all rather incidental, are given over to non-white actors.[32]

As a way to get at the second, converse, point, concerning the politics and economics of casting, perhaps it would do to shift to one of Branagh's other Shakespearean films, *Much Ado About Nothing* (1993), set in a stylized Italian pastoral vaguely redolent of the eighteenth century. It cannot be claimed that this movie relegates non-white actors to vanishingly small roles, since the African-American actor Denzel Washington is cast as the noble Don Pedro of Aragon. Interestingly, however, his bastard brother Don John is played by Keanu Reeves, an actor whose mixed Hawaiian descent still allows him to be read as white. Here, as in *Hamlet*, Branagh is gesturing towards cinematic realism, however uneven its application: although the principals' hair, for instance, is decidedly twentieth century in style, the location shots seem consonant with a bucolic and Italianate pre-industrial languor. Thus there is an element of surprise in making the legitimate offspring black, and the illegitimate one white. (Indeed, such impeccably conscientious casting reads as a symbolic negation of the far more likely possibility that, in the eighteenth century, any black offspring of the aristocracy, should one have existed, was likely to be a bastard.) Given Branagh's penchant, manifested here as well as in *Hamlet*, for casting Hollywood stars in supporting roles, does Washington's status as star outweigh as signifier his raced body to the audiences of the film, given that many of Washington's star roles engage with race?[33] And assuming such circumstances can be rationalized into existence through a liberal suspension of disbelief – it's only a movie, and on some level the pleasure on offer is to see an unlikely star do a star turn – how then to recuperate Beatrice's rejection of Don Pedro's proposal?

As played by Emma Thompson, Beatrice offers a graceful refusal of Don Pedro's offer of marriage, in keeping with the script's characterization of the Prince as 'too costly to wear every day', and with her own covert affection for Benedick. Indeed, that the Prince stands mostly as spectator to the various erotic interactions between Beatrice and Benedick, and Hero and Claudio, is a function of the playtext. But it is a function that Branagh's casting and directing, intentionally or not, have exacerbated. Given that Don Pedro's substitute (and suspect) wooing of Hero for Claudio takes place while he is masked – as well as Branagh's lavish climax, which just barely records the Don's isolation from the happy denizens of the villa as the camera cranes over the ever-expanding nuptial festivities – it becomes difficult not to colour Beatrice's rejection of the black Don as evidence of the film's covert perception of racial difference and its significance. And it is a perception that runs precisely counter to Branagh's avowed intention to offer an inclusive, all-encompassing instantiation of Shakespeare. While Washington the Hollywood star might appeal erotically to spectators of many races, within the diegesis of Branagh's film its only black actor is repeatedly denied access to amorous subjecthood. That Thompson's reaction *is* graceful occludes the subtext of the moment in which she participates. If she had hesitated, made an obstacle of her repudiation in any way, the film might have offered a more overt purchase on what it stages via Washington – and then appears to look away from; Branagh's *Much Ado* might not then have been 'blind' to the restrictive interplay that subtends its mixed-race casting. Because the proposal, shot in close-up, plays off his darker face against her lighter one, contrasts her whiteness with his lack of it, Beatrice's refusal nevertheless makes clear what the other moments to which I've alluded only hint at: *this* Don Pedro, however great his authority, cannot be assimilated to the social realm whose consolidation Shakespearean romantic comedy celebrates – and Branagh's Hollywood spectacle reiterates.[34] (In this Denzel Washington's Don is, perhaps, luckier than most Othellos: denied the fantasy of romance as unassimilable, he is thereby denied the consequences of domestic tragedy.)

Beatrice's refusal of Don Pedro in Branagh's film of *Much Ado About Nothing* constitutes one of the most interesting moments in the movie, since it reveals that it is often the question of hetero-sexual desire across differently raced bodies which reasserts the extra-diegetic reality of the moment of viewing.[35] That is, the nor-mative gender roles so important to Shakespearean drama, when played by men and women of different races, make clear that the liberal, utopian, and integrative aspirations of colour-blind casting might be cancelled out by the pressure to the white Imaginary: hence my reading of the scene in Cyprus. In the wake of the O. J. Simpson trial, which revealed how quickly much of the white population of the United States abandoned its ideological commitment to colour-blindness when the subject of justice concerns cross-racial desire and a prominent black defendant, that race still matters cannot in gen-eral be a surprise. The Simpson trial made abundantly clear that scenes of abstract justice at the turn of the millennium are readily turned into spectacles of embodiment, with the letter of the law – or the text – seemingly secondary to the antique play of black and white, and the haunting spectre of miscegenation.

It is not solely because O. J. Simpson was frequently referred to as an Othello figure that he seems apposite to my argument, however.[36] Both the casting of this production and the proceedings in Los Angeles derive their meanings from the failures of colour-blindness as project within a society committed to integrationist reforms: indeed, the legal scholar Kimberlé Williams Crenshaw has suggested that Simpson is himself 'the essential symbol of the colour-blind ideal'.[37] Crenshaw's words give us a way to read the white outrage that attended the jury's finding that Simpson was not guilty. Despite the evidence of racism as well as questionable procedures on the part of state agents, the verdict was made apprehensible only when it was deemed that *Simpson*'s lawyer, Johnnie Cochran, was the one who introduced 'race' into the proceedings. In acknowledging that race mattered in the case against him – implicit, indeed, in the melancholy comparisons that yoked him with Othello – Simpson was perceived to have violated a tacit contract, an understanding that he was liv-ing and operating in a world where colour did not matter; at the same time, he was being judged within a system where racial bias was also tacitly normalized.[38] Such a contradiction, by and large invisible to white spectators, suggests that the failures of the colour-blind ideal are not operational, a matter of uneven deployment and enforcement; rather, they are conceptual and material. Hence the importance of reading the Washington *Othello* in light of critical race theory, which holds that critical attention to race, and hence scepticism about the discourse of integration and colour-blindness, are not incompatible with a progressive racial politics.[39] Thus Crenshaw's characterization of civil rights agendas of the recent past: 'the rejection of ideologies of black exclusion and inferiority was not met with any rethinking of the nature and legitimacy of white dominance in American institutions. Racism was framed only in terms of the formal exclusion of nonwhites, not in terms of the privileging of whiteness'.[40]

It goes without stating that there is much to separate theatre as an institution from the legal system, although it is clear that both have notably pursued liberal strategies designed to correct inequities of representation, themselves born out of a history of racist practices. But my abbreviated analysis of the monolithic Shakespearean voice enjoined upon the actor suggests that the implicit 'privileging of whiteness' Crenshaw detects as the structural flaw in integrationist projects is not entirely remote from the theatrical mark. Reinforced in varying degrees by the material infrastructure that supports both systems – the juridico-disciplinary apparatus in the case of one, directors, producers, voice and movement coaches, and technical workers in the case of the other – is the *symbolic* persistence of whiteness as the unacknowledged dominant. And nowhere is that made more apparent than in the spectacle of Stewart's 'photonegative' Othello.

III

Casting Patrick Stewart in a Shakespearean role is a canny move from a box-office standpoint – perhaps as canny as Branagh's enlisting Billy Crystal as the gravedigger or Robin Williams as Osric. Unlike those actors, however, Stewart combines both the popular name recognition conferred by his seven years of playing Captain Jean-Luc Picard on *Star Trek: The Next Generation* with an estimable pedigree as a Shakespearean actor. This pedigree was often alluded to within the science fiction television show; Picard, for instance, keeps a First Folio in his twenty-third-century private quarters, and there are a few episodes in which he helps the android Data perform the discourse of 'humanness' by acting in *The Tempest* and *Henry V*.[41] Although such grace notes did not constitute an important thematic of the series, the evidence they provide of Shakespeare's universal pertinence and durability link Stewart imaginatively with a potentially reactionary view of Shakespearean subjecthood.

Stewart's presence, while it guaranteed the staging a great deal of public interest, could not do the same for its conceptual plausibility. As I have already suggested, there were scattered snickers from the audience at Stewart's intoning 'Haply for I am black'; yet the reaction, surely unintended on the director's and actor's parts, cannot simply be blamed on the audience's lack of imaginative sophistication. To accept the undeniably pale Stewart as black demands that the power of the script's fiction – what I've already termed the authority of the Shakespearean text – override all the cues to the contrary that the actor playing Othello is *not* black, nor is he making any somatic attempt to impersonate blackness, vexed, indeed, as that possibility would be. Acceptance demands a rarefaction and idealization of the site of viewing perhaps unlikely ever to have been achieved by any audience at any time, but certainly not to be achieved when part of the point of casting Stewart is presumably his fame, either as a mass-culture icon, or as a British Shakespearean actor. The discourse of the star system as elucidated in cinema studies analyses what is, perhaps, the inevitable case with respect to the theatrical star: that a star is one to the extent that she or he exceeds the role being acted, that she or he is perceived and, indeed, appreciated as *not* wholly absorbed in the role, as signifying beyond it. Thus when Patrick Stewart plays Othello, his characterization as Captain Jean-Luc Picard may constitute an inevitably resonant resource for those segments of the audience that view him as a star. Indeed, given the extent to which Stewart's prior experience as a Shakespearean actor was itself written into *Star Trek: The Next Generation*, it is possible that the boundary between one type of performance and another becomes increasingly hard to chart.

Further complicating the reading of Stewart as Othello are his prestige and cultural capital as a *British* actor and sometime member of the Royal Shakespeare Company. If, via the casting of well-known actors with American accents and less elite training, Branagh models the symbolic diversification of Shakespeare via the discourse of Hollywood, casting Stewart in DC has the reverse effect: rather than making his Britishness a meaningful sign of the exoticism that the part carries along with it, his very presence on an American stage can be read to confer the restrictive legitimacy of Shakespeare's originary culture. Indeed, the effect of casting him is to consolidate many species of institutional power in the person of the actor, and so to turn him – rather than, strictly speaking, Othello – into the centre of gravity for the production.[42] And in the space between those two lies the production's main obstacle.

Even for those segments of the audience not particularly conversant with facets of Stewart's prior career, there remains the issue of whiteness as a cultural dominant, given greater effectivity for the problem's not being addressed directly, as a problem of visuality for the theatre. In speaking of spectacle over script throughout this essay, I have focused on what may be seen, what is put on display, so as to correlate with the idea of 'blindness' with respect to colour. Stewart's performance, highly competent as it naturally was within the traditional markers of Shakespearean acting, could not avoid confronting the audience with the brute irreducibility of the articulating subject in collision with a language that would have him be seen as different from what he is, and apart from a theatrical tradition that turns all hues to white. Nor could it avoid having that difference involve a deconstruction of whiteness-as-privilege, a privilege both material and discursive, motivated solely by adherence to the script's letter, insofar as the lead actor is concerned.

At any rate it is not on the level of linguistic signification that the most telling, most chilling instance of the recalcitrance of whiteness – its obstinate resistance to being rendered discursive – occurred. That definitive demonstration was provided by a passing interaction in the final act. Preparatory to Othello's murder of Desdemona, Stewart rages and flings Patrice Johnson about the stage, at one point pushing her up against the wall, speaking at her, as the lines indicate, with a combination of desire and fury. But to be made to see this vulnerable Desdemona as a vulnerable *black* woman, one thus forced and abused by an ineluctably *white* man, is to see the plot's contrary figment of the white racial Imaginary displaced by a primal scene in American history the more disturbing for its failed repression at this critical moment in the production. Instead of the dangerous and desirous black male assaulting a white woman, the play enacts, reiterates, the attacks on powerless black females by masterful white men that constitute the seldom-acknowledged event on which much racial discourse in the United States is founded. Throughout the play, Johnson offered a strong and graceful portrayal of Desdemona; her demeanour well suited a young woman of aristocratic privilege. But in the final act, the spectacle of Stewart's white rage, white desire, obliterated whatever sense of privilege might have accrued to her, whatever specificity of class or person Johnson's acting earned in the part. More than abused Venetian wife, the spectacle rendered her emblematic chattel, the objective correlative of a prolonged cultural repression.

As must be clear, such a resonance could precisely not have been intended within the fiction of the photonegative, which asks, however incompletely, that race be taken as performance rather than as endowed with significance because of a material history of dominance and exploitation, because of an uneven distribution of power that persists despite the occasional reverse-discrimination argument to the contrary. Thus, in some sense, a white Othello's violence towards a black Desdemona responds to, indeed, falsifies, both a textual fantasy and a proximate stage one. Engaged is not only the hoary myth of black male rage and erotic frenzy that *Othello* may well inaugurate, but also the scene of black Venetian menace among the white Cypriots that I have analysed elsewhere in the essay, which recalls the 'rape and rescue' scenario made infamous by *Birth of a Nation*. If that earlier insertion serves as a 'guilt-ridden denegation of White man's history of raping Black women', then this scene comes clean about what the production denies as the very fantasy it mobilizes plays itself out, that we are enough 'beyond' colour to deploy it as a formal property of the stage.[43] Unlike the white Cypriot woman saved from a fate worse than death, an invention, presumably, of the director, Desdemona is inexorably condemned by plot, by a fidelity to script that is unlikely ever to be violated. And since the climax of the play is also the climactic moment of inevitably raced violence in the production, the corrective staging of white laying hands upon black is inserted in the position of revealed psychic truth. What it reveals, however belatedly, is the bad conscience of the production.

IV

In a discussion of 'antiliteral' casting practices, Ella Shohat and Robert Stam ask: 'What is wrong with non-originary casting? Doesn't acting always involve a ludic play with identity? Should we applaud Blacks playing Hamlet but not Laurence Olivier playing Othello?'[44] They pose these 'irreverent' questions provocatively, the better to argue for a context-sensitive casting practice: 'The casting of Blacks to play Hamlet, for example, militates against a traditional discrimination that denied Blacks any role, literally and metaphorically, in both the performing arts and in politics, while the casting of Laurence Olivier as Othello prolongs a venerable history of bypassing Black talent'.[45] Given the generous amount of work it provided for African-American actors, the Washington *Othello* surely cannot be accused of having perpetuated the material exclusion Shohat and Stam note, and that is part of the history of mainstream Shakespearean production in the United States. But its casting was schematic, symbolic, with fair labour practices onstage an apparent by-product, if a fortunate one, of a 'photonegativity' inflected by the casting of Patrick Stewart in the title role. To understand my point, consider the difference between this production and a *Hamlet* with a largely African-American court, one whose production crew was also dominated by African-American personnel.

Looking for new ways to play old texts is part of the business of performance, when it comes to Shakespeare or to other classic dramatists. But there are some texts whose unpalatable propositions mean that any attempt at innovation needs to be taken with a keen eye to the resonances those propositions still retain: *Othello* is surely one, *Taming of the Shrew* is another. Far too seldom, even now, is the symbolic violence of either play addressed in dominant production practice; what obtains instead is a sense that these plays can be rescued from their worst tendencies in the name of preserving an aestheticized and performatively innocuous Shakespeare. So *Shrew* is played as though the brainwashing of Kate might not in fact have defined humour for some audiences, and *Othello* as the tragedy of a distant racism whose continuing truth is belied by the usual presence of non-white actors on the mainstream stage. (The same point might, of course, be made about *The Tempest*.) Hence the casting of Stewart becomes a parody of affirmative action, a parody that befits this dangerous moment in the discourse and material practices of race in the United States, when an ideological clamour suggests racial parity is an accomplished fact, and calls any further attention to race itself a form of racism.

To consider race as a matter for discursive manipulation, of representation and public visibility, is to fall into the limitations of colour-blind casting as I have described them. My students' first reading of Desdemona's line in Act I that she '[sees] Othello's visage in his mind' is to suggest that she somehow discerns him truly, which for them signifies seeing beyond his colour to the disembodied truth of interiority. But of course at least one other reading is possible: that her love for him is not beyond race but cognizant of it, as Othello is of himself. The former line reading reveals how easy, how 'natural' it is, for conscientious post-civil rights subjects to imagine that seeing race means seeing wrong. Instead, I would guess that we have barely begun to perceive it rightly, in theatre as everywhere else.

From *A Feminist Companion to Shakespeare*, ed. Dympna Callaghan (Oxford, 2000), pp. 226–47.

NOTES

[Denise Albanese argues that the consequence of 'colour-blind' casting is that all actors are meant to be read as white. This normalizing process is compounded by the homogenization of voice and movement that results from contemporary training in and expectations for classical acting. In a 1997 production in Washington, DC that is less well known than those which Hodgdon discusses and that has not been more widely distributed through videotape, director Jude Kelly defied conventional wisdom on the casting of *Othello* with a 'photonegative' production. If the fiction of colour-blind casting is that race no longer matters, at least in what Albanese calls the 'utopian' space of the theatre, this production demonstrated the powerful ways in which race continues to signify even on stage. The reversals did not 'work' either in the arena of 'imaginative representation' (as a production of *Othello*) or in the sphere of reception (as it incited conditioned responses of racial and sexual fear in some members of the audience). 'Black and White, and Dread All Over' is included in a collection called *A Feminist Companion to Shakespeare*. It does not position itself as a piece of feminist work – its immediate concern is race – but it is illustrative of the directions now taken by third-wave feminist scholars. Ed.]

1. This essay has benefitted from conversations with Devon Hodge, Robert Matz, Zofia Burr, Susan Snyder and Caleen Jennings.

2. The programme notes for *Othello* written by Miranda Johnson-Haddad refer to the production as 'photonegative', as did the actor Ron Canada (who played Iago) on the Diane Rehm show, broadcast over National Public Radio ('Reader's Roundtable on *Othello*', November 1997). The part of Bianca (who in the event turned out to be well named) was cast with a white actor, Kate Skinner. According to Ron Canada, the director Jude Kelly was inverting the British theatrical tradition, in which Bianca is cast as a woman of African descent. The other white actors in the production played soldiers from Cyprus.

3. I take as a given that all production decisions, for good or ill, may not be available to analysis in terms of directorial intention. Nor, given the

collaborative nature of staging, does it seem wise to hold a director wholly accountable for what is (to be) seen, still less what may be experienced by various segments of the audience.

4. For information on Shakespearean programmes that also contained minstrel shows, see L. Levine, *Highbrow, Lowbrow: The Emergence of Cultural Hierarchy in America* (Cambridge, MA: Harvard University Press, 1998), pp. 21–3.

5. A partial bibliography stressing issues of stage and screen performance would include S. Barnet, '*Othello* on Stage and Screen', in Alvin Kernan (ed.), *Othello* (New York: Signet, 1998); E. Hill, 'Shakespeare and the Black Actor', in *Shakespeare in Sable: A History of Black Shakespearean Actors* (Amherst: University of Massachusetts Press, 1984), pp. 1–16 (especially pp. 7–12); D. Callaghan, ' "Othello was a white man": Properties of Race on Shakespeare's Stage', in Terence Hawkes (ed.), *Alternative Shakespeares 2* (New York: Routledge, 1996), pp. 192–215; J. Singh, 'Othello's Identity, Postcolonial Theory and Contemporary African Rewritings of *Othello*', in Margo Hendricks and Patricia Parker (eds.), *Women, 'Race', and Writing in the Early Modern Period* (New York: Routledge, 1994), pp. 287–99 (reprinted as chapter 7 in this collection); B. Hodgdon, 'Race-ing *Othello*, Re-Engendering White-Out', in Lynda E. Boose and Richard Burt (eds.), *Shakespeare the Movie: Popularizing the Plays on Film, TV, and Video* (New York: Routledge, 1997), pp. 23–44 (reprinted as chapter 8 in this collection).

6. See, for example, J. Butler, *Gender Trouble: Feminism and the Subversion of Identity* (New York: Routledge, 1990); Judith Butler, *Bodies That Matter: On the Discursive Limits of 'Sex'* (New York: Routledge, 1993); M. Garber, *Vested Interests: Cross-Dressing and Cultural Anxiety* (New York: Routledge, 1992); K. Bornstein, *Gender Outlaws: On Men, Women and the Rest of Us* (New York: Routledge, 1994).

7. Here and elsewhere, I do not claim to speak authoritatively about the play's reception. I have tried to be cautious about generalizations, and have based them on discussions and interviews with people who also attended the production.

8. In one sense, this substitution commemorates a long history of the part's being performed by white actors, albeit white actors in blackface. Indeed, given that 'the cultural performance of alterity' is a precondition of the Shakespearean stage, there is a sense, as Dympna Callaghan has argued, in which Othello is ineluctably white (p. 193).

9. The extent to which a director honours, or not, the text is an aspect of the way in which directors define their practice in relation to the authority of 'Shakespeare'; see W. B. Worthen, 'Shakespeare's Auteurs: Directing Authority', in *Shakespeare and the Authority of Performance* (Cambridge: Cambridge University Press, 1997), pp. 45–94.

10. I do not have time to do justice to the point, but I take the laughter as potentially significant evidence that the cultural formations around Shakespeare variously described by (e.g.) Lawrence Levine and Graham Holderness have begun to recede in influence. For Shakespeare as an elite icon in the United States, see Levine, *Highbrow, Lowbrow*; for 'Bardolatry', see G. Holderness (ed.), *The Shakespeare Myth* (Manchester: Manchester University Press, 1988), especially pp. 2–15.

11. The practice of colour-blind casting is not without its own historicity. Since I cannot speak authoritatively about how, for instance, Joseph Papp's breakthrough productions might have disposed and directed integrated casts, I have thought it best to restrict myself to recent productions. However, I'd venture a guess that what might once have been radical theatrical practice has now become the unremarkable demotic of Shakespearean theatre – and in that passage from innovation to commonplace lies much of the impetus for my argument.

12. For a brief but suggestive analysis of how conventions of voice are taken to be 'natural', see S. Bennett, *Performing Nostalgia: Shifting Shakespeare and the Contemporary Past* (New York: Routledge, 1996), pp. 42–3.

13. Linklater, as quoted by W. B. Worthen, *Shakespeare and the Authority of Performance* (Cambridge: Cambridge University Press, 1997), p. 117.

14. Ibid., p. 99.

15. John Simon in *Commonweal* magazine, 1963; quoted in H. Epstein, *Joe Papp: An American Life* (Boston: Little, Brown, 1994), pp. 290–1. Conversely, the possession of such a voice by an actor of brown skin can be viewed as a stupendous achievement. Errol Hill, who is from Trinidad, notes that the principal of the Royal Academy of Dramatic Art assumed he was from 'darkest Africa' and considered Hill's 'cultivated English accent ... remarkable' (see E. Hill, *Shakespeare in Sable: A History of Black Shakespearean Actors* [Amherst: University of Massachusetts Press, 1984], pp. xix–xx).

16. Errol Hill, in a chapter called 'How Relevant Is Race?', notes, and even echoes, the stance of critics who found African-American actors in Shakespearean productions not equal to the task. I take such words as evidence that the display of a particular training is longed for, evidence, that is, of a normativity when it comes to how Shakespeare should be acted (see Hill, *Sable*, especially pp. 146–8 and 152–3). Indeed, when African-American actresses were praised for their performances, the words can seem suspiciously exoticizing: Walter Kerr refers to Jonell Allen (in John Guarre's 1971 musical *Two Gentlemen of Verona*) as an 'untamed enchantress' (quoted in Hill, *Sable*, p. 155).

17. Hence, even the criticism of Baz Luhrmann's film of *Romeo and Juliet*, for destroying the sound of the verse: the actors speak their lines

'prosaically', that is, without an attempt to declaim or sound magniloquent. The resultant performances render Shakespeare both demotic and American.

18. Both Dorn's Emilia and Johnson's Desdemona were particularly impressive performances.

19. Of course, this argument depends to some extent on a normative view of the audience: 'whiteness' can have a very different resonance for a largely black audience; for but one illustration, see bell hooks, 'Representing Whiteness in the Black Imagination', in Lawrence Grossberg, Cary Nelson and Paula Treichler (eds.), *Cultural Studies* (New York: Routledge, 1992), pp. 338–46. Based on my experience over several years of attending Shakespeare productions in Washington, DC, it would be fair to say that adult audiences are mainly white. However, the frequent presence of school groups at productions can change the demographics, and inflect the texture of audience response.

20. I am aware that my summary is far too schematic. For one, it neglects the extent to which current oppositional agendas around affirmative action in the United States are not conducted along the axis of black-white, but also engage with the very different places and problems of Asian-Americans and Latins. For another, it is not clear that even places like California, which have been considered the 'wave of the future' when it comes to voter-driven challenges to affirmative action programmes, offer a coherent depiction of frustration with the 'privileges' of minorities.

21. For a provocative and problematic suggestion that affirmative agendas, by instituting a Foucauldian regime of the statistical normalization of the workplace, have unintentionally offered a blind to racist hiring practices, see M. Yount, 'The Normalizing Powers of Affirmative Actions', in John Caputo and Mark Yount (eds.), *Foucault and the Critique of Institutions* (University Park, PA: Pennsylvania State University Press, 1993), pp. 191–229.

22. Errol Hill credits Joseph Papp, in his early efforts to bring Shakespeare plays to residents of New York City who were by reason of race or class not seen as target audiences for classic theatre, as the first to cast the plays without regard to the race of the actors; see Hill, *Sable*, pp. 143–76, especially pp. 143–55.

23. John Simon's 1963 piece in *Commonweal*, quoted in Epstein, *Joe Papp*, pp. 290–1 (ellipses in original). On Papp's commitment to integrated casting (which went back as far as a 1952 production of a Sean O'Casey play), see Epstein, pp. 77, 92–4, 168–9.

24. A similar objection to interracial casting that offers itself as an attempt to preserve the integrity of Shakespearean drama is cited by Errol Hill: in 1965, Bernard Grebanier wrote that 'when the Vivian

Beaumont Theater gives me a black Orsino and Maria, I am upset – not out of racial prejudice but out of respect for Shakespeare's plays. After all, a white man doing Othello blackens face, arms, legs and hands. Is there any reason why a black actor should not whiten his when doing a white role?' (*Sable*, p. 3.)

25. Hodgdon's words come out of an essay in which she considers two different televised versions of *Othello* with black actors in the title role (see 'Race-ing *Othello*', p. 31). This is the place to acknowledge my general indebtedness to Hodgdon's essay: although much of my own essay was conceptualized in advance of my having read hers, we come to many similar conclusions.

26. Edward Gero, in discussion of the production at George Mason University, October 1997.

27. James L. Loehlin provides a handy characterization of my claim that Branagh's films draw on the conventions of cinematic verisimilitude: 'The realist Shakespeare film is characterised by the sort of mid-range naturalistic acting, cinematography and editing that is used in most Hollywood films. The characters are presented as "real people", in plausible make-up and costumes, and the film relates the narrative straightforwardly, without calling attention to the medium' (J. L. Loehlin, ' "Top of the World, Ma": *Richard III* and Cinematic Convention', in Lynda E. Boose and Richard Burt [eds.], *Shakespeare the Movie: Popularizing the Plays on Film, TV, and Video* [New York: Routledge, 1997], pp. 67–79, p. 67).

28. That Laurence Olivier's 1948 filmed version also presented the star with extremely blond hair is also a likely factor in Branagh's tonsorial decision, given that Branagh has seemed to make his film career as a Shakespearean actor in emulation of – and rivalry with – Olivier.

29. My truncated analysis is partly inspired by Susan Bennett's work on Shakespearean productions and their stagings as part of the past as a form of ideological correction; see *Performing Nostalgia*, especially pp. 1–38.

30. Branagh's words occurred in a public discussion on 21 December 1996, moderated by Susan Stamberg of National Public Radio, and itself a part of the Smithsonian Institution's 'Stella Shakespeare Weekend'. I am grateful to Diane Williams for making her transcript of the discussion available to me.

31. In the same discussion, Branagh denies that his casting of Americans has anything to do with box-office considerations – although his desire to make Shakespeare more broadly appealing is surely a matter, if not a purely instrumental one, of expanding audience demographics.

32. During the Royal Shakespeare Company's summer 1998 visit to Washington, DC, two of the productions it offered, *Hamlet* and *Cymbeline*, also cast non-white actors in comparatively minor roles.

33. For instance, Washington has starred in several of Spike Lee's movies, among them the title role in *Malcolm X*.

34. Of course, neither can Don John – but then he's the bastard.

35. I specify the desire I am concerned with as 'heterosexual', in part because I am unsure whether the argument can be extended to same-sex eroticism (and I have not attempted the demonstration), and in part because the historical fears of miscegenation that come into play are specifically engaged with my privileged dynamic.

36. For instance, the poet Anthony Hecht felt impelled to write a letter to the *Washington Post* regarding the notable parallels between the two figures. Such comparisons betray both a suspect desire to ennoble a potential wife-killer (who in this event was deemed guilty before a trial had even occurred), and a limited conceptual repertory for understanding the complexities of race. Playing off this obsession with O. J. as Othello, Ann duCille has analysed a complementary positioning of Nicole Brown Simpson as the 'browned' woman of captivity narrative; see A. duCille, 'The Unbearable Darkness of Being: "Fresh" Thoughts on Race, Sex and the Simpsons', in Toni Morrison and Claudia Brodsky Lacour (eds.), *Birth of a Nation'Hood: Gaze, Script, and Spectacle in the O. J. Simpson Case* (New York: Pantheon, 1997), pp. 293–338.

37. The following analysis is much indebted to K. W. Crenshaw's essay, 'Color-Blind Dreams and Racial Nightmares: Reconfiguring Racism in the Post-Civil Rights Era', in Toni Morrison and Claudia Brodsky Lacour (eds.), *Birth of a Nation'Hood: Gaze, Script, and Spectacle in the O. J. Simpson Case* (New York: Pantheon, 1997), pp. 97–168.

38. In reading the case as I have, I do not of course dismiss the evidence of spousal abuse in the case of Simpson – any more than I would the violence against Desdemona in my reading of *Othello*. At the same time, I want to stress that it is precisely because of Simpson's race that the violence against Nicole Brown Simpson mattered as much as it did.

39. For a representative collection, see K. W. Crenshaw, N. Gotanda, G. Peller and K. Thomas (eds.), *Critical Race Theory: The Key Writings That Formed the Movement* (New York: Free Press, 1995).

40. Crenshaw, 'Color-Blind', p. 106.

41. For more on the various connections between Shakespeare and *Star Trek*, see the special issue of the science fiction journal *Extrapolations* for Fall 1995.

42. In an interview conducted during *Othello*'s run with Arch Campbell, the film and drama critic of the local NBC network affiliate WRC,

Stewart spoke of his long-standing desire to perform the part, and his fear that it would prove impossible to do so until this production came round. I do not have unequivocal evidence that Stewart was cast first, but in a sense it does not matter: the effect of casting Stewart was to turn him into its focus.

43. The quotation comes from Ella Shohat and Robert Stam's discussion of *Birth of a Nation*; see E. Shohat and R. Stam, *Unthinking Eurocentrism: Multiculturalism and the Media* (New York: Routledge, 1994), p. 159.

44. Ibid., p. 191.

45. Ibid., p. 191.

Further Reading

TEXTS

Especially because *Othello* survives in multiple texts, each edition of the play constitutes an interpretive approach to it. For years, the gold standard of single-volume editions was the 'New Arden' series, for which *Othello* was edited by M. R. Ridley (London: Methuen, 1958). Ridley's choice of the First Quarto of 1622 as his copy text (rather than the First Folio of 1623) was controversial. What now seems unforgiveable is his discussion of Othello's race. Newer single-volume editions include the Arden 3 *Othello*, which has superseded the New Arden. Its editor, E. A. J. Honigmann (Walton-on-Thames: Thomas Nelson, 1997), has also authored *The Texts of 'Othello' and Shakespearian Revision* (London and New York: Routledge, 1996). Therein, Honigmann defends a text conflating the Quarto and the Folio on the grounds that both incorporate authorial variants, or revisions, and both demonstrate corruption.

Norman Sanders has edited a conflated text for the New Cambridge Shakespeare (Cambridge: Cambridge University Press, 1984). As he has done for other volumes in the Cambridge series, C. Walter Hodges has drawn speculative but enlightening suggestions for early staging and stage movement; in the case of *Othello*, the re-creative emphasis is on the last two scenes of the play. Cambridge has also published *The First Quarto of 'Othello'*, edited by Scott McMillin (Cambridge: Cambridge University Press, 2001), a scholarly edition of the 1622 text of the play. Nick de Somogyi has reproduced a facsimile of the First Folio version, *The Tragedie of Othello, the Moore of Venice*; on facing pages, the 1623 text is reproduced in modern type (London: Nick Van Hern Books, 2002). *Othello* has not yet appeared in the New Oxford series (as of 2002), but it is in preparation by Michael Neill. Neill's essays on the play go to suggest that this edition will make an important contribution. An edition that can be hard to find but that has some uniquely valuable glosses is Lawrence J. Ross's *The Tragedy of Othello, the Moor of Venice* (Indianapolis: Bobbs-Merrill, 1974). For a sense of eighteenth- and nineteenth-century interpretive preoccupations, readers should also consult the New Variorum *Othello*, edited by Horace Howard Furness (Philadelphia: J. B. Lippincott, 1886), with its thorough, line-by-line review of scholarship to that date. This will in due course be succeeded by a twenty-first-century Variorum, to be published by the Modern Language Association of America.

Also worth consulting are the various collected editions of Shakespeare, which include: *The Arden Shakespeare Complete Works*, gen. eds. Richard Proudfoot, Ann Thompson and David Scott Kastan, 3rd series (Walton-on-Thames: Thomas Nelson, 1998); *The Riverside Shakespeare*, gen. eds. G. Blakemore Evans et al., 2nd edition (Boston: Houghton Mifflin, 1997); and the three Oxford volumes edited by Stanley Wells and Gary Taylor, *William Shakespeare: The Complete Works*, *William Shakespeare: The Complete Works, Original-Spelling Edition* (both Oxford: Clarendon Press, 1986), and *William Shakespeare: A Textual Companion* (Oxford: Clarendon Press, 1987). *The Norton Shakespeare*, edited by Stephen Greenblatt, Walter Cohen, Jean E. Howard and Katharine Eisaman Maus (New York and London: Norton, 1997) is based on the Oxford edition.

Other important essays on the vexed issues of revision and corruption in the texts of *Othello* are Thomas L. Berger's 'The Second Quarto of *Othello* and the Question of Textual "Authority" ' (in *Othello: New Perspectives*, a collection edited by Virginia Mason Vaughan and Kent Cartwright and further described among other collections, below) and Scott McMillin's 'The *Othello* Quarto and the "Foul-Paper" Hypothesis' (*Shakespeare Quarterly*, 31 [2000], 67–85).

GUIDES TO CRITICISM

There are several guidebooks to *Othello* that include reviews of the play's critical history. The most current is Joan Lord Hall's '*Othello*': *A Guide to the Play* (Westport, CT: Greenwood, 1999), with chapters on textual history, contexts and sources, dramatic structure, major characters, themes, critical approaches and the play in performance, as well as a narrative bibliography. Nicholas Potter's *William Shakespeare: 'Othello'* (New York: Columbia University Press, 2000) is more introductory, an inventive patchwork of critical history, short extracts from selected authors, and comments upon and explanations of those extracts (though these can be over-solicitous). Peter Davison's '*Othello*': *An Introduction to the Variety of Criticism* (Houndmills: Macmillan, 1988) is brisk and accomplished, although it shows its age with interpretive categories that predate the advents of poststructural theory and political approaches: 'genre criticism', 'historical and social criticism', 'dramatic convention and decorum', 'character and psychological criticism', 'the play as dramatic poem' (i.e., formalist criticism) and 'archetypal criticism'.

Margaret Lael Mikesell gives a thumbnail sketch of *Othello* criticism in the introduction to the Garland *Annotated Bibliography* she compiled with Virginia Mason Vaughan (cited below); in the same volume, Vaughan reviews material on *Othello*'s texts, sources, performance history, and adaptations. Also worth noting are Helen Gardner's '*Othello*: A Retrospect, 1900–67', in *Shakespeare Survey*, 21 (1968), 1–11. This focuses on the issues of character and theme in reviewing earlier criticism and is an act of interpretation itself. Martin Orkin's '*Othello* and the "Plain Face" of Racism', *Shakespeare Quarterly*, 38, 2 (1987), 166–88, provides a more specialized review of the racist assumptions betrayed in some earlier criticism of the play.

Faith Nostbakken's *Understanding 'Othello': A Student Casebook to Issues, Sources, and Historical Documents* (Westport, CT: Greenwood Press, 2000) excerpts relevant historical documents as well as some performance reviews and a rather dated cluster of critical writings. The documentary selections include Gaspar Contareno and Lewis Lewkenor on Renaissance Venice, Richard Knolles on Turkish history, Leo Africanus and John Pory on Moors, John Dod and Robert Cleaver on marriage, and William Garrard on the arts of war. Nostbakken also relates themes in *Othello* to the O. J. Simpson trial, the Unabomber case, and the Monica Lewinsky scandal. For more advanced scholars, this volume will undoubtedly be superseded by the Bedford Shakespeare Series *'Othello': Texts and Contexts* now (in 2002) being readied for press by Kim F. Hall.

CRITICAL MONOGRAPHS

The two most important monographs for further study of *Othello* and its reception are Edward Pechter's *'Othello' and Interpretive Traditions* (Iowa City: University of Iowa Press, 1999) and James L. Calderwood's *The Properties of 'Othello'* (Amherst: University of Massachusetts Press, 1989). Even those works that constitute what we have thought of as a late twentieth-century critical 'revolution' continue to play out the debate between A. C. Bradley and F. R. Leavis, according to Pechter, who is willing to seem politically incorrect in discussing the particular jeopardies of interpreting *Othello*. For Calderwood, the concept of 'property' ramifies to incorporate early modern land law, men's property in women and its relationship to violence against them, Othello's identity and the play's cultural capital.

Other single-authored volumes are cited in chronological order. (1) G. R. Elliott's *Flaming Minister: A Study of 'Othello' as Tragedy of Love and Hate* (Durham, NC: Duke University Press, 1953; reprinted by AMS Press, 1965), is a scene-by-scene close reading of the play that is informed by a theatrical consciousness and suggests possible stage business and gesture. Elliott argues that the tragedy results from the 'self-concealed pride' of Cassio, Desdemona and, especially, Othello, not from Iago's 'concealed deviltry', and that Othello's final self-recognition makes the play a great love tragedy. (2) Robert B. Heilman's *Magic in the Web: Action and Language in 'Othello'* (Lexington, KY: University of Kentucky Press, 1956) also takes a New Critical approach and also discusses the theme of love in the play. Heilman finds no motive for malignancy in Iago and argues that there are flaws and vulnerabilities in Othello. He is especially interested in images that originate with Iago and then spread out into the play. (3) Martin Elliott's *Shakespeare's Invention of 'Othello': A Study in Early Modern English* (Houndmills: Macmillan, 1988), is another close reading that emphasizes syntax and diction. Elliott turns his observations to character analysis and to the question he considers to be most central: how can it be that the noble Othello of the first part of the play can become the murderer of his wife? (4) Jane Adamson's *'Othello' as Tragedy: Some Problems of Judgment and Feeling* (Cambridge: Cambridge University Press, 1980) was, according to the author, completed in 1976, and so it is still very much preoccupied with A. C. Bradley and F. R. Leavis. Adamson argues that each critic says something important about the play and each says something insufficient to it. She refuses to declare *Othello* a 'lesser' tragedy, and she locates its greatness in the way it forces its readers and audiences to recognize what we share with each of its characters. (5) Virginia Mason Vaughan's *'Othello': A Contextual History* (Cambridge: Cambridge University Press, 1994), though not exclusively a performance history, is discussed more fully in that category. The first section of the book considers four 'Jacobean contexts' for the play: global, military, racial and marital.

COLLECTIONS ON *OTHELLO*

With a number of collections on *Othello* already in print, one goal of this volume was to select essays not already made easily available in the volumes listed below. The most comprehensive and useful collection for the history of *Othello* criticism is Anthony Gerard Barthelemy's *Critical Essays on Shakespeare's 'Othello'* (New York: G. K. Hall, 1994). Extracts from A. C. Bradley and Eldred Jones are included (though not F. R. Leavis or T. S. Eliot), as are the key essays by Lynda E. Boose ('Othello's Handkerchief'), Carol Thomas Neely ('Women and Men in *Othello*'), Joel Fineman ('The Sound of O in *Othello*'), Karen Newman ('"And wash the Ethiop white"'), Thomas L. Berger ('The Second Quarto of *Othello*'), Ania Loomba ('Sexuality and Racial Difference'), and Michael Neill ('Unproper Beds'). The editor contributes a new essay.

Earlier scholarship is handily represented in three collections: (1) Leonard F. Dean, ed., *A Casebook on 'Othello'* (New York: Thomas Y. Crowell, 1961). A text of the play is complemented by selections from Thomas Rymer, Samuel Taylor Coleridge, William Hazlitt, G. B. Shaw, A. C. Bradley, Elmer Edgar Stoll, T. S. Eliot, Leo Kirschbaum, Winifred M. T. Nowottny and Robert B. Heilman. There are also some essays on performance history. (2) John Wain, ed., *'Othello': A Casebook* (1971; rev. ed. London: Macmillan, 1994). Wain includes such frequently cited work as that by Rymer, Samuel Johnson, Coleridge, Bradley, Eliot, G. Wilson Knight, William Empson, F. R. Leavis, Helen Gardner, John Bayley, W. H. Auden and Neville Coghill. (3) Kenneth Muir and Philip Edwards, eds., *Aspects of 'Othello': Articles Reprinted from 'Shakespeare Survey'* (Cambridge: Cambridge University Press, 1977). This includes Helen Gardner's important 'Retrospect' on criticism from 1900 to 1967; such frequently cited essays as those by S. L. Bethell ('Shakespeare's Imagery: The Diabolic Images in *Othello*') and Barbara Heliodora C. de Mendonça ('*Othello*: A Tragedy Built on a Comic Structure'); and a superb selection of stage photos.

Another good introduction to the history of *Othello* criticism is provided by Susan Snyder's collection, *'Othello': Critical Essays* (New York and London: Garland Publishing, 1988). Included are the standard essays and extracts from Coleridge, Bradley, Leavis, Gardner and others, but there are also selections from Kenneth Burke, Edwin Booth, Ellen Terry and Konstantin Stanislavsky. With essays by Edward A. Snow and Peter Stallybrass, the collection ends on a forward-looking note. The contributions to *Autour d'Othello*, edited by Richard Marienstras and Dominique Goy-Blanquet (Amiens: Presses de l'UFR de Langues, Université de Picardie-Jules

Verne, 1987), were first presented at a conference organized by CERLA at the Institut Charles V. Richard Marienstras, Pierre Iselin and François Laroque (among others) take up such topics as genre, translation, negation and perversion. Ann LeCercle's 'The "Unlacing" of the Name in *Othello*' and Lynda E. Boose's ' "Let It Be Hid": Renaissance Pornography, Iago, and Audience Response' (an early version of the chapter included in this collection) are the only essays in English. Linda Cookson and Bryan Loughrey have edited *William Shakespeare: 'Othello'* for the Longman Critical Essays Series (Harlow: Longman, 1991).

There are also three collections of new, not reprinted, work. (1) Especially interesting is Mythili Kaul's *'Othello': New Essays by Black Writers* (Washington, D.C.: Howard University Press, 1997). Kaul commissioned and collected pieces from 'theater persons', 'creative writers' and 'academic critics'. The actor Earle Hyman describes ego as the play's central theme; director Sheila Rose Bland imagines an all-white, all-male cast to emphasize themes of racism and homoeroticism in the play; dramatist Ishmael Reed writes *Othello* into a scene between two college professors; memoirist Maryse Condé describes how *Othello* helped her recognize racism and understand the construction of her own identity; and more. (2) Virginia Mason Vaughan and Kent Cartwright are the editors of *'Othello': New Perspectives* (Rutherford: Fairleigh Dickinson University Press, 1991). Among the essayists are Thomas L. Berger (on the second quarto text), Thomas Moisan (on iteration), Joseph A. Porter (on speech acts), James Hirsh (on perception), Frances Teague (on stage properties), and Martha Tuck Rozett (on teaching the play). (3) The most recent collection is edited by Philip C. Kolin: *'Othello': New Critical Essays* (New York and London: Routledge, 2002). Kolin's extended introduction on *Othello* criticism is organized by character (Othello, Desdemona, Iago) and then by performance medium (stage, film, television, other media). Contributors include David Bevington, Peter Erickson, Jay L. Halio, Sujata Iyengar, Scott McMillin, James Schiffer and Daniel J. Vitkus.

PERFORMANCE CRITICISM

In the introduction to *'Othello': New Essays by Black Writers* (see above, under collections), Mythili Kaul describes 'Stage Representations of Othello from 1604 to the Present', focusing on the skin colour ('Black or Tawny?') of the actor. This is a much-discussed issue in the performance history of the play, but far from the only one, as a group of excellent volumes attest. (1) In *'Othello': Plays in Performance* (Bristol: Bristol Classical Press, 1987), Julie Hankey annotates a text of the play with line readings, blockings and cuts recorded in prompt books, contemporary descriptions and reviews from past performances. She shows how the performance history of *Othello* interacts with its critical history, discussing, for example, the influence of F. R. Leavis's reading of Othello's character on Laurence Olivier's performance of the role. (2) Lois Potter's *'Othello' in Performance* was released just as this volume went to press (Manchester: Manchester University Press, 2002). Potter's extensive experience as a theatre reviewer and historian give promise that this will be an important contribution in the field.

More introductory are (3) Martin L. Wine's *'Othello', Text and Performance* (London: Macmillan, 1984) with plot synopsis and analysis of key characters, themes, speeches, sources and theatre productions; and (4) John Russell Brown's *William Shakespeare: 'Othello'* (New York and London: Applause, 2001), with line-by-line expositions of the kinds of decisions actors have to make.

The great pioneer in performance history, Marvin Rosenberg, made *Othello* his starting point with *The Masks of 'Othello': The Search for the Identity of Othello, Iago, and Desdemona by Three Centuries of Actors and Critics* (Berkeley: University of California Press, 1961). Rosenberg's first purpose, to validate performance history as a fit scholarly subject by showing that stage renderings can yield interpretive insights, scarcely needs arguing now (thanks in no small part to his own work). His second mission, to prove that Othello is noble because actors over the centuries have intended him to be, holds less water. Rosenberg established a canon of the most noteworthy performances of *Othello* that other historians have followed. Among the other production histories worth consulting are Kenneth Tynan's *'Othello': The National Theatre Production* (New York: Stein and Day, 1966), a scene-by-scene record of rehearsals for the production that famously starred Laurence Olivier, and Carol Jones Carlisle's *Shakespeare from the Greenroom: Actors' Criticisms of Four Major Tragedies* (Chapel Hill: University of North Carolina Press, 1969), with a chapter on *Othello*. *Stanislavsky Produces 'Othello'*, translated by Helen Nowak (London: Geoffrey Bles, 1948), is a collection of notes Konstantin Stanislavsky sent back to the Moscow Art Theatre Company while in Nice under doctor's orders in 1929. In *'Othello': A Contextual History*, Virginia Mason Vaughan emphasizes the historical context for each of the productions she studies from the Restoration to the late 1980s. She updates the canon with a discussion of Trevor Nunn's 1989 production for the Royal Shakespeare Company, for which a new category of evidence survives: a video recording.

The first single-authored book devoted to the making of a Shakespeare film is about *Othello*: Micheál MacLiammóir's *Put Money in Thy Purse: The Diary of the Film of 'Othello'* (London: Methuen, 1952), re-issued as *Put Money in Thy Purse: The Making of 'Othello'* (London: Virgin Books, 1994). This volume excerpts the diary of Orson Welles's 'Iago'. *Othello* also features largely in major volumes like Jack Jorgens's *Shakespeare on Film* (Bloomington: Indiana University Press, 1977); Anthony Davies's *Filming Shakespeare's Plays* (Cambridge: Cambridge University Press, 1988); and Susan Willis's *The BBC Shakespeare Plays: Making the Televised Canon* (Chapel Hill: University of North Carolina Press, 1991).

OTHELLO AT THE CRITICAL FOREFRONT

The suggestions for further reading, above, have included sources of traditional scholarship because there is ample evidence that the next critical turn may involve their rediscovery and revaluation. For a history of the role *Othello* has played in the newer criticisms of the 1970s and 1980s, however, a core group of ten essays (many mentioned in the Introduction to this volume) is essential. They include: (1) Lynda E. Boose, 'Othello's Hand-kerchief: "The Recognizance and Pledge of Love"', *English Literary Renaissance*, 5 (1975), 360–74; (2) Stanley Cavell, 'Othello and the Stake of the Other', chapter 3 of *Disowning Knowledge in Six Plays of Shakespeare* (Cambridge: Cambridge University Press, 1987), pp. 125–42; (3) Joel Fineman, 'The Sound of O in *Othello*: The Real of the Tragedy of Desire', *October*, 45 (1988), 76–96; (4) Stephen Greenblatt, 'The Improvisation of Power', chapter 6 of *Renaissance Self-Fashioning: From More to Shakespeare* (Chicago and London: University of Chicago Press, 1980), pp. 222–54; (5) Carol Thomas Neely, 'Women and Men in *Othello*: "What should such a fool / Do with so good a woman?"', in *The Woman's Part: Feminist Criticism of Shakespeare*, ed. Carolyn Ruth Swift Lenz, Gayle Greene and Carol Thomas Neely (Urbana: University of Illinois Press, 1980), pp. 211–39; (6) Michael Neill, 'Unproper Beds: Race, Adultery, and the Hideous in *Othello*', *Shakespeare Quarterly*, 40 (1989), 383–412; (7) Karen Newman, '"And wash the Ethiop white": Femininity and the Monstrous in *Othello*', in *Shakespeare Reproduced: The Text in History and Ideology*, ed. Jean E. Howard and Marion F. O'Connor (New York and London: Methuen, 1987), pp. 142–62; (8) Patricia Parker, 'Shakespeare and Rhetoric: "Dilation" and "Delation" in *Othello*', in *Shakespeare and the Question of Theory*, ed. Patricia Parker and Geoffrey Hartman (New York and London: Methuen, 1985), pp. 54–74; (9) Peter Stallybrass, 'Patriarchal Territories: The Body Enclosed', in *Rewriting the Renaissance: The Discourses of Sexual Difference in Early Modern England*, ed. Margaret W. Ferguson, Maureen Quilligan and Nancy J. Vickers (Chicago and London: University of Chicago Press, 1986), pp. 123–42; (10) Valerie Wayne, 'Historical Differences: Misogyny and *Othello*', in *The Matter of Difference: Materialist Feminist Criticism of Shakespeare* (Ithaca: Cornell University Press, 1991), pp. 153–79.

A number of these are republished in Anthony Gerard Barthelemy's *Critical Essays on Shakespeare's 'Othello'*, cited above under 'Collections'.

RACE AND COLONIALISM

Othello anchors many discussions of race and colonialism in early modern history and early modern literature. See especially Eldred Jones's *Othello's Countrymen: The African in English Renaissance Drama* (London: Oxford University Press, 1965); Ruth Cowhig's 'Blacks in English Renaissance Drama and the Role of Shakespeare's *Othello*', in *The Black Presence in English Literature*, ed. David Dabydeen (Manchester: Manchester University Press, 1985), pp. 1–25; Anthony Barthelemy's *Black Face, Maligned Race: Representations of Blacks in English Drama from Shakespeare to Southerne* (Baton Rouge: Louisiana State University Press, 1987); Ania Loomba's *Gender, Race, Renaissance Drama* (Manchester: Manchester University Press, 1989); Jack D'Amico's *The Moor in English Renaissance Drama* (Tampa: University of South Florida Press, 1991); and Virginia Mason Vaughan's *'Othello': A Contextual History*. Also discussed above is *'Othello': New Essays by Black Writers*, edited by Mythili Kaul. In the introduction, Kaul notes that 'opinion is almost equally divided between those contributors who see [*Othello*] as a racist play, written by a racist playwright, for a racist audience, and those who see it as a play *about* racism, with Iago (and not the playwright or the play itself) as the embodiment of racist attitudes'.

A monograph to be consulted is Kim F. Hall, *'Things of Darkness': Economies of Race and Gender in Early Modern England* (Ithaca: Cornell University Press, 1995). Important collections include *Women, 'Race', and Writing in the Early Modern Period*, ed. Margo Hendricks and Patricia Parker (London: Routledge, 1994); *Post-Colonial Shakespeares*, ed. Ania Loomba and Martin Orkin (London: Routledge, 1998); and *Shakespeare and Race*, ed. Catherine M. S. Alexander and Stanley Wells (Cambridge: Cambridge University Press, 2000).

GENDER AND SEXUALITY

Othello similarly features prominently in major works on gender studies. See, for example, Coppélia Kahn's *Man's Estate: Masculine Identity in Shakespeare* (Berkeley: University of California Press, 1981); and Peter Erickson's *Patriarchal Structures in Shakespeare's Drama* (Berkeley: University of California Press, 1985). Collections to be consulted include *The Woman's Part: Feminist Criticism of Shakespeare*, ed. Carolyn Ruth Swift Lenz, Gayle Greene and Carol Thomas Neely (Urbana, IL: University of Illinois Press, 1980); *The Matter of Difference: Feminist Criticism of Shakespeare*, ed. Valerie Wayne (Ithaca: Cornell University Press, 1991); and *Shakespearean Tragedy and Gender*, ed. Shirley Nelson Garner and Madelon Sprengnether (Bloomington, IN: Indiana University Press, 1996).

Queer theorists have been slower to write about *Othello*, perhaps because it is difficult to validate a critical practice through the unsavoury character of Iago. There are a few exceptions: Graham Hammill adds a long and provocative footnote on *Othello* to 'The Epistemology of Expurgation: Bacon and the Masculine Birth of Time' (in *Queering the Renaissance*, ed. Jonathan Goldberg and Margaret Hunt [Durham, NC: Duke University Press, 1994]); and Robert Matz has published 'Slander, Renaissance Discourses of Sodomy, and *Othello*' (*ELH*, 66 [1999]: 261–76).

FURTHER BIBLIOGRAPHY

For more comprehensive suggestions than are possible here, readers should consult: (1) the annotated World Shakespeare Bibliography, edited by James L. Harner and now available both as a printed annual supplement to the *Shakespeare Quarterly* and also, at many libraries, as an online database of criticism, book and theatre reviews, dissertations and other materials; (2) the Bibliography of the *Publications of the Modern Language Association*, also available both in printed version and as an online enumerative database (readers should be warned that *PMLA* policy precludes listings for a single chapter on *Othello* in a book considering other topics, as well); (3) the annual reviews of 'critical studies', 'editions and textual studies', and works on 'Shakespeare's life, times and stage' published in *Shakespeare Survey*; (4) a similarly discursive and evaluative survey of the year's work in each Spring's issue of the quarterly journal *Studies in English Literature*; (5) *'Othello': An Annotated Bibliography*, covering the years 1940 to 1985 and compiled by Margaret Lael Mikesell and Virginia Mason Vaughan (New York and London: Garland Publishing, 1990); and (6) for earlier material, the enumerative *Shakespeare's 'Othello': A Bibliography*, compiled by John Hazel Smith (New York: AMS Press, 1988). Many of the works cited throughout this guide to 'Further Reading' also include selective bibliographies on *Othello*.

Notes on Contributors

Denise Albanese is Associate Professor of English and Cultural Studies at George Mason University. Author of *New Science, New World* (1996), she has also published on Juan Luis Vives, Tudor mathematics, and Shakespeare films and commodity culture. She is currently finishing a book on Shakespearean formations outside academia, called 'Extramural Shakespeare'.

Emily C. Bartels is an Associate Professor of English at Rutgers University and the Associate Director of the Bread Loaf School of English (Middlebury College). Her publications include *Spectacles of Strangeness: Imperialism, Alienation, and Marlowe* (1993), an edited collection of essays on Christopher Marlowe (1997), and a number of essays on Marlowe, Shakespeare, and Renaissance representations of Africa, Moors and race. She is currently working on a book entitled 'Before Slavery: English Stories of Africa'.

Harry Berger, Jr. is Professor Emeritus of Literature and Art History at Cowell College at the University of California, Santa Cruz. His books on Shakespeare include *Imaginary Auditions: Shakespeare on Stage and Page* (1989) and *Making Trifles of Terrors: Redistributing Complicities in Shakespeare* (1997). His most recent books are *Fictions of the Pose: Rembrandt Against the Italian Renaissance* (2000) and *The Absence of Grace: Sprezzatura and Suspicion in Two Renaissance Courtesy Books* (2000).

Lynda E. Boose is Professor of English at Dartmouth College, where she also teaches in the War and Peace Studies and the Women's Studies Programs. She is co-editor with Betty Flowers of *Daughters and Fathers* (1989), co-editor with Richard Burt of *Shakespeare the Movie: Popularizing the Plays on Film, TV, and Video* (1997) and is currently working with Burt on the sequel, 'Shakespeare the Movie, II: Popularizing the Plays on Film, TV, and DVD'. She has also written on 'Bosnian Rape Camps, Turkish Impalement, and Serb Cultural Memory' (SIGNS, 2002).

Michael D. Bristol, Greenshields Professor of English at McGill University, is the author of *Carnival and Theater: Plebeian Culture and the Structure* *of Authority in Renaissance England* (1986), *Shakespeare's America, America's Shakespeare* (1990) and *Big-Time Shakespeare* (1996). He has edited *Print, Manuscript, and Performance: The Changing Relations of the Media in Early Modern England* with Arthur F. Marotti (2000) and *Shakespeare and Modern Theatre* with Kathleen McLuskie and Christopher Holmes (2000).

Elizabeth Hanson is Associate Professor in the Department of English at Queen's University in Canada. She is the author of *Discovering the Subject in Renaissance England* (1998), as well as essays on early modern English literature.

Barbara Hodgdon, Adjunct Professor of Drama at the University of Michigan, is the author of *The End Crowns All: Closure and Contradiction in Shakespeare's History* (1991), *'The First Part of King Henry the Fourth': Texts and Contexts* (1997) and *The Shakespeare Trade: Performances and Appropriations* (1998). She is currently editing *The Taming of the Shrew* for the Arden 3 Shakespeare and co-editing, with William B. Worthen, the 'Blackwell Companion to Shakespeare and Performance'.

Lena Cowen Orlin is Professor of English at the University of Maryland, Baltimore County and Executive Director of the Shakespeare Association of America. Her book *Private Matters and Public Culture in Post-Reformation England* (1994) has a chapter on *Othello*. She is also editor of *Elizabethan Households* (1996) and *Material London, ca. 1600* (2000) and co-editor, with Stanley Wells, of *Shakespeare: An Oxford Guide* (2003). She is at work on a book entitled 'Locating Privacy in Tudor England'.

Alan Sinfield is Professor of English at the University of Sussex. His recent books include *Literature, Politics and Culture in Postwar Britain* (1989), *The Wilde Century: Effeminacy, Oscar Wilde, and the Queer Moment* (1994), *Cultural Politics – Queer Reading* (1994), *Gay and After* (1998) and *Out on Stage: Lesbian and Gay Theatre in the Twentieth Century* (1999).

Jyotsna Singh is Associate Professor of English at Michigan State University. She is the author of *Colonial Narratives/Cultural Dialogues: 'Discoveries' of India in the Language of Colonialism* (1996) and co-editor of *Travel Knowledge: European 'Discoveries' in the Early Modern Period* (2000). She is currently working on a book project with the working title 'The Economy of the Gift in the Early Modern Period'.

Index